TAMU

A GUEST AT THE BORNEAN TABLE

BRYAN KOH

TAMU

A GUEST AT THE
BORNEAN TABLE

Published by Xochipilli

ISBN: 978-981-18-0480-9
Editor: Meena Mylvaganam
Graphic Design: Nay Zaw Lin
Art Direction, Design and Layout: Bryan Koh

National Library Board, Singapore Cataloguing in Publication Data
Name(s): Koh, Bryan.
Title: Tamu : the guest at the Bornean table / Bryan Koh.
Description: Singapore : Xochipilli, [2021] | Includes bibliographical
references and index.
Identifier(s): OCN 1260166007 | ISBN 978-981-18-0480-9 (paperback)
Subject(s): LCSH: Cooking, Malaysian. | Cooking--Malaysia--Sarawak. |
Cooking--Malaysia--Sabah. | Cooking, Indonesian. | Cooking--Indonesia--
Kalimantan. | Cooking--Brunei. | LCGFT: Cookbooks.
Classification: DDC 641.5959--dc23

Location photographs © 2021 Bryan Koh
Studio photographs © 2021 Bryan Koh
Author photograph © 2021 Darren Gabriel Leow
Map of Borneo © 2021 Wilson Wang

Printed in Singapore by Markono

**The book cover motif is inspired by the array of shields used by
various Dayak groups across Borneo, their designs intended to ward
off evil spirits.**

KALIMANTAN

BRUNEI

I remember a friend's mother once saying in response to a slumber-related gripe years ago, that she found the notion of elusive sleep unfathomable. She believed that all one needed was discipline. "It all has to do with the mind…empty it…" she sang, snapping the fingers of one hand while those of the other turned her black coffee into a milk pond. "…and let nothingness take over," she concluded, raising the vessel to meet her supercilious countenance. At times I wonder if she had it wrong, as the nature of my problem seemed more circadian than existential.

Yet her words have come to visit me as I hover in blackness, despite all efforts to silence memories swirling around in the home they have made behind my eyes, like leaves in a freshly brewed teapot. The errant flashes of hut and broad gashes of river. The soft hiss of tapioca filings cajoled into fat discs on hot iron. The flames of turmeric and white bullets for chillies as granite pestles ripped them asunder. The sight of silver-skinned fish getting jiggled down bamboo culms with wild ginger and alien berries. The aroma of unknowable game acquiring a deep tan over burning wood, the wafts of smoke deranged and delightful. A GIF of endless sheets of turquoise and sapphire, trembling beneath a steady breeze, punctuated by a solitary crystal kayak, its burly occupant incapacitated by disreputable rum.

Unfortunately, it is the jagged, cascading tune of an alarm that brings the performance to a halt. I peel open my eyes and reach for my cellphone. Through its icy glare, I discern that it is about a quarter past four. My companion, Ken, unaffected by the minor din, is sound asleep in the driver's seat. Stale in the residual chill of the dormant vehicle, and groggy from the minimal oxygen permitted by almost-shut windows, I decide to get some fresh air.

I open the door and step out of the vehicle to kiss the molasses-deep darkness on its lips. The sky is a sprawl of undecorated teal this morning, the silence of the surroundings so deathly that even the rattle of a cicada would prove comforting. I feel the temptation to check the boot, for there lies a modest, and quite precious, cargo of dried octopus and stingray, mummified in multiple layers of *The Borneo Post* and masking tape. The folks back at Lahad Datu warned against taking these desiccated creatures on our long drive through the wilderness, along vast stretches of unlit road. They believe their scent to attract all kinds of unexplainable mischief. Despite having made it this far, I decide not to tempt fate. Much can happen before the arrival of dawn.

The yellow lights of the car's interior have suddenly popped open. Ken sticks his head out, ruffling his hair, wiping his eyes. "Think it's time," he says, and I respond by returning to the vehicle. It leaps into life, illuminating the *Arecaceae* enveloping the sandy space. Ken takes his foot to the pedal and we set off in the direction of the airport, which turns out to be an amusing five minutes away.

To our chagrin, the building is still shut, save for several signages and fluorescent beams lighting up the arrival hall. A security guard appears at the entrance and, as if battling a somnolent stupor, staggers towards us. Ken calmly lowers his seat window. Shaking his head and wagging his finger, the guard explains that they have decided to open a little later as the flight has been delayed. Before turning his back and heading off, he sweetly urges us to get something to eat in the meantime, reinforcing one of life's greatest axioms, that when food is not a solution, it makes a welcome distraction. But with the closest *kedai kopi* being in Tawau city, a solid hour away, we decide to stay put. The engine is silenced and we return our seats to full recline, poised for another round of waiting.

If there is one thing I have picked up during the making of this book, it is the art of waiting. Waiting for the right contacts to be made, for rapports to be struck, for itineraries to be sketched. Waiting for these itineraries to be fulfilled, hopefully in alignment with the seasons of crucial fruit and vegetables. Waiting, with baited breath and frayed nerves, for a research trip to go as planned – a rarity, in these parts. Waiting for a response to fresh queries, of which there tend to be numerous, involving techniques, words and ingredients gleaned off-site. Truth be told, the coming together of this book thus far has been anything but piecemeal. The chapters began their existences at vastly different times and matured at their own, often languid, pace on parallel paths, tugging at my sleeves every now and then, and taking months to arrive at utter completion. A friend based in Brunei, in response to my voiced frustrations, quipped, "The Gods must think you unready." Now, close to four years since my maiden excursion to Kuching, where I gloried in the resiny *Canarium odontophyllum* and boorish *Mangifera pajang*, I am pleased to be almost finished. Almost.

THE BORNEAN KITCHEN

When broaching the food of Borneo, a connection is promptly established with its indigenous folk, often referred to as Dayaks, the exonym largely applying to the island's non-Malay ethnic groups. There are at least fifty such peoples excluding subgroups, in itself a somewhat understudied and sensitive topic. I have decided to focus on the more prominent, more accessible, groups, such as the Iban, Bidayuh, Melanau, Lundayeh and Kelabit in Sarawak; the Murut, Kadazan, Dusun and Rungus in Sabah; the Ma'anyan, Ot Danum, Ngaju in Kalimantan.

I first learned about the food of these groups through a friend from Sarikei, a civil servant in the education sector who works closely with the Bidayuh and Iban in the area. His tales of golden, sour aubergines and sweet forest butter, of durian flowers and black ginger, set my imagination ablaze, and I was thrilled to get the chance to explore the world of bamboo cookery, of fermented and smoked meats, of starch-laden roots and palm shoots, of river fish and bivalve, of wild greens and fruit, many of which I had never before encountered. For me, the natural world has always been a rich source of intrigue and fascination, and I feel terribly fortunate to have been able to work with some of the edible wonders of this island, the third largest in the world, whose climate and various vegetations, from mangrove to montane forest, provide the ideal conditions for a mind-boggling array of species to flourish.

But there is more to Borneo than that. As I ate my way across the island, I found myself enchanted by the foods of its Muslim ethnic groups, from the *ambuyat* of the Bruneian Malays, a translucent gruel of sago typically consumed with an array of viands, to the *nasi subut* enjoyed by the Tidung of East Kalimantan, these days eaten with *sate pari*, barbecued skewers of stingray. Despite claims that Islam first reached these shores in the 10th century with merchants from China, it was likely only until the 15th century that it secured something of a foothold, travelling with Indian Muslims via Sumatra. As tempting as it is to tap on our notions of the cuisines and parties involved and draw links, the lack of evidence makes these attempts nothing more than clever guesses. For instance, while the prominence of cumin, coriander and fennel in Bornean Muslim kitchens is undeniable, as is their ubiquity in Indian and Arab realms, when and how these spices arrived, and how they wended their way into local dishes, remain largely unknown.

There was, I admit, the initial decision to exclude the foods of non-indigenous folk, the groups who only arrived and settled in Borneo in the past millennia or so. This, however, was overturned as soon as it became clear the great extent to which these cuisines have been sown into this island's culinary fabric, seams fading, even melting away, at points. The Javanese is one such group. They established contact with Borneo since the days of the Srivijaya and Majapahit empires and migrated over in thick swathes with the Madurese under the Dutch-initiated *transmigrasi* in the early 20th century. Their influence rings clear as bells in many foods in Kalimantan, especially those prepared by the Banjarese, from *soto* and *laksa* to certain *wadai* (or *kue*).

There are also the Southern Chinese, namely the Hakka, who mined for gold in the areas around Bau, and the Foochow, encouraged by James Brooke to migrate over and work in farms along the Rajang in Sarawak. Both parties brought with them their respective cuisines that though distinct generously overlap, sharing dishes of chicken, pork and noodles laced with rice wine or rice wine lees. One such dish, *huang*

jiu ji, chicken braised with ginger and sweet, straw-coloured rice wine, has become a favourite among many Dayak groups in Sarawak and Sabah.

There are also the Bugis who have been moving to these parts from Sulawesi from as far back as the 17th century, after the fall of Makassar. Their contributions assume the form of rice gruels flecked with corn and banyam (*barobbo*), sago dumplings swimming in pools of aromatic broth (*kapurung*) and twice-fried flattened bananas (*sanggarak pappe*). And of course mention must be made of the Iranun, Suluk, Kagayan, Ubian and Bajau, whose earliest ancestors are believed to have migrated southwards from Mindanao and the Sulu Archipelago centuries ago. They brought with them sunlit dishes of flaked stingray, soups of burnt coconut and steamed cakes of tapioca. Being given the opportunity to learn more about the foods of the last group has been especially fulfilling, somehow serving as a coda to research I started nearly a decade ago, the findings resting in my Philippine book, *Milkier Pigs & Violet Gold*.

TAMU

To study a cuisine is to attempt to understand people, so a book about the food of an area is ultimately a window into the lives of its residents, both past and present, where my role is merely that of a medium, a channeller of ideas and voices. This rings especially true here, as it could not have been born without the kindness and openness of others.

The bulk of Borneo's culinary treasures lie far beneath its lush surface. It is certainly true that a decent glimpse may be stolen at certain specialist restaurants, such as those run by Kelabit in Miri, Lundayeh in Kuching, Kadazandusun in Kota Kinabalu and Ngaju in Palangkaraya, establishments I have had the fortune to visit, whose owners I have had the privilege of speaking with. But for the unfiltered, undiluted spirit required for this slow-simmering assembly, I had to travel away from the big cities and glittering coasts and head towards the island's infuriating heart, where nature dictates diet and one's wit survival, where the forest is both the grocer and pharmacy, where a trespasser may still be extinguished by a venom-laced dart. It would have been folly to show up uninvited or unprepared, and access to such areas would have been impossible without the assistance, enthusiasm, even involvement, of kindred spirits.

The auspices were not always in my favour. Shortly after touching down in Kota Kinabalu for my first proper research trip, my guide was struck by Hantavirus Pulmonary Syndrome and had to be hospitalised for a week. Excursions to Papar, Kundasang and Ranau, along with meetings to establish a network of contacts to

facilitate future trips, were dashed, and what had already seemed like an immense –
and entirely self-imposed – undertaking, suddenly felt insurmountable. Crestfallen,
confused and lost, I reached out to Pison Jaujip, whom I had only met on Instagram,
through his wonderful page *@ropuhanditanakwagu*. Without hesitation, he agreed to
accompany me, and in the days that followed, I found myself visiting his family's rice
mill on the fringes of Kota Belud and shopping at my very first *tamu* in Tamparuli.
There, I was introduced to several species of wild durian and fern, the dried, liquid-
sharpening, fruits of *Garcinia forbesii* and *tarap* leaf parcels holding treasures of sweet
ground corn and glutinous rice.

For centuries the *tamu* has been a venue for members of various ethnic groups
from different parts of the region to gather and barter. In today's context, they are
best described as farmer's markets, those in cities usually relegated to unprepossessing
concrete boxes tucked in among the urban sprawl. Unlike markets, however, *tamus* are
usually open for only a few days a week, beginning their trade at a wicked hour and
bereft by the time lunch has descended. I have visited many other *tamu* since, such as
those in Bintangor, Donggongon and Kudat. Indeed, any trip to Sarawak, Sabah and
Brunei would be incomplete without at least one such pilgrimage.

It was only rather recently that I discovered the word *tamu* exists across the
Malaysian border, though attached to a slightly different meaning. Over a breakfast
of *bubur pedas* in Singkawang, in West Kalimantan, Chef Yudha Pramanto, who has
since become a dear and fierce friend, shared with me that in Indonesian, *tamu* means
"guest". It then struck me, like a thunderbolt, that there did not exist a more fitting
title for this book, not just because it highlights my place in this foreign world, but
for the invitation it seems to warmly connote, an invitation that I, and the people by
whom I have only been enriched, rather excitedly wish to extend to you.

I had been warned about travelling to Sarawak in January. From November to February, the monsoon rains liberally water the East Malaysian state, together with most of West Borneo, giving it the dampness of a summer pudding, though unfortunately none of its lusciousness. Despite this technically being the tail-end of the season, the past week in Kuching has been a tale of aqueous mornings, cigarette-stained clouds and dimmed foliage. Mist hugs the bases of hills and mountains like woollen scarves around necks at Christmas. What this phenomenon provides in terms of mystique and romance it judiciously balances by casting the safety of motorists to the winds.

It is another early morning for me in the capital city. The hour is several minutes shy of seven and I am already where I begin most of my culinary investigations, deep in the bowels of a market. Today, I am not alone but in the voluptuous company of Amy Ting, to gather the wherewithal for dinner at her house later this evening.

Little melamine saucers cover sections of the rude cement floor, an army of bright, retro-hued discs lit with calamansi, candy-coloured bird's eye chillies, rumpled tomatoes and sweet-looking shallots. Some bear winged beans and black ear fungus that look as if they were recently freshened with Evian Mist.

Each section of this plant-based parade has been marked by gauchely arranged rectangles of cardboard, likely ripped from boxes, prices blaringly inked in marker pen. Sometimes the marker is left at the scene of the crime. On my maiden trip here, I found the contrast between life-giving bounty and cold, haphazard signages rather jarring but have since learned to accept it as a bit of a cultural quirk. As a Kuchingnite friend once joked, "they serve to remind you that this is Borneo."

We find large rattan baskets spilling over with *buah dabai*, their skins dusty purplish-jet, their pale yellow sepal wounds like cyclopean panther eyes, glaring at us. *Canarium odontophyllum* is very much a seasonal treat, arriving and disappearing with the big rains. The Hokkiens call it *or-kana*, "black olive", which has more to do with its taste than any true botanical connection with *Olea europaea*.

Dabai is unpalatable in its raw state, sappy and tongue-itching. A brief immersion in hand-hot water does the trick softening it, but getting the temperature right is tricky business. Too hot and they will be tough and uncooperative. Too cold and nothing will happen. What divas they are. In Bicol, Philippines, the pili nut, which is of the same genus, is given the same treatment, the result called *tinolang pili*. I know a friend who "cooks" his *dabai* by chucking them in a plastic bag and leaving it under the sun, or in the back of a warm car, for several hours.

While scalded *pili* is dipped into *balao*, Bicolano fermented *Acetes*, *dabai* is sprinkled with salt or dressed in dark soy sauce, sugar and, for those craving heat, sliced bird's eye chilli. You suck and ingest the creamy, pale primrose flesh, which has the flavour of artichoke and banana heart as well as texture – though a tad more fibrous than either. As with most fruits, its seed is to be expelled, although the kernel hidden within it can be boiled and consumed. Given its limited availability, Chinese cooks make the most of their haul by preserving them with salt or dark soy, pounding and adding their fermented, deep puce, flesh to woks of fried rice.

Amy's eyes fall upon compact Styrofoam nurseries of *midin*, young specimens of bracken fern, *Stenochlaena palustris*. These are elfin creatures, their stalks a deep, lacerating green, fine as wires, their fronds whipped into tight, fragile curls. It is heart-breaking to know they will not survive a night in the fridge. Amy buys half a kilogram, intent on frying them with garlic, shallots, chillies and a little nugget of chocolaty *belacan* (fermented shrimp paste), the best of which is said to come from Bintulu, further up the coast. This is the most popular treatment for *midin* in Borneo, transcending boundaries set by ethnicity. The vegetable fern *Diplazium esculentum*, known as *pakis* in several local tongues, is also thoroughly enjoyed this way.

An unkempt bundle of star gooseberry leaves (*Sauropus androgynus*), tamed by a rolled sheet of newspaper, finds itself quietly slipped into her shopping trolley. In Malaysia and Singapore, this is called *cekur manis* or *sayur manis*. Here, it is known as *cangkok manis*, *mani cai* and, perhaps most specific of all, "Borneo vegetable". After being massaged with salt and wrung to relieve them of bitterness, the leaves are fried with garlic, egg and a little chicken broth until they turn into a slippery, sweetly herbaceous, mess and the eggs seize into fine blossoms.

Over the course of the next half-hour, the shopping trolley gets fattened with soil-dampened fingers of black-and-red-skinned gingers, said to have been harvested in the wild; furry tongues of sand ginger leaf; a hacked-up *kampung* (free-range) chicken; shimmering grey prawns; and several packets of *bihun* (*bee hoon*), rice vermicelli. The last three ingredients play crucial roles in the star of tonight's feast: the local *laksa*. Close to every state in Malaysia has its own rendition of the noodle dish, and Sarawak is no exception, its contribution dulcet with coconut milk, gently honed with tamarind and invigoratingly spiced with coriander and cumin among other things.

There are various tales concerning its origins. One claims it was invented by a Teochew immigrant from Guangzhou, using just six ingredients; "lak" and "sa" sound like the Hokkien words for "six" and "vermicelli". Another suggests the concept was brought to the region after the Second World War by a Cantonese man who had previously lived in Indonesia. The consensus seems to be that it is a fairly recent addition to the state's culinary sphere, arriving at some point in the 1940s, and only becoming more widely consumed from the late 1970s when halal eateries and hawkers began serving it.

The vermicelli used for the local *laksa* also features in another highly popular dish, *belacan bihun*, accompanied by beansprouts, cured cuttlefish and century eggs, and drenched in a broth trilling with dried shrimp and the obvious fermented shrimp paste. Shavings of coconut sugar (*gula Melaka*) and a dollop of tamarind water are added to achieve the desired sweetness, acidity and tang. While the availability of *laksa* seems state-wide, it is uncommon to find *belacan bihun* beyond the thresholds of Kuching.

THE HAKKA

Elsewhere in the market, we come across fat bundles of coriander, lemon basil and mint. These, combined with mugwort and green tea leaves, sometimes Oolong, also available here, form the basis for the opaque, emerald liquid central to *lui cha*, "thunder tea", so named for the noise emitted as the herbs are reduced to a pulp with a pestle and mortar.

Lui cha is linked to the Ho Po, a subgroup of the Hakka people. Although the exact year the first Chinese came to Borneo remains undeterminable, records show that labourers from the Southeastern coast of China set sail for West Borneo during the mid-18th century to work in the gold mines for the sultans. This was the seed for the first *kongsi*, a new overseas Chinese organisation that would come into being in subsequent decades. It has also been documented that the vast majority of labourers who worked in the gold mines around Bau in the early 19th century were of pure Hakka ancestry. The continual migration of their relatives and clansmen to Sarawak has resulted in the Hakka comprising approximately a third of the state's Chinese population, residing primarily in rural areas surrounding Kuching.

For the most part, Sarawakian Hakka fare is strikingly similar to its West Malaysian counterpart. Commonly found in coffee shops and food courts are dishes like *yong tau foo*, stock-blanched vegetables stuffed with a paste of pounded fish; *zhu jiao chu*, pig trotters braised with ginger and black vinegar; and *huang jiu ji*, chicken braised with ginger and sweet, pale gold, glutinous rice wine. Prepared without salt, the trotters and chicken are two good examples of "confinement dishes", food consumed by mothers to aid the physical recovery of their post-partum bodies.

There is one Hakka dish however, also associated with confinement periods, that seems to be unique to Sarawak, in particular Kuching, and that is *manuk kacangma*. The star ingredient is the titular *kacangma* or motherwort, *Leonurus cardiaca*, a kind of mint with a bitter, herbal taste made more pronounced by dehydration – *kacangma* is only ever used dried. The leaves are warmed in a pan and crushed, as is an astonishing quantity of roughly grated ginger, both of which are then added to a heatproof bowl with a jointed *kampung* chicken, toasted sesame seed oil and yellow glutinous rice wine. A steamer does the remaining work. While women under confinement have to consume this boldly unseasoned, it may be eaten by others with saucers of sugar and salt.

While the majority of Hakkas historically lived on the outskirts of Kuching, the mercantile Hokkiens, the other major dialect group in this part of Sarawak, mostly resided in the city. The situation is quite different today. It is now common to find urban areas occupied by both parties, as well as other dialect groups, such as the Henghua, Hainanese, Teochew, Foochow and Cantonese, all of whom are considered minorities in Sarawak. Interestingly, one of these minority groups is responsible for one of Kuching's most well-known and beloved dishes, and it is this that lies on the cards for breakfast on this ominous-skied morning.

DRY MIX

A short drive smoothly conveys us from the market to a coffee shop, from one brand of chaos to another. Amy and I wade through the sea of ravenous early risers towards a marble table flushed against a fabulously grimy, white-tiled wall, a large fan whirring throatily above us. Amy heads for the counter to place our orders while I do my part and space out, watching life unfold around me.

Dimpled glass mugs of *kopi* are perfunctorily ferried from counter to various tables, the dark columns of liquid lined with floors of condensed milk. Near the entrance, plumes of steam rise rapidly from an aluminium pot so large it could house several litters of kittens, while a mere metre away, plastic-protected hands are tearing at mounds of fine, straw-coloured noodle crammed against the glass window of a cabinet, a laminated sign bearing the word "*kolo*" spelled out in engine-red tape.

Amy soon returns with two plates, each bearing a mop of those fine noodles, their colour dimmed from blanching, topped with slivered *char siu* and verdant segments of *choi sum*, accompanied by bowls of clear broth and boiled wantons. According to my host, the wheaten strands were dressed in lard, soy, white pepper, chicken powder, crisp-fried shallots, a dash of the ubiquitous monosodium glutamate and a heady daub of chilli sauce.

Compared with the Sarawak *laksa*, *kolo mee* seems an even newer addition to the Sarawak repertoire. As ever, creation myths abound and one claiming that it came from a Cantonese cook seems the most plausible, as the dish is ineluctably similar to the Cantonese *wanton mee* – it was probably derived from it. *Kolo* comes from *gon lo*, which in Cantonese means "dry mixed".

The noodles used in Sarawak are marginally thicker than most of the fine egg noodles (*mee kia*) back home, at times possessing a shoddy perm. They also seem to be devoid of lye (or contain it in undetectable amounts). There is a joy-inducing springiness about them, and a modicum of bite, but there is no serious crunch nor soapiness. I know Singaporean and West Malaysian friends who fly boxes of the stuff back with them for their family and friends.

On our way out of the *kedai kopi*, we greet families applying themselves to plates of what appears to be a kind of *hor fun*, a tangle of wide, soy-dimmed, rice noodles, cuttlefish and prawns, drenched in a thick, reddish sauce, streaked with egg blossoms. This, Amy tells me, is another, if unseemly, Kuching institution, *tomato kueh tiaw*, with quintessential tomato-iness supplied by dollops of ketchup and tomato paste. Its template is believed to be *wat tan hor fun*, wok-seared rice noodles napped in a gravy thickened with cornstarch and egg. Again, a rather famous Cantonese idea.

Innumerable versions of this spice paste exist throughout Sarawak. Some are throbbing with cumin, some are devoid of fennel. Some insist upon dried shrimp. Some add fermented shrimp paste (*belacan*) for a prick of fetid pungency.

REMPAH SARAWAK LAKSA

MAKES APPROX. 900G

FOR THE SPICE POWDER
25g raw peanuts, skinned
20g cumin seeds
50g coriander seeds
15g fennel seeds
1 tbsp black peppercorns
3 star anise
4 candlenuts
2 nutmegs
8 cardamom pods
6 cloves
30g dried red chillies
25g sesame seeds

FOR THE WET INGREDIENTS
125g shallots, peeled
50g garlic cloves, peeled
125g galangal, peeled and sliced
6 red chillies, sliced
10g dried red chillies, softened
  (page 520)
3 lemongrass stalks, tender
  portions only, sliced

TO COOK
250ml vegetable oil
1 tbsp salt
25g coconut sugar, shaved
  (page 524)
2 tbsp caster sugar
250ml tamarind water (page 524)

1 Preheat the oven to 180°C. Place the peanuts on a small roasting dish and toast for 10 minutes or until fragrant and light gold. Tip these into a medium-sized bowl.

2 In a medium-sized frying pan over medium heat, dry-roast the cumin, coriander and fennel seeds, black peppercorns, star anise, candlenuts, nutmegs, cardamom and cloves until aromatic and lightly coloured. Add these to the peanuts.

3 Break the dried red chillies into the frying pan and push them around over medium-low heat until they deepen in colour and crisp up slightly. Be cautious as they burn easily. Add them to the peanuts and spices. Do the same for the sesame seeds, toasting them in the pan until golden. Let these cool down, then blitz in a coffee or spice grinder into a fine powder. Tip into a bowl and stir in 200ml water to obtain a thick paste.

4 In the cosy blender, grind the wet ingredients in batches, adding a little water if necessary. You want this as smooth as possible.

5 Heat the oil in a large saucepan over medium heat. Once hot, add the paste of wet ingredients. Fry for several seconds, lower the heat, and continue frying, stirring constantly, until fragrant and a richer red, separating from the oil. Add the paste of roasted spices and fry for 5 minutes over low heat to awaken it, stirring to prevent burning. Add the salt, coconut and caster sugars and tamarind water. Continue frying, stirring yet again, for another 15-20 minutes or until you get a rich chocolate-brown paste veiled in red oil. Cool, decant into a jar or some such container and chill until you need it. (I make a huge batch, divide it into packets and freeze these for future use.)

I recommend making the soup, taking it up to the addition of the coconut cream, a couple of hours before eating time. Its flavour profile develops and fattens as it rests, which will enable you to season it more judiciously and calmly later on.

In the Eighties, the most common herb with which to embellish this *laksa* was coriander, in particular its fine sprouts, and it is these that I have used here. Of course, regular coriander may be used, as may sawtooth coriander. Even mint.

SARAWAK LAKSA

SERVES 8

FOR THE SOUP
750g medium shrimps
1kg chicken bones
400g chicken thighs, skinned
3 litres water
1 portion (900g) Sarawak laksa
   paste
400ml coconut cream
Salt, sugar and tamarind water
   (page 524), to taste

FOR THE OMELETTES
3 eggs
Pinch of salt
A little vegetable oil

TO SERVE
400g rice vermicelli (*bihun*)
200g beansprouts, picked over
A handful of coriander sprouts
Calamansi limes
Sambal belacan (page 495)

1 Remove the shells and heads of the shrimp but leave their tails on. Devein the shrimp, put these in a bowl and keep in the fridge for now. Fry the shells and heads in a large saucepan over medium heat until coral and redolent of hot beaches. Add the chicken bones and thighs and water. Bring to a boil, cover and simmer for 1 hour, removing the thighs at the 45 minute-mark.

2 Remove and discard the chicken bones. Blend the shrimp heads and shells with the stock in batches in a liquidiser, then crush through a fine mesh strainer into a large pot; you should get approximately $2\frac{1}{2}$ litres' worth and any deficit may be made up with water. Bring to a boil over medium-high heat and stir in the *laksa* paste. Lower the heat, cover, turn the heat down to its lowest setting and simmer for 30 minutes.

3 Meanwhile, shred the meat off the chicken thighs. Make 2 thin omelettes by lightly beating the eggs with the pinch of salt and frying these into thin discs in a lightly oiled 23cm frying pan over medium heat. Roll these up and slice into $\frac{1}{2}$cm ribbons. Set aside.

4 When the gravy has had its 30 minutes, add the coconut cream and simmer for another 10. Adjust seasoning with salt, sugar and tamarind water. It should taste especially emphatic as its intensity will be diffused once it is poured over the noodles.

5 Remove the deveined shrimp from the cold. Bring a large pot of water to a boil and cook the rice vermicelli according to the packet's instructions. Drain thoroughly, rinsing them under a running tap and divide among 8 serving bowls. Bring the gravy to a boil, then add the deveined shrimp. Once these curl up and go opaque, turn off the heat and ladle the gravy over the noodles. Adorn with the shredded chicken and omelette, beansprouts and coriander sprouts. Serve with calamansi limes and *sambal belacan*.

This is one of the most common vegetable dishes one will find in Sarawak and Sabah.

As you weigh the leaves, you will undoubtedly think I have made an error: it is a veritable mound. But once you rub them with salt to expel their bitter juices and cook them, all you end up with is a modest bowlful.

SAYUR MANICAI

SERVES 4

250g star gooseberry leaves
2 tsp salt
4 tbsp vegetable oil
3 garlic cloves, finely chopped
75ml chicken stock
3 medium eggs, lightly beaten

1 Roughly tear the star gooseberry leaves and place them in a large bowl. Rub them with the salt and leave for 5 minutes, by which time they would be damp, having released their bitter juices. Squeeze them to expel these juices, then wash thoroughly to rid them of surfeit salt. Give the leaves a final squeeze to dry them and set aside.

2 Heat the vegetable oil in a wok over high heat. Shoot in the chopped garlic, stir with a pair of tongs or chopsticks until fragrant and lightly coloured, then add the prepared leaves. Continue frying, stirring until they are oil-slicked, then pour in the chicken stock. Once the leaves are tender and the liquid has evaporated, create a well in the middle of the heap and pour in the eggs. Leave for a few seconds, then gradually stir the egg into the leaves, among which they should set into fine blossoms. Taste and adjust seasoning with salt.

This is also mighty fine prepared with *kangkong* (water convolvulus) or *pakis* (fern fiddleheads).

MIDIN GORENG BELACAN

SERVES 4

250g young bracken ferns
3 tbsp vegetable oil
4 garlic cloves, peeled and minced
1 red onion, peeled and sliced into
    thin half-moons
2 heaped tsp fermented shrimp paste,
    grilled (page 522)
¼ tsp salt
¼ tsp sugar
100ml anchovy stock (page 520) or water
1 red chilli, sliced on a gentle bias

1 Pick over the young bracken ferns, snapping off any tough portions. Cut into 4cm sections.

2 Heat the oil in a large frying pan over medium-high heat. Once hot, add the garlic and stir until light gold, which will take just a few seconds.

3 Stir in the red onion and the moment they acquire translucency, add the fermented shrimp paste. Stir it into the oil, then add the salt, sugar and anchovy stock. Once the liquid bubbles, add the *midin* and red chilli. Lower the heat slightly and cook until the *midin* is tender. Taste and adjust seasoning with salt.

The most common (if not only) way to eat *dabai* is to immerse them in bowls of hand-hot water, covered, for 15 minutes. This takes their skins further into blueish-black territory and softens their flesh, which would have attained the texture of braised banana hearts. Then dip into saucers of viscous dark soy, sugar and sliced bird's eye chilli and suck on them salaciously.

Because *dabai* season is short, stretching from December to February, there is a great need to preserve them. Wash and dry the fruits and drown them in sterilised jars of brine. I use a ratio of 1 litre water to 35g salt, sometimes adding a swig of dark soy. The jars are then kept in a cool, dark place for at least 2 months. (I have kept some for as long as 10.) The flesh of the fermented fruits are then ground into a thick paste and contained in bottles that will gladden the interiors of fridges for up to 3 months. The most common function of this magenta condiment is to tint and titillate woks of fried rice.

NASI GORENG DABAI

SERVES 4

FOR THE SPICE PASTE
4 shallots, peeled
3 garlic cloves, peeled
2 red bird's eye chillies
1 tbsp dried shrimp, soaked and drained (page 521)

TO FRY
8 tbsp vegetable oil
75g dried anchovies, washed and dried
¼ tsp salt
5 tbsp fermented *dabai* paste (see above)
500g cold cooked jasmine rice

1 Crush the spice paste ingredients with a pestle and mortar into a fine pulp.

2 Heat half the oil in a large wok or concave frying pan over medium heat. Once hot, but not smoking, add the cleaned dried anchovies. Lower the heat and fry until they are pale gold and lightly crisp. Remove them to a sheet of kitchen towel where they will crisp up further.

3 Discard the oil in the pan, replacing it with the remaining half. Get it hot over medium heat, as before, then add the spice paste. Fry for a minute, then lower the heat and cook, stirring until it splits and deepens in redness, about 3-4 minutes.

4 Stir in the salt and fermented *dabai* paste, until the latter turns a subfusc kalamata purple and begins to separate from the oil. Add the cold jasmine rice and fry, turning the grains in the dark paste with a metal spoon or frying slice, until they are evenly coated and begin to crackle deliciously. Fling in the fried anchovies and remove from the heat. This is lovely eaten with fried eggs.

This is truly an acquired taste, almost hot with ginger and searingly herbal with the titular *kacangma*, dried motherwort. It should be noted that this recipe contains salt, which is not usually done for mothers under confinement.

A sweet yellow rice wine is ideal here. (A recipe for it rests on page 169.)

MANUK KACANGMA

SERVES 8

30g dried motherwort leaves
1½kg free-range chicken, jointed into ten
    pieces
3 garlic cloves, peeled
4 shallots, peeled
30g young ginger, peeled and sliced
3 tbsp vegetable oil
200ml yellow rice wine
450ml water or light chicken stock
Salt

1 Toast the dried motherwort leaves in a deep frying pan. They will crisp up slightly, lose some of their dull greenness to brown and adopt a warming aroma, one of roasted rice and hot wood. Crush these leaves into a fine powder with a pestle and mortar and set aside. Do not wash or keep your frying pan just yet; you will need it again.

2 Prepare your steamer, filling its lower compartment with plenty of water and bringing it to a rolling boil over high heat. Rub the chicken portions with a generous smack of salt. Pound the garlic, shallots and young ginger into a rough paste.

3 Once your steamer is on the cusp of boiling, begin the cooking. Heat the oil in the recently used frying pan over medium-high heat. Once hot, add the paste and fry until fragrant and lightly coloured.

4 Add the chicken and fry, shaking the pan and stirring, until well sealed and lightly browned. Stir in the crushed motherwort and half the yellow rice wine. Cover, reduce the heat and leave to steam for 5 minutes.

5 Pour in the water or stock and once this boils, tip into a deep heatproof dish. Gingerly lower this into the waiting steamer, cover and cook for 45-60 minutes or until the chicken is very tender. Splash in the remaining rice wine, cover and give it a final 3-4 minutes.

IN
FOURS

It is barely eight of the clock and already the Weather Gods have been out achieving some remarkable things. A sky devoid of feather. A bright, brutal sun. Air so still you could slice it with a knife. In the *kedai kopi* where breakfast is to be had, every patron has a countenance buttered with discomfort and annoyance, their shirts plastered onto slouched backs. Another hour in this meekly ventilated space and I may have to be scraped off my stool.

The mood improves with the arrival of a pair of shallow bowls. While *laksa*, *kolo mee* and *belacan bihun* have received international acclaim, little has been spoken about *mee jawa*, one of the most popular breakfast foods among Sarawakian Malays. Frankly, there is nothing not to like: egg noodles, chunks of boiled beef and a solitary hardboiled egg, doused in a sauce with the colour and viscosity of roast gravy. While the beef stock forming its base, rich and muscular, imbues the liquid with comforting familiarity, the presence of certain ingredients refracts it through an undeniably Southeast Asian prism. These, according to Zainal's uncle, include dried shrimp, fermented shrimp paste (*belacan*), chilli, lemongrass, ginger and galangal and dry spices, like cumin, coriander and fennel seed. Its appearance, and to some extent taste, seems reminiscent of the *mee rebus* in Singapore and West Malaysia. I read somewhere that as with *mee rebus*, it is sweet potato that is responsible for *mee jawa*'s spoon-coating sauce. "My uncle always used cornflour, though. And it's not supposed to be sweet," Zainal tells me, pushing a bowl in my direction. "His recipe also featured coconut milk".

A native to Kuching, Wan Zainal relocated to Brunei in the early years of adulthood. His father is of Arab descent while his mother identifies as Bruneian Malay. It has been suggested that most Sarawakian Malay families possess Bruneian Malay or Minangkabauan roots, their seafaring ancestors living in stilted dwellings along rivers in Sambas and Sarawak.

Embarrassingly, when this book was in its early stages of planning, little thought was given to the Malay foods of Sarawak. During the first couple of research trips, most of the Malay foods I encountered in eateries were, though delicious, not terribly unique; no matter how celestial the *roti canai*, how smoke-suffused the satay, how fragrant the *nasi lemak*, these were items that were common in Singapore, throughout West Malaysia and beyond. The same can be said of the repasts I had in Malay households in the state that, bar the odd *lempeng*, *kari* and *sambal*, were dominated by halal renditions of Chinese and Iban dishes. It was only later that I learned that the most colourful and compelling creatures prefer to reserve their time for festive occasions.

A wedding *pengilan* makes a fine example. Guests are led to sheets of white cloth laid across the floor of a tented space and invited to sit in fours around strategically placed platters of food that are to be consumed communally. This manner of serving and eating is known as *saprah*, the cloth on which the activity occurs *kain saprah*. The spread for a wedding *pengilan*, nearly always a lunch, is lavish, vividly hued and something of a carnivore's dream. Meat is viewed as an extravagance and its rare appearance at daily Malay meals is compensated on these occasions where it assumes many delectable forms.

There are several standards. A *kurma* or *kari* made of chicken or beef. *Daging masak hitam*, beef cooked in dark, sweet soy, that Malay families of Arab blood would enrich with pureéd raisins. *Dalca tulang*, a tamarind-honed, coconut-sweetened stew of beef marrow and yellow split peas. *Sambal goreng perut*, ox tripe redly cooked with crushed chillies, shallots, garlic and lemongrass. The supporting cast may include *keceni nenas*, sometimes mystifyingly referred to as pineapple chutney; an *acar* of salted fish, bamboo shoots or jewel-bright preserved fruit; and unifying plates of *nasi minyak*, rice cooked with ghee and several breath-sweetening spices. If the couple were especially well heeled, the menu may also include a shoal of *ikan terubok*, bronzed in hot oil, to be eaten with smudges of *sambal belacan* and squirts of calamansi lime juice. "It happens to be quite expensive," Zainal says of the *toli shad* as the final strands of yellow noodle vanish from my plate.

Kain saprah are also laid out for religious functions, like *tahlil* (prayers for the departed) and *doa selamat* (thanksgiving), with the food only consumed after *asar*, late afternoon prayers, or *isyak*, the final prayer for the day. The food served at these events are usually simple and unfussy. While the menu is never fixed, it often involves discs of turmeric-tinted glutinous rice (*pulut kuning*) sprinkled with grated coconut either cooked in coconut sugar (*inti*) or lit with crushed spices (*sambal nyiur*). There may also be saucers bearing tiles of buttery, Western-style, cake. Before departing, the most senior at the *kain* would take it upon themselves to oversee the *kandong* – the distributing and packing of leftovers.

Another occasion that spells great feasting is Hari Raya Aidilfitri, which marks the end of the fasting month. It is often as grand as those for weddings, and although the menu is seldom fixed, there seems to be a pool of dishes from which to choose, one that also applies to the Muslim Melanau and Dayak communities for whom this event is also significant. The aforementioned *daging masak hitam*, *keceni*, *dalca*, *nasi minyak* and *acar* are examples of some. There may also be *rendang*, that hauntingly spiced and much-too-famous beef preparation; *ayam masak panggang*, braised-then-grilled chicken with coconut milk, cumin and white pepper; and *lemang*, cylindrical cakes of glutinous rice and coconut milk cooked in the hollows of bamboo poles placed near a fire.

But it is sweets that consummate the occasion. For a whole week following Aidilfitri, coffee tables in Malay households will find themselves weighted down with several sorts. There may be sweets glassily set with agar-agar, such as the eponymous *agar-agar guling*, for which hard-set sheets of jelly are rolled into batons and turned in granulated sugar, served sliced into the most mesmeric, retro-looking, medallions. There may be steamed ones, like *kek hati pari*, the fruit-studded "stingray liver" cake, a title inspired by the severe shade of brown caused by caramel and bicarbonate of soda, as well as *kek lumut*, "green moss cake" and rainbow-hued *kek lapis bumi*, both essentially vessels for the combined goodness of malt chocolate powder, condensed milk and coconut jam. A keen participant will be *kek lapis*, derived from the Indonesian *lapis legit*, made with sensational quantities of egg yolk and butter and cooked layer by layer beneath a hopefully efficient grill. It is hard on the nerves but effortless on the palate.

In recent years, many commercial *kek lapis* have, with the help of E-numbers and clever slicing techniques, had their plainly striated cross-sections transformed into mosaics and stained-glass windows. They make rather popular (and eye-watering) souvenirs. And although it has become increasingly common to find even the regularly hued ones cast in an array of flavours, from chocolate to prune, mocha to cheese, as recently as the Eighties there were only two versions, *kek lapis rempah*, the "original", fragrant with cinnamon and nutmeg, and *kek lapis masam manis*, that has papery, carmine, hawthorn wafers embedded in between their many leaf-fine layers.

Not all cake is destined for general visitor consumption however. The especially effortful and aesthetically pleasing ones serve as *kueh palak meja*, "head of the table cakes", reserved for special guests. While households may differ in opinion as to which cakes make the cut, those fortunate enough to have *kek wilmina* gracing their tables will undoubtedly have it fulfil this role.

Kek wilmina is a layered confection of egg pastry, first shaved into fine noodles, a sugared rubble of roasted peanuts, condensed milk and a generous amount of butter. Mostly served during engagement dowry ceremonies and Hari Raya, it has become something of a rarity among Sarawakian Malays, not only due to the effort required, but also because the recipe has always been closely guarded by the Sharifahs, all of whom are of Arab ancestry – its striking resemblance to *baklava* made with *kadaif* is not coincidental.

Despite not being a festive occasion, rather a period of reflection, penitence and community, Ramadan itself has some treats to offer. For *sungkai*, the breaking of one's fast, there is the balm that is *bubur roti kapal*, made by allowing *roti kapal*, Osbourne biscuits, to unwind in a warm bath of coconut milk and coconut sugar, perfumed with pandan leaves. This is very much something that is enjoyed at home.

There will be several stalls at Ramadan bazaars dedicated to *bubur pedas*, whose appeal is undermined somewhat by its ingredient list that reads as if it were the result of a Kondo-triggered kitchen clear-out. It includes meat, usually chicken or beef, or shrimp; vegetables, such as yardlong beans, potatoes, aubergine, carrot, *midin* and *daun singkel* (*Premna*); herbs like turmeric leaf and Vietnamese mint; and other items like dried beancurd, black fungus and coconut milk. This excludes the crucial *bumbu* or spice blend, which is a riot of garlic, shallots, dried chillies, lemongrass, galangal, ginger, turmeric, coriander seed, black and white peppercorns, cinnamon, cloves, cardamom, star anise and dry-roasted rice and coconut.

There will certainly be vendors selling *kueh* in its many magical forms. While most of their kind are available all over the whole of Malaysia, one that seems unique to these parts is *kueh cangkir*. This unites two layers of steamed pudding, for want of a better term, one flavoured with coconut sugar (*gula Melaka*), another of pandan, in dainty Chinese teacups. *Cangkir*, in Sarawakian Malay, means "cup".

There too would be *renjis*, also spelled *renjes*, once known in these parts as *kueh tuala*, essentially a fine, lacy crêpe or pancake, struck gold with turmeric. The Indonesian word *renjis* means "to sprinkle", a likely nod to how the batter lands on hot metal. It is known more commonly throughout Malaysia and Singapore as *roti jala* and *roti kirai*, *roti* as in bread, *jala* meaning "net" and *kirai* the circular motion the cook's hand has to assume for these pancakes to be produced.

Besides serving as a mop for pools of *kari*, *renjis* may be used as a vehicle for boisterous fillings and rolled into fat, stout cigars. Today this usually means potatoes liberally doused with curry powder, sometimes boosted with minced meat. I recently found out that in Sarawak the pancakes were once commonly filled with a fragrant potpourri of dried shrimp, shallots, chilli and lemongrass. This, unfortunately, has become a rarity.

Or as it is known throughout most of West Malaysia, *serunding kelapa*.

SAMBAL NYIUR

MAKES APPROX. 300G

15g garlic cloves, peeled
20g shallots, peeled
2 lemongrass stalks, tender portion only
15g ginger, peeled and sliced
8 dried chillies, softened (page 520)
15g dried shrimp, softened (page 521)
125ml vegetable oil
300g grated coconut
½ tsp salt
1 tbsp sugar

1 With a pestle and mortar, pound the garlic, shallots, lemongrass, ginger and softened dried chillies and dried shrimp into a fine paste.

2 Heat the oil in a large wok or deep saucepan over medium heat. Once hot, add the spice paste. Fry for a minute, then lower the heat and continue frying until it is a darker red and has just split from the oil. Stir in the grated coconut until evenly coated in the red paste. Lower the heat and continue cooking, stirring regularly, until the coconut has dried out and the resultant mixture feels light and is milk chocolate in colour. Stir in the salt and sugar, cook for a further minute, then take off the heat. Using a rolling pin or pestle, lightly crush the *sambal* in its pan, breaking the filings into a faintly oily, more cohesive, rubble.

PULUT KUNING

MAKES APPROX. 600G

500g glutinous rice
1 tsp turmeric powder
4cm turmeric (root), sliced
1 lemongrass stalk, bruised
200ml coconut milk
   (second extract; page 521)
75ml coconut cream
½ tsp salt
2 tsp sugar

1 Wash the glutinous rice three times or until the water runs clear. Put in a bowl with the turmeric powder. Cover with 2cm of water and leave overnight or at least 8 hours.

2 The following day, prepare your steamer, lining the perforated compartment with muslin. Drain the rice and place it with the turmeric root and lemongrass in the compartment. Conceal with the excess muslin, cover and steam for 30 minutes. Stir in the coconut milk, then steam for another 25 minutes or until tender. Finally, fork in the coconut cream, salt and sugar and steam for a final 5 minutes. The turmeric root and lemongrass are to be discarded.

Modern recipes for *mee jawa* seem to include crushed boiled sweet potatoes, which makes it taste awfully like *mee rebus*. This version, heavily based on a recipe supplied by my friend Wan Zainal, who learned it from his father, uses cornflour as a thickening agent and is sweetened with just a little light brown sugar. It also uses a rich beef stock, a thrilling combination of spices, fermented shrimp paste, a highly unusual addition, and a glug of coconut cream.

The amount of sauce this recipe makes will likely stretch to feed 8 people (in the Southeast Asian context, anyway). As with all recipes here however, I have erred on the side of caution and stipulated 6. You could make the sauce a day in advance, but only add the coconut cream the following day before serving.

Mee jawa is often consumed with small fried squares of firm tofu (*tau kwa*) and sliced red chillies. I find the beef, beansprouts, Chinese celery, hardboiled egg and fried shallots really quite sufficient, but if you feel it still needs some bulking up, by all means do so.

MEE JAWA SARAWAK

SERVES 6

FOR THE BEEF STOCK
500g beef shortribs, cut into 4cm
    chunks
1½ litres water
4 spring onions, roughly cut
4cm ginger, bruised
1 star anise
4cm cinnamon stick
6 cardamom pods, bruised
4 cloves
1 tsp black peppercorns
1 tsp white peppercorns
1 tsp salt

FOR THE SPICE POWDER
2 tsp cumin seeds
1 tbsp coriander seeds
1 tbsp fennel seeds
1 tsp turmeric powder

FOR THE SPICE PASTE
75g shallots, peeled
20g garlic cloves, peeled
40g galangal, peeled
2 lemongrass stalks, tender
    portions only, sliced
6 dried red chillies, softened
    (page 520)
15g dried shrimp, softened
    (page 521)
1 tbsp fermented shrimp paste,
    grilled (page 522)

TO COOK
100ml vegetable oil
100ml coconut cream
1 tbsp light brown sugar
2 tsp cornflour, made into a slurry
    with 2 tbsp water

TO SERVE
700g fresh yellow egg noodles
75g beansprouts
25g Chinese celery leaves,
    chopped
3 hardboiled eggs, halved
1 quantity fried shallots
    (page 524)

1 Begin by making the beef stock. Place everything in a large saucepan, bring to a boil over high heat, then lower the heat, cover and simmer for 1½ hours or until the meat is tender. Scum that has accumulated on the surface of the stock should be removed with a slotted spoon.

2 Meanwhile, lightly toast the whole spices for the spice powder in a frying pan over medium heat. Once aromatic and lightly coloured, tip into a mortar and cool slightly before crushing into a powder with a pestle. Tip into a small bowl, then mix in the turmeric powder and 3 tbsp water, to obtain a loose paste. Also use this time to pound the ingredients for the spice paste with a pestle and mortar until fine and smooth. Alternatively, grind the ingredients in a cosy blender, adding a little water if necessary.

3 When the stock is ready, strain it through a sieve or colander into a large jug. You should have approximately 1.2 litres. Of the solid contents, discard everything except the shortribs. Harvest their meat, breaking them into bite-sized pieces and set aside.

4 Heat the oil in a large saucepan over medium heat. Once hot, add the spice paste. Fry for several seconds, lower the heat, and continue frying, stirring, until it is fragrant, a deeper red and separating from the oil. Add the paste of ground spices and fry for 2 minutes over low heat, stirring to prevent burning. Pour in the stock, summon to a boil, then cover, reduce the heat to its lowest and simmer for 30 minutes.

5 As the sauce bubbles, tend to the serving components. Blanch the egg noodles in boiling water, drain and rinse under a cold tap. Divide them among 6 shallow bowls. Pick over the beansprouts, chop the Chinese celery leaves. Hardboil, peel and halve the eggs if you have not. I shall assume that you have already fried the shallots.

6 When the sauce's simmering time is up, stir in the coconut cream, light brown sugar and cornflour slurry. Simmer for just 2-3 minutes, until it thickens and arrives at a velvety consistency. Taste and adjust seasoning with salt and sugar.

7 Nap the bowls of noodle with several ladles of gravy – you want a splash pool. Divide the harvested beef, beansprouts, Chinese celery leaves, hardboiled eggs and crisp-fried shallots among them. Serve at once.

Daging masak hitam may be considered standard Malay fare, but what makes this version so unusual is its inclusion of black raisins, ground into a paste and dolloped into the dish towards the end of its time on the stove.

DAGING MASAK HITAM

SERVES 4-6

FOR THE SPICE POWDER
1½ tsp cumin seeds
1 tbsp coriander seeds
2 tsp fennel seeds
2 tsp black peppercorns
4 cardamom pods
4cm cinnamon stick
6 cloves
2 star anise

FOR THE SPICE PASTE
60g shallots, peeled
20g ginger, peeled
20g galangal, peeled
2 lemongrass stalks, tender
   portions only
6 dried red chillies, softened
   (page 520)

TO FINISH
100ml vegetable oil
750g beef shank meat,
   cut into 4cm pieces
4 tbsp sweet soy sauce (*kecap*)
½ tsp salt
650ml water
125g black raisins

1 In a dry frying pan over medium heat, toast the ingredients for the spice powder until fragrant and lightly coloured. Remove from the heat, cool and blitz in a coffee or spice grinder into a fine powder. Tip into a bowl and stir in 100ml water. Set aside.

2 Pound the ingredients for the spice paste with a pestle and mortar. Alternatively, blend them in a cosy blender, adding a little water if necessary.

3 Heat the oil in a large saucepan over medium heat. Once hot, add the spice paste (of wet ingredients). Fry for several seconds, lower the heat and continue frying until fragrant and a deeper red. It should also begin to split from the oil. Add the paste of toasted spices and fry for 2 minutes over low heat, stirring to prevent burning.

4 Raise the heat. Add the beef, sweet soy and salt. Fry for 1-2 minutes to seal the meat. Pour in 500ml of the water, bring to a boil, then cover, reduce the heat to its lowest and simmer for 2 hours or until the meat is tender.

5 Towards the end of the cooking time, place the black raisins in a small saucepan with the remaining 150ml water. Simmer for 5 minutes, so they soften and swell, then blend the contents of the saucepan into a smooth paste. Stir this into the meat and simmer for 5 minutes without a lid so the sauce thickens slightly. This tastes even better the following day.

Also known as *chutni nenas* or *pacheri nenas*, this is not unique to Borneo or Sarawak. In fact I provided a recipe for it in *Bekwoh, Stories from Peninsular Malaysia's East Coast.* My decision to include it here is not just due to this version being different – the pineapples are cut into rough slivers and little sugar is used – but because the *daging masak hitam* on page 52 truly blossoms in its company.

KECENI NENAS

SERVES 4-6

2 tbsp vegetable oil
1 garlic clove, peeled and chopped
2 shallots, peeled and thinly sliced
2cm ginger, peeled and finely grated
½ tsp turmeric powder
2 star anise
3 cloves
4 cardamom pods
4cm cinnamon stick
400g pineapple flesh, cut into
    rough slivers
2 tbsp demerara sugar
½ tsp salt
2 tbsp water

1 Heat the oil in a deep frying pan over medium heat. Once hot, add the garlic, shallots and ginger and fry until light brown and aromatic.

2 Add the turmeric powder, star anise, cloves, cardamom and cinnamon. Push them around for about 30 seconds to cook out their rawness, then stir in the pineapple, demerara sugar, salt and water. Lower the heat, cover and cook until the pineapple is tender without having disintegrated, stirring occasionally. It should have also deepened in colour.

Although its title literally translates into "oil rice", do know that the fat used is usually ghee, clarified butter, sometimes margarine. More than vague, the title is also inadequate, for there is no mention of the spices that perfume it nor any suggestion of the garlic, shallots and ginger that ground and fatten it.

While not everybody uses basmati rice, I think its grains, svelte and sharp, are perfect here. The presence of evaporated milk may raise several brows, but it is both traditional and necessary, affording a truly unique salinity and richness. (Some cooks add a dollop of condensed milk, too.) And while it is normal to cook the turmeric with the other spices, I sizzle it in a little ghee and sprinkle it over the rice towards the end of its cooking time. The uneven tonality, the various shades of yellow amid the white, is glorious.

NASI MINYAK

SERVES 4-6

250g basmati rice
1 tbsp ghee, plus 1 tsp
1 garlic clove, peeled and crushed
3 shallots, peeled and thinly sliced
2cm ginger, thinly sliced
2 star anise
3 cloves
4 cardamom pods
4cm cinnamon stick
¼ tsp salt
500ml light chicken stock or water
3 tbsp evaporated milk
¼ tsp turmeric powder

1 Wash the basmati rice three times or until the water that runs from it is clear. Place in a bowl, cover in 2cm of water and set aside for 30 minutes.

2 Drain the rice thoroughly, allowing it to sit in a sieve suspended over a bowl. Heat 1 tbsp of the ghee in a medium saucepan over medium heat. Once hot, add the garlic, shallots and ginger and fry until light gold and aromatic.

3 Add the star anise, cloves, cardamom and cinnamon. Push them around for about 30 seconds, then stir in the drained rice and salt. Fry the rice in the spiced ghee for another 30 seconds, then pour in the stock or water and evaporated milk. Give it a final stir, then cover, turn the heat down to its lowest setting and allow the rice to cook for about 20 minutes or until the grains are tender. Resist the urge to stir.

4 Meanwhile, heat the remaining 1 tsp ghee in a tiny saucepan and add the turmeric powder to it. Let it sizzle for several seconds, then remove from the heat.

5 Uncover the rice and sprinkle over the turmeric-tinted fat. Cover and leave to cook for just 2 more minutes, then take the pan off the heat and leave it to stand covered for another 30 minutes before fluffing the grains with a fork.

I have to thank Wan Zainal for kindly sharing his grandmother's recipe with me. This manner of eating *renjis* has grown elusive in Sarawak, where it used to be commonly made by the Malay community. In recent decades, the fragrant filling of dried shrimp, lemongrass and Chinese celery has been replaced with a more convenient one of spiced potatoes, which is the version I have encountered in Peninsular Malaysia. So far, I have not found a Malay cook from the peninsula who has heard of this sprightly, potpourri-like, filling. The Malay community in Thailand do make it, however, usually with coriander instead of Chinese celery.

I use Tipo '00' flour as I think it produces the finest pancakes. Some cooks add a dash of limestone water or slaked lime (*air kapur*) to make the pancakes crisp, but I omit this. Worry not about the confetti-like filling falling out of the holes in the *roti*. Most of it rather magically manages to remain contained.

RENJIS

SERVES 4-6

FOR THE FILLING
100g dried shrimp, softened
  (page 521)
1 red chilli, sliced
4 red bird's eye chillies
5 tbsp vegetable oil
4 shallots, peeled and thinly
  sliced
5 lemongrass stalks, tender
  portions only, thinly sliced
¼ tsp salt
¼ tsp sugar
3 tbsp Chinese celery leaves,
  chopped

FOR THE PANCAKES
225g Tipo '00' flour
¼ tsp salt
½ tsp turmeric powder
2 eggs, plus 1 yolk
325ml water
100ml coconut cream

1 Begin with the filling. Pound the softened dried shrimp into a rough floss with a pestle and mortar. Tip out into a bowl, then crush the regular and bird's eye chillies into a rough paste. Scrape this out into a separate bowl.

2 Heat the vegetable oil in a large frying pan over medium-low heat. Add the shallots and fry until light gold and fragrant, then remove to a plate. Add the pulverised dried shrimp and fry until fragrant and reddish brown, about 7-10 minutes. Stir in the chillies and fry for another 3-4 minutes to remove any rawness. Return the fried shallots to the pan and add the lemongrass, salt and sugar. Fry for 2 minutes, so the lemongrass softens and infuses the shrimp with its perfume. Finally stir in the Chinese celery leaves and remove from the heat. Taste and adjust seasoning with salt and sugar if need be.

3 Now make the *renjis* batter. Combine the flour, salt and turmeric powder in a large mixing bowl, then whisk in the eggs and yolk, water and coconut cream until a smooth batter is obtained. Cover and leave to rest for 30 minutes.

4 Lightly lubricate a 22cm frying pan with vegetable oil and put it over medium heat. Stir the *renjis* batter, then scoop a little of it into a *renjis* or *jala* funnel. The presence of holes makes it difficult to be precise about how much to fill the funnel with, so just ensure that the batter covers the perforated base by approx. $\frac{1}{2}$cm. Do not overfill it as the pressure results in thick lines and splodges. When the pan is hot, swiftly bring the funnel over it. Holding the implement about 2cm above the hot metal, steadily move it in concentric circles, rotating your wrist as you do so, thereby covering the pan with a lacy net. Once the batter sets, which should take about 30 seconds, slide it off onto a large tray with a palette knife or spatula lined with a sheet of greaseproof paper. Make all the *roti* this way, keeping them separate between sheets of greaseproof paper.

5 Gingerly take one *roti* and arrange it on a work surface. Sprinkle 2 tbsp of the dried shrimp filling over its middle, then fold it into a rectangular parcel in the same way one would a duvet. Do the same for the rest of the *roti*.

As with the previous few, I am indebted to my friend Wan Zainal for this heirloom recipe.

The fine noodles here are made from a yolk-laden pastry, which makes them both tender and rich, and are layered with a startling quantity of sweetened crushed peanuts. Some people add raisins to the rubble, others hawthorn flakes, to stave off monotonous heaviness. Here, the only hint of fruit is the customary arrangement of glacé cherries lighting up its roof.

Traditionally, *kek wilmina* is baked large and tall, as with the other 8-10 cakes weighting down coffee tables at Hari Raya open houses, although these are usually only cut for special guests. The cake this recipe produces is small but will still feed up to a dozen generously. Moist, sumptuous and slightly crumbly, it is to be savoured in dainty slices with cups of hot bitter coffee.

KEK WILMINA

SERVES 10-12

FOR THE NOODLES
8 egg yolks
Pinch of salt
Approx. 225g Tipo '00' flour

TO FINISH
200g skinned peanuts
75g caster sugar
¼ tsp salt
Approx. 150g unsalted butter
Approx. 150g condensed milk
8 glacé cherries, halved

1 Before embarking on the noodles, toast the peanuts in an oven preheated to 180°C for 15 minutes or until aromatic and golden. Cool completely before blitzing into a fine-ish rubble – you want a healthy combination of fine confetti and sand – in a food processor, then tip into a bowl and mix in the salt and sugar. Set aside.

2 In a large bowl, lightly beat the egg yolks with a pinch of salt. No major aeration is required: you just want them to lighten a shade. Incorporate the flour in batches until you get a smooth, supple but firm dough that should leave the bowl clean. Cover and leave it to rest for 30 minutes.

3 Meanwhile, melt the butter and let it cool slightly. Halve the glacé cherries and give them a rinse-and-dry if they are too wet with syrup. Lightly butter the interiors of a 15cm round cake tin that is approx. 6cm in height and comes with a removable base. Line its base and sides with greaseproof paper, ensuring its collar rises approx. 1cm above its walls.

4 Now for the fun bit. Divide the lump of dough into 8 balls. With a pasta machine, roll these into 1mm-thick sheets, arranging them haphazardly on a large tray. Lightly dust both the tray and their surfaces to prevent any sticking. Then, with a fierce knife and great patience, cut these sheets into smaller sections and then ravage these sections into thin noodles. The exact length of the noodle is unimportant, but you want most of them to be approx. 4cm long. As you slice, convey the noodles to a fresh tray and toss with a little flour to prevent them from sticking. (The whole process takes me about 20 minutes to complete.)

5 Preheat the oven to 170°C. Clear your work surface and have about your person the noodles, sweetened peanuts, melted butter, condensed milk, glacé cherries and of course the lined tin.

6 Divide the noodles into 7 portions. On the floor of the prepared tin, place 2 of these portions, spreading them evenly but without compacting them. Drizzle with 2-3 tbsp melted butter, sprinkle over a quarter of the sugared peanuts. Gently level the surface, then drizzle over 2 tbsp condensed milk. Lay over 1 portion of the noodles, then 2-3 tbsp melted butter, another quarter of the sugared peanuts and 2 tbsp condensed milk. Repeat this noodle-peanut layering process two more times, finishing with the final 2 portions of noodle, spreading them out. This final layer should rise just above the walls of the tin (hence the need for the high collar.) Try to make this layer as beautiful and even as possible as it is the only one guests will see. Give the tin several light taps against the work surface to expel any pockets of air.

7 Brush its surface generously with butter – you want all the strands oiled – paying particular attention to the edges. Arrange over the sliced glacé cherries in whatever configuration you fancy. I usually go for a simple but smart cross.

8 Sit the tin on a baking tray. (Do not skip this as oil tends to bleed from the tin.) Bake the *kek* on a centre shelf for 40-45 minutes. The roof should be pale gold, its edges a-sizzle with melted butter. It should have also shrunk slightly. Leave to cool completely before freeing the cake from its ring, then slip it off the base with a cake slice onto a serving platter. Its collar of baking paper may be removed, but I recommend leaving the one lining its base on. If you have let it cool overnight and returned to it to discover that it has somehow adhered to the tin despite all that contraception, do not stress: simply sit the tin on a ring of timid flames at the stove. The aroma of melted butter and a soft sizzling sound are indications that the cake has been released from the metal. (If you catch yourself whinging over any butter that may have leaked onto your stove top, please rethink your priorities.)

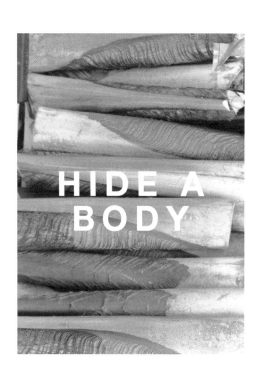

Somewhere along the highway between Sarikei and Sibu, Kew Ming has decided that he has found the perfect place for lunch. He manages to find a sandy spot on one side of the road, most of the stretch devoured by wild vegetation. "It's a hike, but we'll get there", he says. The 10-minute trek that follows takes us past a string of vegetable and food stalls operated by Iban folk to a piece of property that seems to be in the process of finding its voice.

The gaping toolboxes on the edge of the tarmac afford a succinct explanation for the property's ramshackle state. Even a diplomat would struggle to tag "roadside shack" onto it, a playground of plank, timber, chip and nail from which over a dozen wood columns rise. Half of these columns, situated further from the road and closer to the foliage, demarcate a space with timber flooring, similar to those found in saunas. In the middle of this floored area rests a solitary plastic stool, and on it, a circular tray, one of those used for pints and pitchers in pubs, its generous lining of newspaper – several crumpled pages of *The Borneo Post* – obscured by an inferno of bird's eye chillies.

Put out to sun, these bullets of scarlet, jade, mustard and orange may be the property's chief source of colour but are not its sole source of vibrancy: where the timber flooring surrenders to warm, grass-blotched earth, lies the kitchen, with a patchwork of corrugated plastic and tarpaulin propped up by the remaining wood columns serving as shelter.

The kitchen is open and skeletal. It comprises a deep barbecue pit facing the road; a sink and counter running perpendicular to it, almost encroaching the shrubbery; and a lopsided wooden picnic table, where I find Kew Ming and Ling Huong sitting, already wearing glazed expressions. I lower myself gingerly onto one of the table's benches, meekly anticipating a splinter. Here, the three of us sit, quietly baking in the beige heat, like potatoes roasting in too low an oven. Both my companions soon begin scrolling through their phones while I, a closet arsonist, find myself entranced by the smoke dancing wildly from the barbecue pit occupied by a row of bamboo culms (*buluh* in Malay, *ruas* in Iban) resting against one side of it.

Every *ruas* has a scroll of banana leaf shoved down its opening. A compact, severe-looking, cook watches over the culms, fanning the coals. A portly, affable lady, who reveals herself to be the cook's wife, hoists several hefty trays of darkly grilled meat – wild boar, possibly? – onto the sink-side counter and informs us that lunch will be a little longer. While his wife orders another tepid Coke, Kew Ming and I stroll back down the road to the short string of stalls we walked past earlier. "Let me show you what the Ibans eat,", he says, smiling.

The Iban are a people indigenous to Borneo, their population concentrated in Sarawak, West Kalimantan and Brunei, and divided into subgroups based on the geographical location of their settlements. Those living further inland, near Sri Aman, for instance, are known as Balaus, those from Serian district, Remuns, those from Lundu, Sebuyaus, those from Miri, Rajang, so on and so forth. These groups are united by tongue, though numerous dialects are spoken, all of which are mutually intelligible.

They got their name "Sea Dayaks" from the British who first encountered them in the 16th century as many were once fishermen and pirates, living in settlements along main tributaries. They are more popularly known, however, for being headhunters, although this tradition has been all but gradually extinguished since the arrival of the Europeans in the mid-19th century. They have since worked on pepper farms and rubber, cocoa and oil palm plantations. They were all once animists but many have converted to Christianity through interactions with missionaries from the Western World.

When travellers think of the Iban, images of their wooden longhouses, *rumah panjai*, immediately spring to mind. Sadly, few of these magnificent structures remain. The few that do are mostly reserved for tourism-related purposes, like homestays or museums. Now, even in rural areas, Ibans live in concrete houses.

The stalls are leanly stocked, as expected. It is early afternoon, after all, and these vendors begin their trade in the wee hours of the morning. Occupying the counters and floors of a couple of them are several bundles of palm shoots or hearts, *umbut* in Malay and *upat* in Iban. Besides being easily mistaken for kindling wood, palm hearts are important sources of fibre, vitamins and minerals.

Several kinds of palm shoots are eaten in Sarawak (and throughout Borneo). *Umbut asam paya* or *asam kelubi* (*upat maram*) comes from *Eleoidoxa conferta*; a species of palm with a predilection for swamps. *Umbut kelapa sawit* are the shoots from the oil palm *Elaeis guineensis*; *umbut kelapa*, the coconut palm; *umbut rotan* (*upat lalih*), rattan palms belonging to *Calamoideae*, adored for their bitterness; and *umbut nibong* (*upat pantu*), the wild sago palm, *Eugeissona utilis*, whose oleaginous, fibrous fruits are favoured by macaques, squirrels and rats.

Skinned and cut into thin chips, any of these may be stir-fried with garlic, dried anchovies (*ikan bilis*) or added to all kinds of soupy stews and coconut-mellow Malay *gulai* (spiced braises) with pointy *tengkuyu* (*Pachychilidae*), chubby *siput remoi* (*Ampullariidae*) and dark malachite *kedunkang* (freshwater mussels) collected from rivers. In the past, the Ibans, as with all indigenous folk, would prepare them simply, by boiling them in water with salt and bulking them up with whatever meat, game, fish or fowl they happen to have to hand. Many in the villages still cook this way, while those in the city, exposed to other cuisines and techniques, would augment the aromatics, use stock and even brown their meat.

On the counter of a fruit stall, manned by a jubilant Iban gentleman, calamansi limes, tight clusters of *asam paya*, *asam kembung* and *terung Iban* bulge out from plastic baskets blue, pink and red. Also known as *buah kelubi*, *buah asam paya* are the fruit of the above mentioned *Eleoidoxa* palm. They wear red snakeskin armours and are skimpily enrobed in a soft fragrance reminiscent of longans. Beneath their skins lie crisp, cream-coloured segments of astringent flesh that make a wonderful *sambal* when pounded with chilli, sugar, salt, dried anchovies and *belacan* (fermented shrimp paste). The fruits may also be pickled in brine, unpeeled, or added to soupy braises, especially ones with fish, that require souring.

The dark-skinned *asam kumbang*, literally meaning "sour beetle", is a wild species of mango, *Mangifera quadrifida Jack*. It has a rather peculiar scent that hovers between that of ripe mango and jackfruit. Its golden flesh is succulent, fragrant and slightly sour, rather like a greengage. It is most commonly eaten as is or pounded, as with *asam paya*, into *sambals*.

Terung Iban or *terung Dayak*, botanically *Solanum ferox*, is a species of nightshade. They are most commonly found smooth, lustrous and gamboge, as they are now, in their prime, though at times you will spot some fiercely wearing their aspirations of aubergine and tiger's eye when they are less ripe. They come in a variety of sizes, some as small as clementines, some as large as grapefruits. These magnificent creatures possess flesh the hue of palest persimmon and a colony of sour-tasting seeds; their third name is *terung asam* — sour aubergine. In these parts, segments will be pushed into stews of chicken or wild boar, fragrant with turmeric leaves and torch ginger. It features in a simple soup that is hugely popular among the Ibans, resonant with wafery, barky shards of *ikan lumek salai*, essentially smoked Bombay duck or bummalo, which happens to be sold at another stall here, alongside various kinds of smoked catfish: walking catfish (*keli*); *lajong*, a pink-skinned catfish known as *supak* by Ibans in Bintulu; *Dimena* catfish (*lais*); and *Ariidae* catfish (*duri*; *mayong*).

There are other forms of preserved fish here. Salted stingray (*pari*); the salted bodies and roes of yellow puffer fish (*buntal kuning*), *Xenopterus naritus*; and plastic pouches of *kasam ikan*, fish fermented in ceramic jars with rice, salt and several blades of *daun bungkang* (*Syzygium polyanthum*), a flavour enhancer, much like monosodium glutamate. Sultan fish, tilapia and silver rasbora (*enseluai*) are several choice candidates for *kasam ikan*, but the one sold here is made with white-fleshed wallago (*tapah*), a species of catfish harvested from the Baram and Rajang rivers. The salty, soured fish is usually relished as is, perhaps with some crushed bird's eye chilli, but it can be fried in oil with garlic and shallots. Sharp on both snout and palate, *kasam* can be tricky terrain for the uninitiated. Game such as wild boar may also be fermented like this, as may *ensabi*, a mustard green endemic to Borneo. *Pekasam ensabi* is quite delicious as a salad, with slices of sweet white onions tossed in, or stir-fried with *buah empayang* (*Pangium edule*; *buah kepayang*). The mud-brown, rough-skinned fruits have to be steeped in water overnight, boiled for several hours, peeled, sliced and soaked yet again, to expel the toxins that can result in wooziness – the root of the Malay phrase *mabuk kepayang* – or, in some extreme cases, death.

This *salai* and *kasam* stall is also selling leis of *ciping*, the yeast tablets with which cooked glutinous rice may be fermented into *tuak*. I am more familiar with its distilled kin, *langkau*, sometimes called *arak pandok*, "cooked spirit", having experienced an especially cruel hangover on my last trip to Sarawak.

We trudge back up the road and arrive at the roadside eatery in time to witness a bamboo culm hoisted from the coals. As the severe-looking Iban cook removes the banana leaf scroll from the *ruas*, his wife explains the cooking procedure to Kew Ming. Chicken pieces were massaged with crushed onions, garlic, ginger, galangal, a dash of monosodium glutamate and several blades of *daun bungkang* before getting loosely packed into the *ruas* with a halved torch ginger bud and a shattered lemongrass stalk. In went a fat bunch of tapioca leaves, then a trickle of water, and finally the rolled-up banana leaf, that served as a stopper. Sections of *upat tepus* (*Etlingera coccinea*) are sometimes added, bringing with it notes of ginger, coriander and Vietnamese mint. This high-pitched ingredient is often called, in these parts, "wild ginger". The loaded *ruas* was then plunged into the bed of white coals at an angle maintained by the wall of the barbecue pit and abandoned for an hour or so.

The tangle of *pucuk ubi*, now deliciously soft and sodden, is extricated with a pair of tongs and popped into a bowl, or rather, a repurposed ice cream container lined with plastic. With a heave and a ho, the culm is promptly lifted, tilted and juggered with gusto, producing the most salacious squelches. Out plops the chicken pieces with unceremonious abruptness, followed by a deluge of broth. That St. Vincent tune "Birth in Reverse" begins to ring in my head.

The chicken gets distributed among three melamine bowls of rice, which the cook urgently encourages us to dampen with the broth. The waft of aromas return energy to our fatigued bones. I take a spoonful. I find it remarkable, though by no means surprising, that a simple chicken soup can bring so much joy and comfort even in 36°C heat.

The way in which the chicken was cooked is known as *pansuh* in Malay, *lulun* in Iban. It is perhaps the food the Ibans are best known for. This cooking method is used by many indigenous ethnic groups, alongside grilling, fermenting and stewing, as mentioned earlier. And as with many forms of primitive cooking, there are hardly any rules. Besides chicken, wild boar, fish, crabs, river shrimps and bivalves, even vegetables, from yams to wild banana hearts and *sayur sukar* to *kesindau*, may be cooked *ala pansuh*, retaining many, if not all, of the aforesaid seasonings. Preparing *paku kubuk* or *uban*, hairy sword fern (*Nephrolepis biserrata*) with torch ginger in this manner is supposed to be extremely beneficial for lactating mothers.

THE LAND FOLK

While the Iban were once called "Sea Dayaks", the Bidayuh got the title "Land Dayaks". The term is a broad canopy for numerous indigenous ethnic groups occupying settlements in the Sungai Sarawak basin, particularly in areas of southern Sarawak like Kuching, Lundu, Bau, Serian, Penrissen, Padawan and Siburan, and West Kalimantan, around Sanggau. Most of these communities have their own language and dialect that are, unlike the Iban, not mutually intelligible, and so *Bahasa Melayu* is the tongue that unites them.

The Bidayuh were once predominantly hunters and hill paddy farmers. Some of those who lived in the northern areas of Sarawak were involved in the harvesting of edible bird's nests from the Niah and Tatau limestone caves.

Like the Iban, many Bidayuh have turned their backs on longhouse life, electing instead to forge careers in the towns and cities. From a purely personal standpoint, the feature of their longhouse with the most intrigue has little to do with structure or layout, but the use of durian trees as markers of territory. To discover that the odoriferous fruit lands in many of their foods should thus not come as a surprise. Although its flowers are cooked when in season, fried with garlic and a stock of dried anchovies, the durian's richest contribution to Bidayuh cuisine assumes the form of *tempoyak*, made by combining their flesh with salt and leaving it to ferment for several days. The Bidayuh of Bau would call this substance *tipuyak* and, as with most of their counterparts elsewhere in the state, fry it with spices and aromatics (*tipuyak goreng*), sometimes adding slivered pork or wild boar. They also add it to *sambals*, which they call *samal*, and soups like *ponas*, a broth thickened with grated tapioca, flavoured with *belacan* (fermented shrimp paste) and nutritionally enhanced with whatever vegetables they have to hand.

Besides durian, the Bidayuh apply their fermentation know-how to tapioca shoots, combining them with both salt and cooked rice. The result, *tebah duon bandung*, is best sautéed in a little oil before eating as part of a meal. They also make their version of the Iban *kasam*, which the Bidayuh from Serian call *gires*, those from Bau *tobah*. The Bau Bidayuh have a more elaborate version of this, called *kau'*. Fish is first cured with sea salt for several days to rid them of moisture and undesirable odours. They are then piled into a pot (*gobuk*), topped with tapioca leaves or those of *bikolamp*, a thorny creeper, to prevent insects from laying eggs on them. The pot is then sealed with layers upon layers of *buant* and *manah* leaves that are secured by bark from the *boyuh* tree. After three to four days, the fish is removed, rubbed inside and out with warmed powdered rice, returned to the *gobuk*, this time for a month or so, until the bones of the fish prove no challenge for the milkiest of teeth.

As with the Iban, the Bidayuh primarily cook things in bamboo culms over charcoal. On an afternoon spent with the Bidayuh at Anna Rais longhouse, I learned of *saam*, equivalent to the Iban *lulun*. Into bamboo culms, chunks of chicken (*siok*), pork (*ayo*) and wild boar (*daang*) are pushed, together with handfuls with lemongrass (*serai*) and ginger (*raii*), while bony pieces of wild duck (*tik*) receive prudent helpings of black peppercorns, torch ginger (*sekarih*) and Indonesian cinnamon (*kayu manis*). Handfuls of rice (*tubi*) may be added along with the meat, or just cooked alone. Glutinous rice cooked this way with coconut milk (a relatively new ingredient in the Bidayuh arsenal) results in *lemang*, their more fascinating counterpart being *trambuok*, where pitcher plants (*periuk kera*), serve as individual steamer-bound vessels.

Like the Iban, the Bidayuh are especially keen on alcohol. For *tuak*, rice wine, soaked glutinous rice is first cooked in water tinted with caramelised sugar, not just for burnished hue, but for an additional layer of flavour. After being cooled, the rice is then mixed with crushed yeast and large quantities of water, conveyed to urns and kept in cool, dark places for up to four months before getting distilled. Another moonshine is *tepui*, derived from sugarcane juice. This is sometimes made from *topoi* which, according to one brewer at Anna Rais, requires assistance from shards of *keh* bark so that it fizzes properly and yields something potent.

The Bidayuh have a fondness for flour made from sago palm pith, using it before it has been completely dried into a powder. In this slightly damp state, it is known as *tepung sagu basah*. The Bidayuh of Singai pack this substance into bamboo tubes and cook it over fire to yield *rotung*, fry it into thin pancakes called *kubar*, and stun it with boiling water to get *linut* or *selinut*, a substance so gluey that it has to be wrangled with a pair of thin bamboo chopsticks – neither fork nor spoon seem amenable to it. Both filling and bland, it is treated like any other carbohydrate, as a canvas for other flavours to colour, served with *samal* and a broth fragrant with lemongrass and soured with *tipuyak*.

In truth, I have always associated *linut* more with the riverine-dwelling Melanau than the Bidayuh, although both groups are not the only ones in Borneo consuming it. The word Melanau, as with Dayak, is an exonym, one eschewed by the relevant party for centuries; the Melanau preferred "a-likou", meaning "People of the River". Unlike the Iban and Bidayuh, most of whom have clung onto their identities, the vast majority of Melanau have not only moved to larger town and cities, but assimilated into the fabric of the state's Malay community, going insofar as to identify themselves as such and converting from animism to Islam. Despite the large-scale dispersal of Melanau throughout Sarawak, Mukah remains the centre of their community.

Since ancient times, the Melanau have had a reputation for being skillful fishermen and excellent boat builders. Even prior to the arrival of Christianity and Islam, they celebrated *Pesta Kaul* at the end of April, marking the recession of the monsoon and the arrival of fishing season and voyages into the open waters. Legend has it that it was on such voyages that the Melanau first invented *umai*, as it was the only way to settle hunger pangs without sending their boats up in flames. Essentially a raw fish salad, *umai* is the most well-known Melanau contribution to Sarawak gastronomy. White-fleshed sea fish, like Spanish mackerel, even anchovies, are preferred, though shrimp and even cured jellyfish (*obor obor*), are welcome. The list of spices and aromatics that light up the traditional *umai* is standard, shallots, ginger, chillies, lime and the aforementioned *asam paya*. Modern day cooks like to jazz things up with torch ginger, roasted peanuts and coriander. *Umai* is usually distinguished from *umai jerk*, which is fish served sashimi-style, to be plunged into bowls of *sambal*.

During the monsoon, the Melanau make *pipus* or *pipuh*. For this, flaked fish meat is seasoned with crushed garlic, shallots, dried chillies, galangal, ginger and lemongrass, parcelled into nipa palm blades or banana leaves and cooked over hot coals. The Melanaus' expertise with fish extends to the realm of preservation too. They meticulously straighten their shrimp before sunning them – I thought I was being joked to when told – and make some of the sweetest, pucest, *belacan* in Sarawak.

The Melanau were once also growers of paddy, as well as sago, developing a palate for live sago palm weevil larvae (*siet*), combining sago flour and coconut milk to make airy biscuits of *tebaloi*, these days made by cottage industries in an array of sensational hues. They also turn the sago flour into pearls that, instead of being dried, are roasted in a large pan until crisp and sandpaper-hued. These are most commonly eaten with *umai*. *Sagu nyiur*, a finer version of these beads, enriched with coconut milk, is delectable with torpedoes of ripe banana.

The jellyfish seized in the waters off Kuching, Ulu Kuala Matu and Sematan are usually red (*Rhopilema esculentum*) or white (*Lobonema smithii*). After being cleaned, the celestial beings are pampered with a mixture of salt and alum (now considered toxic), sometimes bicarbonate of soda to encourage out moisture, which is then removed. The treatment is repeated several times before they are finally set out to dry into crinkly, crunchy pads. The entire process can take anywhere between 3-6 weeks.

Several species of jellyfish are available on the market and most should work in this salad. They come in varying degrees of saltiness and dryness, so it is best to check with your fishmonger on how to best treat whichever you have selected. The jellyfish I get from Kuching *tamu* comes already rehydrated, jiggling in a packet slicked with brine.

If you cannot find *asam paya*, simply add 2 more tbsp of calamansi juice.

This *umai* is at its best served chilled. Avoid leaving it to its own devices for more than 30 minutes however, as the jellyfish tends to continue releasing liquid, turning its turtleneck of thrilling flavours into a shapeless blouse.

UMAI OBOR OBOR

SERVES 4-6

200g cured jellyfish (see above)
2 garlic cloves, peeled
5cm young ginger, peeled
4 red chillies, deseeded
Flesh of 4 *asam paya* fruits
4 shallots, peeled and finely sliced
1 habañero chilli, deseeded and finely sliced
1 tsp light brown sugar
3 tbsp calamansi juice
Freshly ground black pepper
2 blades sawtooth coriander, finely shredded
Salt

1 Wash the cured jellyfish and steep in barely warm water for 4 hours, changing the water several times. Drain, rinse well and cut into thin slices. Place in a bowl.

2 Crush the garlic, half the young ginger, red chillies and *asam paya* into a paste. Finely sliver the remaining ginger. Stir the paste into the jellyfish, followed by the slivered ginger, shallots, habañero chilli, light brown sugar, calamansi lime juice and black pepper. Leave to stand for 5 minutes, then adjust seasoning with salt if necessary. Strew with the sawtooth coriander. The Melanau would serve this with baked pearls of sago.

Ponas may be prepared to varying degrees of thickness and with an expandable assortment of vegetables. I like mine barely spoon-coating, like those chicken soups and vegetable broths at old-fashioned Chinese wedding banquets, and healthfully virid with young tapioca shoots.

The dried anchovies I use here are about 2-3cm long and have been cleaned, gutted and split. (Not saying that you can't do these yourself, of course.)

PONAS

SERVES 6

100g young tapioca shoots
1 tsp salt
10g dried anchovies
2 garlic cloves, peeled and crushed
2 shallots, peeled and sliced
2cm ginger, peeled
2 red bird's eye chillies
2 lemongrass stalks, tender portion only
1 litre light chicken stock or water
2 tsp fermented shrimp paste,
   grilled (page 522)
110g tapioca, peeled weight,
   finely grated

1 Lightly bruise the tapioca shoots with the salt in a large pestle and mortar, or in batches in a small one. Place them in a bowl and squeeze out their bitter juices with gloved hands. Place the broken, wrung leaves in a bowl and set aside.

2 Rinse the dried anchovies in several changes of water, to rid them of dirt and excess salt. Drain well and spread them over a sheet of kitchen towel to dry out slightly. Place them in a small frying pan and lightly toast over medium heat so they crisp up and begin to smell warm and appetising, but without colouring.

3 Tip the anchovies into the mortar, then add the garlic, shallots, ginger, bird's eye chillies and lemongrass. Pound into a rough paste.

4 Bring the stock to a rolling boil in a medium saucepan over medium heat. Add the spice paste and the fermented shrimp paste. Let it boil for a further minute, then cover, reduce the heat and simmer for 10 minutes.

5 Stir in the grated tapioca and cook until it turns translucent and thickens the liquid. This should take just a couple of minutes. Finally mix in the tapioca leaves and let the mixture bubble gently for 3-5 minutes, or until the leaves are very soft, adding a little hot water (or stock, if you have extra) if the soup gets too thick.

To the Bidayuh, the title means "fermented durian fried with pork". It is still good without the pork, though functioning more as a condiment than dish.

Although *tempoyak* can be purchased from Malay vendors in markets in Malaysia and Singapore, it is easy to make at home. Combine 300g durian flesh – nothing too pricey – with 1 tbsp salt, mix well and pack into a suitably sized container. Seal and keep in a cool, dark place for 4-7 days. The durian would have exuded some liquid, loosening its palate-coating denseness. Its hoarse, boorish, character would have retreated somewhat as well, tempered, as one would expect, by a pleasantly alcoholic scent.

TIPUYAK GORENG BABI

SERVES 4

4 tbsp vegetable oil
125g pork belly, thinly sliced
3 garlic cloves, peeled
4 shallots, peeled and finely sliced
2cm ginger, peeled and thinly slivered
1 red chilli, finely sliced on a gentle bias
1 green chilli, finely sliced on a gentle bias
250g fermented durian (*tempoyak*; see above)

1 Heat the oil in a large frying pan over medium-high heat. Once hot, add the pork belly slices, frying until light gold and most of their fat has rendered down.

2 Add the garlic, shallots and ginger, and fry for a minute, until just fragrant, then add the sliced chillies. Fry until they soften slightly and release their warm, fruity aromas.

3 Add the fermented durian and fry until it deepens in colour, looking almost like butterscotch, begins to separate from the oil and loosely clings to the meat. Sprinkle in a little water if it has begun to stick to the pan. Taste and adjust seasoning with salt if need be.

The absence of a bamboo culm and a fire pit means this cannot technically qualify as *pansuh*. Still, it is a more than decent approximation, doable in the comforts of a modern kitchen.

Young fingers of tapioca shoot are ideal, but larger, broader blades may be used, although they would require a heavier bashing to break their fibres.

Etlingera coccinea is the scientific name for what is called *tepus* (or *upat* or *umbut tepus*) in Sarawak. Though intimidating in appearance and sound, I stick to this title for recipes throughout this book to avoid confusion, as its name changes from area to area. In its absence, replace it with a torch ginger bud or two.

MANUK PANSUH

SERVES 8

1½kg free-range chicken, jointed
 into eighths
½ tsp salt, plus more for seasoning
2 tbsp vegetable oil
1 red onion, peeled and sliced
4 garlic cloves, peeled and bruised
5cm ginger, peeled and crushed
750ml chicken stock
2 stalks *Etlingera coccinea*
2 fat bunches young tapioca shoots
Black pepper

1 Place the chicken pieces in a large bowl and massage in the salt. Set aside for 30 minutes.

2 Heat the oil in a saucepan over medium heat. Once hot, add the red onion, garlic and ginger and fry until aromatic and lightly coloured. Add the chicken pieces, stir well, then put on a lid and reduce the heat to its lowest. Leave the chicken to steam like this for 10 minutes.

3 Increase the heat to medium-high and pour in the stock. Once it boils, reduce the heat to its lowest once again, cover and simmer for 30 minutes or until the chicken pieces are just tender.

4 Meanwhile, make an incision along each of the *Etlingera* stalks and remove their tough outer casings. Keep stripping away layers of skin until you arrive at their pale, glossy, malleable cores. Cut these into 4cm segments. Lightly bruise the bunches of tapioca shoots with a pestle and mortar, just to break down some of their fibres.

5 Once the 30 minutes are up, add the *Etlingera* and tapioca leaves to the pot. Cover and simmer for a final 10-15 minutes until the leaves are lovely and soft. Taste and adjust seasoning with salt and pepper and eat with disgust-inducing quantities of rice.

The Iban have a deep fondness for this soup. Simple, elegant, spiky yet somehow delicate. *Ikan salai lumek*, bummalo smoked-then-dried into barky, craggy wafers, is the best smoked fish for the job, softening in the simmering liquid into juicy, cotton-textured splinters (in the best possible way). Hot smoked fish will work, I suppose, at least flavour-wise, but its final texture will be really rather different.

I once made a risibly big batch for a dinner party and was faced with a tub of leftover soup. The following day, I strained it, removing the solids, brought it to a feverish boil, then poured it over a mound of wheat noodles and a boiled egg, its yolk waxy and red. I applied myself to it in silent smugness.

SUP IKAN SALAI LUMEK

SERVES 6

4 shallots, peeled and finely sliced
3 garlic cloves, peeled and bruised
2 lemongrass stalks, bruised
1¼ litres chicken or pork stock
500g *terung Iban*, cut into 1cm slices
100g dried smoked bummalo, broken
  into shards
2 red bird's eye chillies, bruised
Salt

1 Place the shallots, garlic, lemongrass and stock in a pot and bring to a boil. Add the sliced *terung Iban*, cover and simmer for 10 minutes or until translucent and tender. Add the smoked bummalo and bird's eye chillies. Simmer for 5 minutes before seasoning with salt. The resultant soup should be sour, smoky and very slightly spicy, but clean on the palate.

As with the *sup ikan salai lumek*, this is a brilliant example of how a small number of modest, mid-toned, ingredients, may be united to create something both familiar and foreign.

The Bidayuh make a version with dollops of creamy, tangy *tempoyak* or fermented durian.

BABI TERUNG IBAN

SERVES 6

4 shallots, peeled and sliced
6 garlic cloves, peeled and crushed
1cm turmeric, peeled and crushed
3 tbsp vegetable oil
600g pork ribs
2 lemongrass stalks, bruised
1 torch ginger bud, halved lengthwise
1½ litres chicken or pork stock
500g *terung Iban*
6 red bird's eye chillies
1 turmeric leaf, roughly shredded
Salt, black pepper

1 Roughly pound the shallots, garlic cloves and turmeric root in a pestle and mortar. Heat the vegetable oil in a saucepan over a medium-high heat and add this rough paste, stirring and frying until fragrant. Stir in the pork ribs, cover, reduce the heat and leave to steam for 10 minutes.

2 Increase the heat and add the lemongrass, torch ginger and stock. Bring to a boil, cover, then reduce the heat once again and simmer for 1½-2 hours or until the meat is tender. Add the *terung Iban*, bird's eye chillies and turmeric leaf. Once the *terung Iban* has turned translucent and soft, adjust seasoning with salt and pepper.

FRUIT
AND
FLAME

My first afternoon in Sarikei is being spent in the abode of Ting Mee Hung, sister to my friend Kew Ming. The six of us – including the host and her two fine children – are seated around a disproportionately large dining table, its calcite-like top hosting a rattan basket bulging with *pulasan*.

There is something both mischievous and flamboyant about the little blighters, like sea urchins of the deepest crimson given a crew cut. The fruit came from this very estate, verily a fruit orchard run by Mee Hung's family for over forty years. At our host's instruction, we hold our fruits with both hands and give them a firm twist. Their scalps snap open crisply and neatly to reveal an orb of translucent flesh, a treasure of silver rose quartz, that we shall soon discover to possess a flavour reminiscent of lychee.

Pulasan, *Nephelium ramboutan-ake*, is of the same genus as the rambutan, many hirsute specimens of which hang redly and yellowly from a cluster of trees outside, their weighted branches infested with ants. Unlike the cultivated rambutan, however, the seed of the *pulasan* does not latch itself onto its flesh, leaving the joy of the latter's consumption unblemished.

The way in which we opened the fruit is apparently how the *pulasan* earned its name – *pulas*, in Malay, means "to twist". The Iban name for it is *buah ma*. In Kalimantan, it is called *meritam*. It is sometimes known as "forest rambutan", which can be misleading as there are numerous species of rambutan endemic to Borneo, especially in its northwestern area. One such species is the fading *buah redan*, that the Ibans call *mujau*, the Melanau *buak seriat*. What distinguishes *redan* from its more popular family members is its utter lack of hair: it is smooth, matte and scarlet. It is also diminutive, the size of a small grape, hiding sweet flesh beneath its cardboardy skin.

We work our way through the *pulasan*, dainty cups of warm chrysanthemum tea serving as lubrication. Our host Mee Hung cautions us against overindulging. "There is more coming. They are still being harvested." What mad privilege in this?

Kew Ming and I had not expected to make it to the orchard today, having been set back by a punctured tire on the way into Sarikei. A highly anticipated lunch of *kompia* had to be foregone and feebly substituted with packets of Jacob's cream crackers while we waited for help to arrive. I sat by the road, nibbling on the flaky, perforated tiles, dreaming of quaking pork and sesame-sprinkled ottomans, commonly nicknamed "Chinese bagels", the breath of the tandoor-like oven still on them. At one point, as if reading my mind, Meng decided to share that the breads have ancient origins, and that the supposed function of their central holes was to allow soldiers to string and carry them around their necks during voyages. I had not

known this but was not hugely comforted.

THE RAJANG

Kompia is a thoroughly Foochow speciality, brought over by migrants from Foochow prefecture in Fujian province. The earliest arrived in Sarawak around 1900, then part of the Brunei sultanate, at the invitation of White Rajah James Brooke and through the mediation of Fuzhou-born Wong Nai Siong. Over a thousand Foochow people – men, women and children – occupied the areas along the Rajang River, their numbers concentrated in Sibu, earning it the title "New Foochow". Unlike the other Chinese dialect groups, who were largely merchants and business owners, most, if not all, of the adult Foochow migrants were experienced farmers. Many continue to work in pepper, rubber, sago and oil palm plantations, vegetable farms and, in the case of Mee Hung, fruit orchards.

Today the Foochow comprise approximately a third of Sarawak's population, and their cuisine is one of the most sought-after and loved. Suffice it to say there is more to it than *kompia*. One of the most commonly eaten Foochow dishes must surely be *soo mee ang chiew*, a birthday staple of wheat noodles, fine as angel hair, in a clear broth the colour of oolong, with shiitake mushrooms and chicken drumsticks first cooked with red rice wine lees. A sedimentary byproduct of glutinous rice fermentation, the thick, carmine paste is core to *ang zao rou,* smothering chunks of pork belly before its steaming time, and also serves as a colouring agent for *pan ngee jeon*, a fermented condiment of small red freshwater crabs usually eaten with rice porridge.

The food found in the public domain, namely Foochow-run restaurants and hawker stalls, usually require more effort or more intense flames. The list includes *chao zhu mian*, stir-fried-then-braised yellow egg noodles with prawns, pork and choi sum, and *zao chai hoon hgan*, thick rice vermicelli in a clear chicken soup, flavoured with mustard leaves first preserved with red rice wine lees. There is also the unusual but comforting *ding bian hu*, for which rice slurry is poured around the edges of wok-borne pools of chicken broth, boosted with pork mince and black fungus. As the slurry creeps and slips into the vociferous liquid, it sets into ragged pieces of pasta. And of course there is the institution that is *kampua mee*, the Foochow version of *kolo mee*, the most significant differences between the two being the noodle and serving style. *Kampua mee* uses a slightly thicker, chewier noodle, seldom contains pork mince and is always served with bowls of clear soup bearing slices of pork liver.

Just as the basket of *pulasan* is depleted, the iron grills of the main door swing open. A pair of hulking workers spill into the living room, their thickly gloved hands heaving a colossal wicker basket abundantly lined with newspaper, bearing yet more spiky fruit, this time in the shape of two species of wild durian.

DURIAN DAYS

Both species of durian are yellow-skinned but of vastly different sizes. The larger one, the size of a soccer ball, is *Durio kutejensis*, sometimes referred to as *pakan*, *ukak*, *pantan* or *nyekak*. The other, nifty as a massage ball, and with pronounced, inch-long spikes, is *Durio oxleyanus*, cutely referred to as *isu* or *isau*.

The men expertly take their knives to the foreboding fruit, prising them open so their flesh-enrobed arils may be admired by everyone in the room. Those of the *pakan* are luscious, dripping with the most sensational shade of yellow. We help ourselves to their treasure. They have a mouthfeel firmer than any kind of durian I have tasted, seized somewhere between Turkish ice cream and avocado. It certainly has the mild sweetness of *Persea americana*, but with notes of ripe jackfruit and artificial butterscotch. The sharp, at times biting, voice so commonly associated with durian is a soft coo here. This is the durian for beginners. The Laughing Cow of the durian world – and in the best possible way.

The smaller *isu* has flesh that is more fiery-hued than the *pakan*, less Colman's mustard, more monk's robes, and also waxier, with the propensity to coat the roof of one's mouth. It has the most intoxicating bouquet as well. Its flavour profile is not too dissimilar to its large counterpart, but is pricked with a pleasing hint of bitterness that makes it taste mildly alcoholic.

There are many other wild varieties of durian endemic to Borneo. There is *durian merah*, *Durio graveolens*, its flesh a sticky, lipstick red, which tastes like a more delicate *pakan*. There is *durian kulit merah*, *Durio dulcis*, like a red-painted *isu* on steroids, with creamy, pale primrose meat. And then there is most elusive *kura-kura*, *Durio testidinarius*, which grows in joyous clusters around the trunks of its trees, its odourless, succulent flesh having an almost demerara-like sweetness. *Kura* means tortoise, and that is what its husk vaguely resembles, shaped like a rugby ball and covered with a mosaic of broad spikes.

Mee Hung grows the more familiar durians in her orchard but has carted those off to markets in Bintulu and Sibu. The cream of the crop are best eaten as is, while those that could do with some help are made into jams or *lempok*, a kind of fudge-like sweetmeat. They could technically be fermented into *tempoyak*, but this is not considered to be especially lucrative.

Unripe durians have a place in the kitchen too, flayed, sliced and dropped into broths and coconut-white stews. Not too long ago, I learned that the filaments

of durian flowers were something of a local delicacy, flung around a hot wok with garlic, dried anchovies and a splash of stock – a thoroughly Chinese approach. I had harboured hopes of trying this, but was told that I will have to wait until September or October, when the blossoms will be luscious and gaping for one munificent week – two if Lady Luck is being benevolent.

If fruit is the main purpose of a visit to Sarawak, then the last two months of the year are the time to come. Part of the giddying entourage will be *Pometia pinnata*, locally known as *matoa* and *kasai*. The fruits that hang off the stalks of this large tropical tree are round, like Christmas balls, with glossy skins that have a vaguely paper-mache feel to them and turn purplish red, green or black when ripe. Some have given it the nickname "dragon eye", because of the translucent, pale yellow flesh enrobing its dark brown seed. It tastes of lychees and longans, which explains its other names, island lychee and crystal longan.

In Malay, longans are called *mata kucing*, "cat's eyes". Sarawak is home to several wild species, the most common of which are *isau* and *kakus*, both having undulating, greenish brown skins, quite unlike the more common sandpaper-skinned ones.

Another member of the welcome wagon will be the mangosteen-like *kapul*, *Baccaurea macrocarpa*. Their thick, somewhat droll, skins encase a tight cluster of chubby segments that are either white or bright orange. In Malay, the former is called *entongon*, the latter *tampoi*, though they both have the same tangy taste. Confusingly, the name *tampoi* is also sometimes used for another fruit, *Baccaurea lanceolata*, whose tartness makes it best eaten with sugar or salt. Its other names are *empawang* and *lepusu*. The Ibans sometimes cook it with fish.

Also available would be the ridiculously photogenic *Baccaurea angulate*, here known as *belimbing merah*, "red starfruit". Like something out of a sci-fi flick, it has an angular, blood red casing, and within it, three, translucent, vein-streaked segments of lip-puckering flesh. The configuration of its interiors is reminiscent of *buah rambai*, which is, unsurprisingly, of the same genus.

And who can forget the splendours of jackfruit, *cempedak* and *terap*? While jackfruit and *cempedak* are more well-known and found in most areas in Southeast Asia, the *terap* seems to be only available in East Malaysia, Indonesia and the southern islands of the Philippines. They all possess similar anatomy and emit somewhat boorish aromas, but the *terap* is the most pungent, redolent of burnt plastic and fried curry leaves. It is not called *Artocarpus odoratissimus* for nothing.

Unlike the durian, however, the controversial pong of the *terap* come from its skin, covered in a layer of thick, pale green bristles, concealing a hive of white balls clustered around a central stalk. In their prime, these arils will be milky and sweet, a real luxury, a cross between mangosteen and jackfruit, but so much better.

Some other members of the *Artocarpus* genus share many features with the *terap*. There is *tekalong*, *Artocarpus elasticus*, favoured more by wild boars than humans, whose bark was once pounded by Dayaks to make traditional clothing. The slightly elongated *langsay*, which the Hakka call *pulong dang*, is known for being the wild ancestor of the common cultivated *terap*, but with sweeter flesh and a less pungent aroma. The whisker-fraught *terap bulu*, *Artocarpus sericicarpus*, which the Ibans call *pedalai*, is similarly odourless, but also has less juicy arils. Kwai Muk, *Artocarpus hypargyreus*, endemic to southern China, looks more like swollen human hearts, with orange or greenish skins and creamy flesh that reportedly tastes of figs, summer stone fruits and berries. Last but not least, there is the incredibly rare *bintawak*, *Artocarpus anisophyllus*, its arils having the colour, fragance and taste of a tropical beach sunset.

An hour later, the fruit detritus is cleared, their space on the table replaced by a stack of cards. A jovial session of blackjack ensues. Outside, the skies have gone Shiraz dark, lit by a single, piercing sliver of silver. Just as Meng suggests we take our leave, Mee Hung insists we stay for dinner. Preempting our looks of horror, she insists it will not be heavy. "It will take another hour anyway," she reassures, urging us to continue playing, furnishing us with cups of viscous mango juice, before returning to the kitchen and melting into it.

This version of *kompia*, or "Foochow burger" as it is often affectionately called, sees the bagel-like buns stultified with chopped-up, redly cooked, pork. I prefer this over the more modern filling of minced meat, which makes it eat like a Sloppy Joe.

The method described here, wherein the *kompia* are baked beneath brutal heat, is designed to mimic the traditional baking process in a tandoor-like oven. Do not be startled by the softness and moistness of the dough. These qualities are necessary to yield bread that is crusty without yet soft and doughy within.

KOMPIA

MAKES 24-26

FOR THE STARTER
175g bread flour
½ tsp instant yeast
250ml lukewarm water

FOR THE DOUGH
350g plain flour
1½ tsp salt
2 tbsp caster sugar
2 tbsp vegetable oil
Lukewarm water

FOR THE FILLING
500g pork belly, cut into slivers
1 tbsp light soy
1 tbsp sweet soy sauce (*kecap*)
1 tbsp dark soy
2 garlic cloves, peeled and
    chopped
2 tbsp vegetable oil
30g rock sugar
500ml water
2 spring onions, cut into large
    sections
Salt

1 The night before, make the dough starter. Combine the bread flour and instant yeast in a bowl, then stir in the lukewarm water until you get a smooth, sticky paste. Cover and set aside in a cool place for 12-16 hours, or until it has swelled slightly and its surface is covered in fine bubbles.

2 Marinate the pork belly the night before as well by mixing the slivered meat with the 3 soy sauces and garlic in a bowl, covering with clingfilm and sticking it in the refrigerator.

3 The following day, sift the plain flour and salt into a large mixing bowl, then stir in the sugar and oil. Mix in the starter dough, taking it as far as you can with a spoon and then going in with your hands, coaxing it into a cohesive, slightly sticky, dough that leaves the bowl mostly clean. Add 1-2 tbsp of lukewarm water if necessary.

4 Convey the dough to a lightly floured surface and give it 10-15 minutes of solid kneading until you achieve a smooth, soft ball that is bouncy, slightly elastic and moist. Plop this ball back into the mixing bowl, cover with tea towel and let it double in size, about 2-3 hours.

5 Meanwhile, cook the filling. Remove the marinated pork from the fridge for about 30 minutes. In a medium saucepan over medium heat, heat the rock sugar in the oil until it melts and turns deep amber. Pour in the water. Once it bubbles, stir in the marinated meat and the spring onions. Cover, reduce the heat to its lowest setting and simmer for 1½ hours or until the meat is very tender. Then uncover and simmer until all the liquid has evaporated. Taste and adjust seasoning with salt. Tip into a bowl, discard the now-wizened spring onions and leave to cool.

6 When the dough has doubled in bulk, preheat the oven grill to 250°C. Place a sturdy baking tray, about 30x40cm in dimension, on the second highest shelf, approximately 10cm from the grill.

7 Unveil your now swollen dough and give it a brief massage. On a lightly floured work surface, roll it into a log and divide it into balls, each one weighing approximately 35g. You should obtain 24-26. Keep half of these beneath a slightly damp tea towel to prevent them drying out. Flatten the remaining half into rough discs about 8cm in diameter and arrange these on another, lightly floured, baking tray. With the aid of a chopstick or the handle of a wooden spoon, drill a hole into each one. Very lightly brush their surfaces with water and sprinkle with sesame seeds.

8 Once the tray in the oven is sufficiently hot, carefully transfer the sesame-sprinkled buns onto it. Bake for 8-10 minutes or until golden brown. Remove these to a basket, return the tray to the oven for several minutes to reheat and bake the remaining dough balls in the same way.

9 Tip the cooked meat onto a chopping board and run your knife through it several times, cutting it into small, irregular pieces. Split the *kompia* and stuff with the chopped meat, giving them a gentle squish so that the juices and fat have a chance to seep into the bread. Apply to face.

The four-wheeler can move no further. The three of us disembark, stepping out into sweater temperature and a darkness the mist has made so fudgy that even the beams cast by our headlights can barely penetrate it. A lethal combination of wet weather and the continuous crunching of large-wheeled monsters has turned the dirt road into a chaos of ridges and folds. As providence would have it, we just had to find ourselves on it in the dead of night, at the tail end of a fourteen hour drive. Turning back is not an option and no calls can be made as telecommunication signals this far into the wilds of Sarawak are tenuous at best.

Our driver inspects the abused path to see how to best navigate it. Andreas, fierce friend and experienced guide, speaks with the driver and passengers of the only other vehicle and discovers they are, or rather *were*, en route to Long Seridan, a settlement in the Kelabit Highlands located even further than our destination, Bario – the two towns have a road through the Tama Abu mountain range between them. The sangfroid with which everyone is handling the situation is, however, encouraging and soon I find myself lowering my shoulders, drinking in the stelliferous sky, nibbling on my umpteenth packet of Julie's peanut butter sandwich biscuits and murmuring casual prayers into the mist-veiled distance.

It would be a lie to say that the road conditions earlier were drastically better. Since leaving asphalt along the outermost rings of Miri, the path has been raw, dusty and undulating. It is not called "abortion road" for nothing. After the second hour trundling over trying terrain, it finally dawned why the Kelabit folks in the city shot one another stifled looks of horror when they learned we were driving instead of flying. I knew it was going to be uncomfortable, just not this nausea-inducing. Before this road came into being just a few years ago, paved for more convenient travel, the journey must have been excruciating. Yet it is precisely the inaccessibility of these distant, isolated settlements that allowed the Kelabit, an ethnic minority indigenous to the highlands of Sarawak, North Kalimantan and Brunei, their numbers trembling around seven thousand, to develop their own culture, far from the glances and influences of foreigners.

The ride up to this point has been a whirlwind of green, blue and brown, with rings run around endless mountains. We sliced through small Kenyah villages, zipped past stretches of naked earth and caught flashes of stilted huts belonging to the Penans, who live in quiet self-sufficiency deep in the jungle, an existence that has been threatened by logging activities in recent years. Andreas, a Tagol Murut, and no stranger to the wilderness, says they are jungle experts. They know that frogs and squirrels eat better than gibbons and macaques, and have apparently discovered a panacea against asthma and snake bites in a bark called *tawanga*. They have also found a long-lasting source of warmth in a wood called *talimbakas*, with the ability to remain kindled for an entire night. And boy, could we do with a bonfire now!

Our driver returns, cigarette in hand, countenance less runkled. It appears he has found a way out of our sticky situation. We hop back onto the vehicle, and he revs the engine. After being hurled through the obstacle course with a series of jerking movements and several precariously sharp turns, we make it to the other side unscathed, even invigorated. The other car follows suit and, with our encouragement, takes the lead. They have far more ground to cover after all.

By the time we arrive at the homestay in Bario, it is several digits past midnight. Its operators, husband-and-wife duo John and Mary, who despite the time appear to be in the highest of spirits, greet us warmly, encouraging us towards a dining table, a basket chunky with pineapples serving as its centerpiece.

The table itself is immense, as if designed for village meetings, a masterpiece of unpolished wood. This rustic, bosky aesthetic applies to most of the house. Even the floors and walls, of stone and brick, have been lavished with thatched baskets and beaded bags, all of them blessed with traditional Kelabit designs.

John assists us with our luggage. Mary offers us mugs of hot ginger tea and rib-sticking slices of a sweetmeat made from *tarap*, the colour of rain-drenched teak, its packaging of corrugated *isip* (*Phrynium*) leaves, wizened and brittle. Mary, perhaps noticing my rapture, says this snack is a rare treat, a food so old, so forgotten, that hardly anybody knows its name. "I think it is *keliking*", she says, one hand tapping the side of her temple. To make it, the flesh from the fruits are first spread over a *rinuh*, through which excess liquid drops during its time beneath a cooperative sun. It takes a day or so before the pulp is adequately dry. The basket's material, rattan, is crucial, as it is heat resistant, a helpful quality for the subsequent step of smoking for a similarly lengthy sojourn over reticently burning wood. Jackfruit, *cempedak* and durian are all apparently very good preserved this way. The time and effort required to make this "*keliking*" has led it to be replaced with less fussy, store-bought options, like candy and chips. "Back in the day, we used to munch on it as if it were chocolate," she says, plaintively.

For all the comfort the sweetmeat provides, it does not quite assuage our weariness and soon Andreas and I have to politely pardon ourselves. We take turns to rinse in icy water, in the company of palm-sized moths, before crawling onto our mattresses and letting slumber take the wheel.

CAVIAR OF THE HIGHLANDS

I rise the following morning to find Andreas having breakfast with John in the backyard. The meal is simple, one of fried eggs, buttered toast and slices of pineapple for which these highlands are rightfully renowned – they are pure nectar. John proudly shares that the *buah kabar*, as they are called here, came from their garden, using his half-drained coffee cup to indicate a cluster of pointy-leafed shrubs near a wire fence, beyond which a chain of sprawling mountains rests, magisterially, picturesquely.

Surfeit pineapples, as well as *tampoi*, are often made into *tuak*, the local moonshine. "Young pineapple shoots are also delicious stir-fried with a little onion and garlic," he informs us, before urging us to hurry along. "The festivities have started. Find my wife. She is already there."

This is the twelfth time Bario is hosting *Pesta Nukenen*, a celebration of Kelabit culture and food that draws people from both East and West Malaysia. By the time we arrive at the town centre, verily no larger than a football field, a bevy of women have taken to the stage to perform a series of traditional dances in their glorious *sapa harit*, a composition of vermillion blouse, black embroidered *kelebong pakai ngarang* ("clothing worn for dancing") and a tomato-red beaded beret. Two stretches of wooden stalls flanking this stage, fed with all kinds of traditional delicacies, are the main lure of the event.

We find Mary amid the frenzy and she motions us towards a modest barbecue pit on the field. On its steel grills, licked by flames gushing from hunks of burning wood, a porcupine, *terutung*, freed of spikes, is getting a mean tan. The cook, languidly fanning the fire, says it needs another half an hour to arrive at perfection.

There is no meat the barbecue is incapable of elevating. For the Kelabit and other ethnic groups with practically unlimited access to forests and jungles, the menu ranges from prosaic chicken, pork and beef, to game, like buffalo (*carubao*), wild boar (*baka*), Malay civet (*payuh*), sambar deer (*bayo*), barking deer (*tela'o*) and mousedeer (*pelanuk*). Samples of each are being sold at one stall here, cast over little plates lined with banana leaf, and Andreas and I apply ourselves accordingly. Other Kelabit cooking techniques include braising, steaming in bamboo culms stationed over hot coals, a process the Kelabit call *nutung*, and more recently, frying.

Given the circumstances under which these beasts are consumed, no part of the animal goes to waste. The intestines (*buri*) of the barking deer, for instance, is exceptional cooked with garlic, ginger, a little salt and not-so-trad soy sauce, while the livers of wild boar are delicious chopped and sautéed with torch ginger buds, *busak luduh*. Incidentally, the word *buri* also points to the contents of the small intestines, that huntsmen in Pa Lugan, Kelapang consider a great delicacy. It is to them what caviar is to the Russians. The *buri* of deer is noted for being quite special, owing to their diet of sweet leaf and forest fruit.

The "waste not, want not" ethos from which *buri* consumption sprung also gave rise to the desire and need to prolong the shelf-life of surfeit meat from a kill. The Kelabit have two main ways of preserving meat. The first is smoking, over softly burning wood, the result known as *labo belatuh*. With firewood being exorbitant in the uplands, the making of such *charcuterie* is usually a secondary activity. The cuts of meat are suspended from the top of the clay hearth (*tetel*) for anywhere between one week to one month, while the fire beneath is used for the daily ritual of family cooking. "Besides lasting longer, smoked meat is also lighter in weight, which makes it ideal for long treks" Andreas adds.

Labo belatuh can be added to soups, even vegetable stir-fries. It has become the star on the menus of the Kelabit eateries that have sprung up in Miri and Kuching in recent years, arriving at tables in ramshackle piles of splinters, having been assailed with a zealous pestle. Young Kelabit have branded this viand *labo senutu'*, "pounded meat". I have been cautioned, however, that *labo senutu'* does not always begin with *labo belatuh*. The modern shortage of time and patience, not to mention hearths in urban areas, has led to cooks grilling or frying their meat instead.

The second preservation technique is good old fermentation. The meat is hewn into chunks, rubbed with salt, sometimes cooked rice, then packed into bamboo culms and left in a cool place for at least a week and up to several months. The Kelabit call the product *senamo*, although the elderly among them would refer to it as *lisam*. The Lun Bawang have their version of this, called *tenu'*. Varying appellations notwithstanding, they all share the same fate, ending in a hot pan with oil, shallots and ginger.

The cooking and preservation methods bestowed upon beasts are valid for finned things as well. Obviously, the selection here is mostly freshwater, including *Mystus* (*luang senien*), mahseer (*luang pelian*), a diminutive variety called *rebaro*, young rock-loving '*semah*' fish (*geraga*), an eel with notoriously sharp teeth (*tuding*), and, despite not technically qualifying as fish, river snails (*akep*). The flesh of these, however sweet, is often sullied with the taste of weed and mud, and so benefit from the presence of a blade or two of *daun lukwa*, the leaf from a species of ginger. Another bugbear is that many of these freshwater fish are mere receptacles of fine bones. Clever cooks have found a way around this however, feverishly inflicting them with incisions along their lengths, cutting right through their fiendish needles, almost turning them into accordions. They then either grill or deep-fry them until golden and crunchy.

There are other ways of mitigating the hazards affecting their enjoyment, albeit at the expense of the cook. Two common ways are to debone and flake cooked fish, then either fry them with torch ginger, making *luang senanum*, or pummel them into floss with *ubud sala'* (*Etlingera coccinea*), yielding *a-b'ang*. Interestingly, in the past, *a-b'ang* was only ever prepared with fish that was salted and left to ferment until almost decadent. "Cooking the fish only happened in recent decades," Mary tells Andreas and me, as she unveils an *isip* envelope to reveal yet another way of fending off consumption woes, in the shape of the increasingly elusive *luang sena'ag*, a smoked parcel of minced fish and banana pith. "This is good made with *tamban*, actually," Mary says, offering us forks. The slightly oleaginous *tamban*, white *sardinella*, is harvested in distant saltwaters.

WING AND SCALE

There appears to be a frisson of excitement several stalls down. Mary urges us along, where we find two men, perched on stools, rapping tiles of some sort of hive, over a plastic basin half-filled with a pick-and-mix of winged things, larvae and cannellini-like eggs. "These are wasps," Mary says, picking up one for me to try. Despite being considered a fad these days, even a source of amusement, the tradition of dining on insects and other, less favourably considered, members of the animal kingdom has been strong among many indigenous groups since time immemorial. "The two wasps we eat are *sibung balang* and *nanan*," Mary says, taking one to nibble on herself.

As we amble our way towards the grain vendor, Mary intimates a fondness for *kelatang*, cicada larvae the absurd shade of forced rhubarb. They are apparently best consumed still wiggling, something with which Andreas concurs. He shares an anecdote of being in Bario several years ago, in the bleakest of chills, eating them freshly winkled from a section of *belinguled* trunk – the tree's Lundayeh name – with shots of brandy to accompany them down the palate. These days, many either blanch the *kelatang* first or drop them into pots of *kikid*, rice gruel.

Occasionally, a snake will slither its way onto menus, the emperor of which must surely be the python (*selengui*). Kelabit cooks handle the enormous serpent as they would fish, hewing it into steaks and braising it with salt, water, ginger and the dried black beads of *buah tenem*, *Litsea cubeba*, which bears the haunting qualities of leather, camphor, cork and tropical citrus. This spice, that locals nickname "mountain pepper" is central to a long-lost blend of spices once used by Kelabit to season almost anything, from soups to noodles, fish to meat dishes. The black beads would be pounded with dried white chillies; lemongrass; *bua' sala*; *daun ipa*, a natural flavour enhancer; *kuboro*, a species of red ginger, *Boesenbergia stenophylla*; and salt, best the greyish grains derived from Bario spring water.

Valued for its delicate salinity and mineral qualities, Bario salt is highly regarded by both cooks and nutritionists. After the water is harvested and evaporated in large vessels called *kawang*, the obtained salt is dried and fed into bamboo tubes, which are then turned over diffident flames for an entire day, which hardens the crystals into cakes. These precious cylinders, freed from tubes, are then wrapped in *isip* leaves and sent to markets across Sarawak where they will fetch a premium.

THE BARIO GRAIN

Even for a vegetarian, the Kelabit Highlands have much to give. The jungles are abundant with edible fern and bracken, pea aubergines and bamboo shoots. There are also pencil-thick stalks of *lanau, Commelina paludosa*, so-called "wild asparagus", best fried with salt and maybe some garlic, and *abang, Setaria palmifolia*, otherwise known as palmgrass, their stems more highly regarded than their foliage by cooks. There is also a splendid array of greens that are hardly known beyond these highlands. *Dure* is especially beloved, its leaves cooked and squelched into slippery mulches in broths of ginger and dried anchovies from the lowlands. The same cooking technique may also be applied to the waxy leaves of *beker iyep* (*Poikilospermum*). The herbaceous *renayun* shines in scintillating broths with water-logged slices of banana pith, to be relished with crunchy, copper curls of fried pork skin. *Tengayan, Hyrtanandra hirta,* from the nettle family, is incredibly good in *kikid*, as is *kerid kuru*, a kind of yellow-flowering mustard so highly appreciated that excess harvests are sunned and kept for rainy days. Once dried, it is called *kerid pering*.

Common split-gill mushrooms (*kulat kedtep*) that appear as delicate, spongy corals on damp, fallen trunks, also end up stirred into pots of rice gruel, while another fungi, *Gymnopilus*, known locally as *kulat lam*, "sour mushroom", prefers to be fried with wild ginger pith (*ubud tubu' buen*; *umbut tepus* in Malay) or that of the torch ginger (*ubud sala'*).

Besides being consulted as an aromatic, torch ginger is also considered an ingredient in its own right in these parts. The buds (*busak luduh*) are halved and cooked with salt and a little water until absurdly magenta and eaten as a viand. The fruit, *bua' sala'*, can be prepared similarly or converted into jams, which I surmise to be a relatively modern invention. Incidentally, *bua' ilang*, a sharp, tangy, purple-red berry that grows wild here, also benefits from being cooked in copious amounts of sugar. The resultant jam has a taste that swiftly summons blackcurrant and mulberry to mind.

To unite their splendid array of viands or *penguman*, the Kelabit require carbohydrate. Their primary source of this is rice, the secondary one *sago*, which seems to be more popular in the areas around Long Seridan, where it is used as an extender for rice, or to make *sinago*, a thick, slimy gruel (essentially *linut* or *ambuyat*).

One need not dig deep into local folklore or mythology to comprehend the significance of this monocot to the Kelabit folk; the existence of numerous culinary terms denoting the simplest cooking processes is evidence enough. *Ngebpa'* is to add water to a pot of rice for cooking, while *ngelaak* refers to the cooking of the grains. *Ngaur* refers to the removal of cooked rice from their pot and wrapping it. *Ngerut* is to scrape out scorched rice with a *gayut,* a spatula-like utensil.

Most of the counter space at the rice stall at *Pesta Nukenen* is occupied by plastic packets of medium grain, white as alabaster, tiny as mouse teeth. This is *bera dari*, one of the two kinds of white Bario rice, often confused with the similarly prized short-grain, *beras adan*, grown in the Krayan highlands of North Kalimantan, bordering Sabah and Sarawak.

Although the term "Bario rice" can technically refer to any rice grown in the town's vicinity, including the beautiful rusty reds, blacks and lilacs, it usually points to *Presidium*, grown by families on their own plots of land, without the use of herbicides or pesticides. The seeds are sown in July and the grains are harvested in January. Once cooked, usually with twice their volume in water, the grains adopt a faintly sticky texture and a wonderful, ghost-of-pandan scent. It is the *terroir*, the altitude, temperature climate and soil, that gives the rice these distinctive qualities, and although many attempts have been made to cultivate it in the lowlands, the results have been largely unsatisfactory.

The other kind of Bario rice, *bera kura*, with its harder, larger grains, is what locals use for *nuba' laya'*, which means "soft cooked rice". For this, the rice is boiled in copious amounts of water and crushed with a pair of wooden oar-like spatulas (*bugo*) until a dense, starchy balm is produced. This is then divided among *isip* or banana leaves that are rolled into pouches. As the filling cools, it sets slightly, achieving a firm, creamy consistency. A packet of *nuba' luya'* is stultifying, somehow tantamount to eating four to five bowls of steamed rice. Ideal for the blue collar worker, less brilliant for sedentary folk.

The Kelabit also plant *bera ubek*, glutinous rice, in shades white and black. These are usually reserved for rice wine (*burak main*), which may be distilled into *burak pa'it*, and several sweet snacks. Two of the most popular are *senape*, for which the grains are lightly sweetened and steamed in slender *isip* parcels, and *urum*, for which they are ground, made into a dough, shaped into chubby fingers and deep-fried. We find them both here at the stall, on a desk by the cash register, calling to us from their bamboo baskets, with the full support of a huge flask of what I assume to be coffee. With Mary busy chatting with the cashier, Andreas shoots me a knowing look. Well. I suppose it would be rude not to...

A variety of fish may be used here, as long as they are white-fleshed and sweet. Most Kelabit will insist upon freshwater varieties as that is what is available to them. They have a favourite in a species of carp called *kelad*.

As previously highlighted, *a-b'ang* has evolved from using salted, rotten fish to their cooked fresh counterparts. With this deviation from tradition, I see no reason to restrict the cooking method one chooses. Many stick their fish in a pot with a little water, salt and ginger, but I prefer the dry heat of the grill or, in this case, the oven.

I also season my *a-b'ang* as many modern Kelabit cooks would, with chillies in addition to the trad *Etlingera coccinea*. Some add shallots, for sweetness and a flicker of allium heat, but I leave this out.

A-B'ANG

SERVES 6

750g carp or other white-fleshed
   freshwater fish (see above), cleaned
½ tsp salt, plus more for seasoning
½ tsp crushed black pepper
2 stalks *Etlingera coccinea*
2 red bird's eye chillies, sliced

1 Preheat the oven to 200°C. Lightly rub the cleaned fish all over with salt and black pepper. Arrange on a cosy roasting tray and bake on a high shelf for 15-20 minutes, or until cooked through. Remove from the oven and allow to cool completely on the tray.

2 Skin the cooled fish and reduce their flesh to flakes, collecting these in a bowl. While Kelabit cooks would often turn a blind eye to whiskery bones, allowing the imminent pestle to obliterate them, I remove all of them, however fine.

3 Make an incision along each of the *Etlingera* stalks and remove their tough outer casings. Continue stripping away layers of skin until you arrive at their pale, glossy, malleable cores. Chop these finely, then pound with the red bird's eye chillies with a large pestle and mortar into a rough paste. The *Etlingera* will make it slightly fibrous. Add the flaked fish and gently pound until you get a moist yet airy floss that threatens to clump. Taste and tweak with salt.

As mentioned earlier, smoked meat is traditionally required for this, with the more rebarbative, leathery specimens requiring boiling before meeting their maker. I use the title *labo senutu'*, "pounded meat" , as my rendition borrows heavily from modern, "lazy" takes, where the meat is grilled, sometimes boiled, and pounded. I cook the meat – I use beef brisket – in a low oven, which makes the final product slightly tenderer than normal, then brown it to get a solid crust.

My meddling does not stop there, though this should by no means suggest thoughtlessness or disrespect. While its typical seasoning is just salt, I have added ingredients associated with the Kelabit kitchen. I cook the meat in a smoothie of garlic, spring onions, ginger, pineapple, dried *buah tenem* (*Litsea cubeba*), that may be exchanged with regular black pepper, and ground cinnamon in place of *tabat borak*, so-called "wild mountain cinnamon".

Speaking of culinary innovations, at a Kelabit eatery in Kuching, I had this pounded beef, fried with garlic, torch ginger, lemongrass, chillies and fine slivers of bamboo shoot. It was unspeakably good and so I do this often at home now. For how to prepare bamboo shoots, kindly refer to page 166.

LABO SENUTU'

SERVES 6-8

750g beef brisket
400g pineapple flesh, peeled weight, cut up
4 garlic cloves, peeled and minced
2 spring onions, sliced
15g ginger, peeled and sliced
1 tsp salt
2 tsp soy
1 tsp ground cinnamon
1 tsp dried *litsea cubeba*, finely crushed

1 Preheat the oven to 150˚C. Place the brisket in a 20x30cm roasting tin.

2 Blend the pineapple, garlic, spring onions, ginger, salt, soy, cinnamon and *litsea*, then pour the resultant liquid over the brisket. Add just enough water so the liquid half-covers the meat. Conceal the tray with foil or a crumpled, fitting sheet of parchment (in other words, a cartouche). Push the tin onto the oven's centre shelf for 4 hours, or until the meat is tender enough to be pulled apart. You do not want baby food; some texture is crucial. Remove the meat from the tin, conveying it to a plate and letting it cool completely. Tip the juices out into a container and freeze it for a rainy day; reduced in a pan slightly, it makes a nice sauce for all manners of grilled or fried meats.

3 Put a frying or griddle pan over high heat. Once smoking, slap on the cooled brisket, and cook for 1-2 minutes per side, to char. Return the meat to its plate and cool slightly. Then, with a pair of forks or keen hands, roughly shred. Put these shreds into a large mortar and lightly whack with a pestle, breaking them further into splinters.

I first encountered this delightful dish of pig's stomach and pineapple at a Kelabit-run eatery in Miri, The Summit Cafe. I only learned a few months after that it was not unique to the Kelabit, but prepared by many peoples in Sarawak. It is a regular feature on feast tables during Gawai, the harvest festival, where it is sometimes prepared with pig's small intestines.

At my request, the Summit Cafe cooks provided the recipe, albeit vaguely, and what lies beneath is an interpretation of their instructions. It does include tomato ketchup and chill sauce. Do not go upmarket: the stuff found at hotdog kiosks is perfect here.

BA'TUAH KABAR

SERVES 6-8

FOR THE PIG'S STOMACH
450g pig's stomach, cleaned
1½ litres water
2cm ginger, crushed
1 tsp salt
1 tsp white peppercorns

FOR FRYING
4 garlic cloves, peeled
5 shallots, peeled
2cm ginger, peeled
8 dried chillies, deseeded,
    softened (page 520)
4 tbsp vegetable oil
1 tsp fermented shrimp paste,
    grilled (page 522)
½ tsp salt, plus more to taste
1 tsp sugar, plus more to taste
150ml light chicken stock or water
350g slightly underripe pineapple,
    peeled weight, cut into chunks
2 tbsp chilli sauce
1 tbsp tomato ketchup
1 tbsp tamarind water (page 524)

1 Place the pig's stomach, water, ginger, salt and white peppercorns in medium saucepan. Bring to a boil over medium heat, then cover, reduce the heat to its lowest setting and simmer for 1½ -2 hours or until the stomach is tender.

2 Drain the stomach, discarding the cooking liquor, ginger and white peppercorns. Give it a rinse, then cut it into ½cm-wide strips no longer than 5cm. Set aside.

3 With a pestle and mortar, crush the garlic, shallots, ginger and soaked dried chillies into a fine paste.

4 Heat the oil in a large frying pan over medium heat. Add the spice paste, frying until it is fragrant, deepens in colour and begins to split from the oil. Stir in the fermented shrimp paste, then the prepared pig's stomach, salt and sugar. Stir for a few seconds, then add the water or stock. Simmer for 3-4 minutes, until most the liquid has evaporated, then stir in the pineapple, chilli sauce, tomato ketchup and tamarind water. Cover and cook until the pineapple is soft but not mushy. Taste and adjust seasoning with salt and sugar.

This viand of fried pig's lung is a signature item of the Lundayeh and Lun Bawang.

I get pig's lung ready-cleaned from the butcher, so all it requires is a bath in a couple of changes of water and a cathartic mincing with a fierce blade.

When I ate this at a restaurant in Kuching, it did not have rice but contained chopped torch ginger. If you have any about your person, they certainly make a welcome addition, added during the dish's final few minutes on the stove.

PARU PARU BABI

SERVES 4-6

1½ tbsp jasmine rice
4 tbsp vegetable oil
4 garlic cloves, peeled and minced
4 shallots, peeled and thinly sliced
½ tsp turmeric powder
½ tsp salt
100ml water
250g pig's lung, cleaned and finely minced
(see above)

1 Put the jasmine rice in a small bowl. Give it a brief rinse, then cover in 1cm water and soak for 2 hours. Then drain and set aside.

2 Heat the oil in a large frying pan over medium-high heat. Once hot, add the garlic and fry until light gold, which will take just a few seconds.

3 Stir in the shallots. Once slightly translucent, add the turmeric powder. Stir, allowing it to sizzle and lose its rawness, then add the minced lung. Fry, stirring gently but constantly, to seal it.

4 Add the drained rice, salt and water. Give it a brief stir, then cover, lower the heat, and simmer for about 15 minutes, until the lung is tender and the grains of rice have swelled.

5 Continue cooking the mixture, without a lid, until all the liquid has evaporated. Taste and adjust seasoning with salt.

It is difficult to be precise about the amount of water here; bags of the same brand of rice vary in thirst. While most Kelabit cooks simply boil their rice for an extended period of time and mash it, I prefer to boil it for a shorter period, then steam it. This two-step process prevents the rice from catching to the base of the pan if the heat is too strong and also grants the cook better control over moisture. This is especially helpful for those of us deprived of the rice the Kelabits use, grains so robust that even a tender mash somehow, eventually, solidifies. Still, there is no point in lying: serious graft is required to get the rice properly crushed into a balm.

If you are lucky enough to find *Phrynium* leaves, brilliant. If not, use heat-softened banana leaves (page 520), brushed with a little vegetable oil. You need not worry about the eventual form of your parcel. As long as it is faintly oblongish and compact, all will be well. By all means roll them into rectangular or cylindrical shapes if you find that easier.

The *nuba' laya'* in the attendant photograph is served with *a-b'ang* (page 110), *sayur manicai* (page 31) and *ba'tuah kabar* (page 114). I also added 1 tbsp purplish black rice (regular, not glutinous) to the pot, resulting in a pleasant lilac shade. Some cooks add common-split gill fungi, thereby producing *nuba' kesip*.

NUBA' LAYA'

MAKES 10

400g jasmine rice
Approx. 1.2 litres water
10 *Phrynium* leaves

1 Prepare a steamer, filling its lower compartment with plenty of water. Wash the jasmine rice three times or until the water runs clear. Tip into a large saucepan or casserole, then pour in the water. Place the cooking vessel over high heat. Once the water boils, stir several times, then reduce the heat and cook until the rice has consumed most of the water. Stir constantly but lazily. This should take about 10 minutes.

2 By now, your steamer should be ready. Scrape the swollen, semi-cooked, rice out from the saucepan into a deep and wide heatproof dish. I use a 22cm round cake tin. Pop this into the steamer and leave it there for 40-50 minutes or until the grains are very soft, their edges blurring, stirring every 10 minutes. Add a little water if the dish looks thirsty.

3 Remove the dish from the heat. Tip the softly cooked rice into a large, sturdy heatproof basin. Rest it on a heatproof mat on your counter or on the floor. Make yourself comfortable. Then, with a large wooden spoon, stir and crush the rice with wild abandon until you get a soft balm.

4 Dollop a cup, 200ml or thereabouts, of this onto the centre of a *Phrynium* leaf. Fold its lengths over the rice, then roll it into a compact, oblong parcel. Make all the *nuba' laya'* this way.

This recipe is modelled after the most sublime *urum* I had just before leaving Bario. It contained coconut from the lowlands and a little black glutinous rice.

The cooks bought their glutinous rice ready-ground from their local market. I soak and grind my own rice as it produces a texture superior than any powder plucked from a supermarket shelf. I did encounter one issue with the recipe that was supplied: the fritters exhibited the proclivity for bursting and distorting as they fried, emerging as distorted limbs, not the plump fingers promised. Their transmogrification is due to the sharp, drastic hike in temperature, which forms a crust that restricts the flesh before it has had the chance to swell. Frying them in big quantities over moderate heat provides amelioration but is only useful for someone running a catering company. The simplest remedy lies in the insertion of an untraditional step: boiling the *urum* before deep-frying. It also makes them softer.

URUM UBEK

MAKES 16-18

250g glutinous rice
2 tsp black glutinous rice
75g caster sugar
½ tsp salt
75g grated coconut
Approx. 2 tbsp coconut cream
    or water, if needed
Vegetable oil, for deep-frying

1 Combine the two kinds of glutinous rice in a bowl. Wash three times or until the water runs clear, then cover in 2cm of water and soak for 6-8 hours.

2 Drain the rice and spread over a tray lined with tea towel. Leave for 20-30 minutes to dry out slightly.

3 Grind the rice in batches in a cosy blender into fine sand; a bullet blender is good. Scrape into a roomy mixing bowl and stir in the sugar, salt and grated coconut, finishing it off with your paws to get a soft, cohesive dough. If it seems thirsty, add the coconut cream or water. Cover and leave for 30 minutes.

4 Divide the dough into 16 balls. Roll these into fat fingers, about 8cm in length, and arrange on a tray lined with tea towel. Fill a medium saucepan with water and place over medium heat. Once boiling, blanch the fingers in batches, until they swell and float. Retrieve them with a slotted spoon and return them to the towel-lined tray to dry off.

5 Discard the water in the saucepan, dry it thoroughly, then fill it with 5cm of vegetable oil. Place this over a medium heat. Once hot but not smoking, deep-fry the *urum* in batches until crisp and the palest shade of gold, gently pushing them around the moment they have developed a crust. Drain on a platter lined with kitchen towel. These are best eaten warm with a modest drizzle of honey.

The term Murut, meaning "People of the Hills", represents an indigenous ethnic group occupying Borneo's impossibly verdant, undulating heart. They may be broken into twenty-nine subgroups, at least ten of which are found in Sabah, including the Paluan, Nabaai, Kolor, Binta, Timugon, Bookan, Tangala, Tenggara Kalabakan, Serudung and last but not least, the Tagol, with whom I shall be spending several days in the village of Marais.

Marais is tiny, a smattering of cement houses flanking a stretch of asphalt so short that you could soft-boil an egg in the time it takes to traverse it on foot. The urban settlement nearest to Marais is the town of Tenom, the gateway to Sabah's lush interior, home to the Murut and Lun Bawang. Despite being a mere half-hour drive away, the Murut of Tenom are of another subgroup, the Timugon.

Tenom is perhaps best known for coffee, the mineral-rich amber of meliponines and the lusciousness of mangosteens, pomelos and bananas, an abundance it owes to the Padas River that blesses the land it slices with sweet fertility. My host warned me against visiting the river alone at night. Those who do either go missing or return unhinged.

The Tagol community in Marais is tightly knit, as one would expect from a settlement of this size. Everyone knows one another and when a foreigner appears, they show up to shake their hand and welcome them. I had not anticipated such warmth or hospitality, as the Murut are generally associated with surliness, simply not to be trifled with. Although it is said of many indigenous groups, the Murut have a reputation for being particularly fearsome warriors. Before the business of headhunting was outlawed, a Murut man had to prove his readiness for marriage and family life by going to battle and returning with the head of his enemy.

On the night of my arrival, after a round of much-needed beer, the village chief invited me to the townhall and showed me some exquisite specimens of *sampayau*, traditional vest-like apparel, made from the fibres of a wood called *puputul* and tinted with plant-based dyes. "Red comes from the *lalandang* tree, black from *ubol* ..." he elaborated, before diverting my attention to the vest's complementary headdresses, flamboyant with the plumage of pheasants and other feathered creatures found in the wild.

Usually reserved for special occasions, each *sampayau* is emblazoned with a pattern that represents the wearer's position in the longhouse. One boasting a pattern known as *lumayau*, for instance, would indicate that he is a warrior, to be equipped with knives, spears and darts, the last typically laced with poison from the *paleh* tree. In what could have been a scene from an Indiana Jones flick, the village chief drew out a tidy stash of darts for my inspection, nattily arranged in a handsome wooden box one might use for Havanas. Brandishing a blowpipe, he mentioned, the chilly

earnestness of his tone only rivalled by his countenance, that even today, these darts are occasionally applied to trespassers.

This morning, I find myself in the outdoor kitchen at one of Marais' road-facing houses, smitten by the company of a dozen cooks. Together, we are making lunch for the whole village. Some cooks are fussing over white chillies (*paras kapular*), others extracting the tiny, pert buds from shut, flamingo-pink parasols of torch ginger (*tikalor*). Two gregarious ladies are busy wringing the milk from a huge basin of grated tapioca, a task a boxy bamboo basket known as a *lanjung* makes light and breezy. Several solid squeezes and the starch-laden juices gush through the cracks of the contraption, leaving its contents spent, hapless. Muslin cloth has nothing on this.

I have been given the task of crushing young tapioca leaves in a pail-sized mortar, with a metre-long pestle, both made of wood, into a consistency the Murut call *sampai hulus* – a fine, fibrous pulp. The resultant emerald mulch of *umbus nu kasila* is going to be fried with garlic, said white chillies and torch ginger buds, and a smidgeon of vegetable oil. Once upon a time, wild boar lard was used, the crisp nuggets of fat, a byproduct of the rendering process, scattered over the cooked greens.

I had no idea the plants of *Manihot esculenta* could grow so tall, even exceeding the height of papaya trees, until earlier this morning, during a jaunt to a nearby forest to gather their tender shoots. We also gleaned banana leaves, in which to contain rice, and a bamboo culm, to cook fish. When it came to selecting the bamboo, our master forager was especially particular, refusing to accept a culm that was not between 4-12 months of age. According to him, immature culms are too narrow, while those that are too old are devoid of perfume and are especially prone to burning. After spending half an hour foraging the wilderness with a machete (*parang*), our man finally spotted a suitable candidate, cast in the most delicious bottle green, the girth of a pencil holder, features that point to suitable vintage, approximately 5 months. Several species of bamboo exist in these forests, but it is the *hulu* variety for which the Murut have a particular fondness.

Just as I finish pounding the last of my tapioca shoots, a cook has begun heating the wrung tapioca starch with water in a large aluminium wok. He continues stirring until it becomes a translucent, rebarbative gel, locally known as *inatok*. This shall be our carbohydrate for the day, along with banana leaf packets of crushed cooked rice, *kanon nilopot*, analogous to the *nuba' laya'* of the Kelabit and Lundayeh.

Another cook takes a cleaver to a massive *ikan lembungao* (tinfoil barb) harvested this morning from a nearby river, reducing it to a platter of steaks. I assist her in smacking these with salt, black pepper and crystals of monosodium glutamate, a modern substitute for the now elusive *apak* leaf, before wrapping them in a sheet of banana leaf with bruised ginger and lemongrass stalks. The loosely formed parcel is fed into the bamboo culm, first washed to prevent itching, then concealed with a scrunched-up blade of *daun tikalor*, torch ginger leaf. The filled, sealed culm is then placed at an angle, over woodfire, for an hour.

Vinulu is the Murut term for cooking food in bamboo culms. As with other groups, this charming though time consuming process has been replaced with stove-bound pots and pans, with any loss of character compensated by augmented aromatics and, if meat is involved, a preliminary browning session. The Tagol Murut from Kampong Meligan in Sipitang, a province adjacent to Tenom, are keen on a braise of coconut palm shoots and beef ribs, something of a luxury given how difficult it is to rear cattle in the conditions set by Borneo's unforgiving belly.

Andreas is a keen huntsman, the wild flowing through his veins. It is he who opened my eyes to the expansive range of game the Murut enjoy, from wild boar (*ulak*; *asi*) to frogs, squirrels to snakes. Silver leaf monkeys, that the Murut nickname "Beckham" due to their Mohawk-like hairdos, are apparently very tasty. Gibbons, macaques and red leaf monkeys are recognised for packing rather undelectable flesh, ranking abysmally on the list of jungle must-eats. The success of a hunt is as reliant on good fortune as skill, and those unfavoured by the auspices may have to (reluctantly) settle for the chunder of their hounds.

When the hunters found themselves with either an insubstantial or motley collection of meats, their solution lay in a gruel known as *pitur*. All they would require is rice, water, perhaps some vegetables. In the event of surfeit meat, excess will certainly have to be preserved. The most straightforward method involves boring old salt, or brine, the resultant pickle known as *inavang avang*. Several Murut cooks here in Marais have told me this is especially good prepared with the flesh and small intestines of wild boars. A similar method, using cooked rice in addition to salt, would yield something called *tamba*.

For foreigners, the most accessible method of preserving meat, especially wild boar and deer, must surely be smoking, best over softly kindled twigs from the mangrove-loving *bakau* tree (*Rhizophora apiculata*). The *sinalah* is usually added to braises, or boiled and assailed with a pestle and mortar, a process known by some Murut as *tinutuh*, meaning "to pound". The Murut of Kampung Tataluan in Nabawan district prepare a more extreme version of this. After smoking the meat once, they leave it out in the open for flies to have their wicked way. Once the eggs have hatched into maggots, they smoke it a second time. It is then ready for eating.

This simple beef soup, served in the accompanying photograph with *rinalau tuhau* (page 156), is usually seasoned with salt and nothing else. I add a little ginger and black pepper. Various vegetables may be added. I use coconut palm, often sold in Thai grocers in neatly sliced slabs, but other kinds of palm shoots, bamboo shoots, banana pith, fern fiddleheads and even yams, may be used instead.

RU' TIAHANG NU SAPI

SERVES 6

1kg beef ribs
2cm ginger, lightly crushed
2 litres water
2 tsp salt, plus more for seasoning
400g coconut palm shoots,
   cut into thin chips
1 tsp black peppercorns, finely crushed

1 Bring a large saucepan of water to a boil over high heat. Add the ribs and boil for 5 minutes. Drain and rinse the ribs, discarding the blanching liquid.

2 Return the ribs to the saucepan. Add the ginger, water and salt, bring to a boil over high heat, then cover, reduce the heat to its lowest and simmer for 2 hours or until just-tender.

3 Add the sliced coconut palm shoots to the soup. Cover and continue simmering until both beef and shoots are very tender, about 20-30 minutes. Add the black pepper. Taste and adjust seasoning with salt.

The Murut make a delicious balm of crushed squash, sweet potato or tapioca, pampering it with a little wild boar lard. Although the title of this dish only mentions *labu*, squash, I have snuck in some sweet potato. It is vital to ensure the varieties used are starchy; you want a soft mash, not a spread. Unable to procure wild boar lard, I use that from a regular pig, best made with fat from either their backs or belly areas.

Andreas Angkaus, who provided me with this recipe, says his mother would make a large batch and parcel them in softened *ikik* or banana leaves for him to take out on forest treks. If you do this – the leaves have the talent for adding the most genteel, appetising aroma to anything they protect – I recommend lightly brushing them with a little lard, too.

LABU SINAANG RA LOMOK NU ULAK

SERVES 6

500g kabocha squash, peeled weight,
    deseeded and cut into 3cm chunks
500g yellow-fleshed sweet potato,
    peeled weight, cut into 3cm chunks
4 tbsp lard
½ tsp salt, or to taste

1 Prepare your steamer. Arrange the squash and sweet potato pieces in the steamer tray. (Although they usually peak at the same time, I err on the side of caution and keep them separate in the tray.) Steam them until just tender.

2 Convey the cooked vegetables from the steamer to a sturdy mixing bowl. Cool slightly, then crush into a pulp with a pestle or rolling pin. A sturdy fork or an electric hand whisk are perfectly reasonable substitutes. You want a smooth and creamy balm, but the odd lump is to be embraced.

3 Gently warm the lard in a small saucepan, then pour it into the mash, mixing it in with gusto. Season with salt.

This method of stir-frying with white chillies and torch ginger is one of the most common ways to cook *pucuk ubi kayu*, which the Murut in Sabah and Sarawak call *umbus nu kasila*. In Borneo, tapioca leaves fine as fingers are preferred over their broader kin. Shoots, delicate and grass-green, are ideal, as they only need to be broken with a pestle and mortar. More mature leaves – the only sort I have access to – need to be truly pummelled to break down their fibres. A lady from Sumatra once taught me to salt and squeeze the crushed leaves, to relieve them of bitter juice, and so I do.

Contrary to what many of us think, the torch ginger is a composite flower or inflorescence, made up of multiple flowers. What people describe – including myself, throughout this book, for the sake of ease – as a torch ginger bud should, in fact, be in the plural. The species used in Sabah, reddish and fat, is especially generous with buds. If you are using the regular pink ones, just chop the entire thing.

This recipe, another gem from my friend Andreas, also features pea aubergines and pork fat. It also uses a touch of dried anchovy stock, in place of the usual water, for extra flavour.

UMBUS NU KASILA SINAANG RA LOMOK NU ULAK

SERVES 6-8

500g tapioca shoots
1 tsp salt, plus more to taste
200g pork fat, cut into 1cm dice
3 garlic cloves, peeled and finely chopped
125g pea aubergines
1 tbsp torch ginger buds (see above)
150g small white chillies
200ml dried anchovy stock (page 520)

1 In a pestle and mortar, crush the tapioca shoots in batches. You want them broken into fragments, not a paste. Place the crushed leaves in a bowl and massage in the salt. Leave for 5 minutes, then squeeze out the bitter juices. Contain the damp mulch of leaves in a bowl.

2 Place the diced pork fat in a deep frying pan or wok and pour enough water to barely cover. Bring to a boil over high heat, then lower the heat and cook until the water has completely evaporated. Continue cooking over low heat, stirring once in a while, until the fat turns into crisp, golden nuggets, in a pond of liquid lard. Remove the chips to a bowl. Resist the temptation to snack on them.

3 Only 4 tbsp of lard is required for frying the leaves, so tip out any excess (which you should strain, bottle and keep for future use). Return the frying pan to a medium heat. When this is hot, add the garlic. Once fragrant and light gold, add the crushed tapioca shoots. Fry for 2 minutes, stirring, then add the pea aubergines, torch ginger buds, white chillies and stock. Simmer for 10 minutes or until the vegetables are tender. Season to taste with salt. Serve sprinkled with the crisp-fried lard.

Nectar. Opulence. Wide-skied summers. The glossy baubles, vivid as clown noses, seem to make the loftiest promises at first glance, but it only takes a single nibble for these to be shot down. Even at its ripest, the rind of *Garcinia forbesii* has the acerbic bite of a bony quince. Its flesh is less astringent, but only fractionally. Vaguely known in English as wild mangosteen, the Kadazandusun call it *takob akob*, using it to sour foods, especially braises and soups, as other ethnic groups might *Garcinia atroviridis* (*asam gelugor*) or tamarind (*asam jawa*).

While *takob akob* may be used fresh, the fruit, or should I say rind, has all its potential unlocked when sun-dried. The darkened, shrivelled fragments resemble ears snapped off desiccated baby mummies, their snappy acidity weighted and broadened by the scent of wine cellars and worn leather wallets. The longer they are dried, the fuller their taste, their perfume. I sit at the lunch table in the porch, running several of these calloused buttons in my hands as if they were marbles, occasionally lowering my snout to them, likely looking quite deranged, waiting for my hosts at the Koposizon Homestay to return and for the feast to commence.

The *takob akob* was fetched from the market yesterday and played a crucial role in *pinasakan*, a tart braise of fish, summerily redolent of turmeric and lemongrass. Most, if not all, fish can be cooked in this fashion, from the freshwater carp (*tuongou*) and catfish-like *kakok* to the marine sardine (*basungan*), for which my hosts have plumped.

The *pinasakan* awaiting eager consumption in this corner of Papar looks quite removed from any I have previously encountered, however. Hendretha, who arrives with a pitcher of iced water, offers an explanation. Instead of simply being simmered until opaque, as is normal, the fish were braised for a loving eight hours over the coyest of flames, left to settle overnight, then fried this morning. The little soldiers now rest on a plate, assembled over a frisson of *ulam raja* (*Cosmos caudatus*), their crisp bodies ravaged, heads absent. Hendretha's husband, William, claims these to be tell-tale signs of a job well done. "You should be able to eat the bones", he chimed upon arriving at the table, one hand bearing a bowl of shredded green mango, another a jar of *onsom tonduguan*, sugar-preserved bilimbi.

The bilimbi came from their garden, a wonderland of flora and fauna. "Growing a vine called *inatawari* in close proximity seems to make the fruit less tart,", highlighted William during a tour around the estate yesterday. From him, I have learned about the gorgeousness of seven-needle flowers and how sumptuous they are simmered with coconut milk and dried shrimp; the *hivu-hivu* that ward off bad spirits; *makota kiwa*, whose plumage and fruit allegedly possess anti-cancer properties; and how bird's nest ferns are thought by villagers to be meeting points for ghosts. "I've seen nothing yet, though...." he reassured me as our feet returned to cool cement.

Today, the *pinasakan* is not alone in its mission to afford sustenance and pleasure. There is *inangsak hobong vogok*, chicken braised with torch ginger and bamboo shoots, and *manuk lihing*, another chicken-based concoction, heaving with ginger and the contents of a whole bottle of sweet yellow rice wine – the *lihing*. Almost every non-Muslim ethnic group in Sarawak and Sabah prepares a version of this dish.

Hendretha made the *lihing* herself. It is a process that requires patience and takes years to perfect; much depends on weather conditions and, well, the mood of the rice. I have heard of housewives swaddling fermenting jars in red cloth and placing knives on their lids to ward off evil spirits. "Having a mint shrub nearby seems to helps the *tinumol* ferment, too", Hendretha adds. *Tinumol* is the old Kadazan word for *lihing*.

THE LAND, THE SHOPS

William is of Hakka ancestry, while Hendretha is a Kadazan from here, Papar.

For its recognition as the largest ethnic group in Sabah, with at least forty subgroups under its canopy, it was not too long ago that the Kadazadusun existed as two. The unifying term was coined in 1989 by the PBS, *Parti Bersati Sabah*, and passed in a resolution by the KCA, Kadazan Cultural Association, which viewed it as the best way to mend an ongoing rivalry between the two peoples that had only served to impede their growth and development. It also helped smooth identity-related bumps: not only are the origins of both words, Kadazan and Dusun, unclear, it has also been theorised by some that the basis for their usage could have been geographical. As historian Owen Rutter, who spent four years with the North Borneo Civil Service in Sabah, wrote in his 1929 book *The Pagans of North Borneo*, "The Dusun usually describes himself generically as a tulun Tindal (landsman), or on the West Coast, particularly at Papar, as a Kadazan."

The dishes at lunch today are exquisite examples of Kadazandusun offerings, though several key figures are missing from the spread. A refreshing concoction of dried *Acetes*, cucumber and bilimbi. *Hinava*, meat, shrimp or fish stunned in acid, the local equivalent of ceviche. *Kinotuan magirorolot piniansak*, sautéed native spring onions, torch ginger buds and white chillies, a tricolour potpourri that market vendors sell in plastic packages, pretty and poised for the pot. *Noonsom bambangan*, chunks of tangy, odoriferous *bambangan* (*Mangifera pajang*) preserved in salt. *Rinalau tuhau*, a searing relish of wild ginger (*tuhau*), red chillies and salt, a preparation that also does justice to the mangrove apple (*Sonneratia caseolaris*; *pedada*).

The Kadazandusun make exceptional soups and liquid-laden stews. Today's *inangsak hobong vogok* is one of many. On previous trips, I have sampled broths cluttered with mangrove clams and yam shoots, dried *kombura* and crisp *touh* melons, and *kouk* from ditches and tender *bambangan* leaves. A Dusun friend introduced me to a soup prepared not with *bambangan* leaves but its fruit, in the company of smoked tinfoil barb (*lampam*). We ate it at his home in Kota Belud, with *vinulu vagas*, rice cooked in a bamboo culm over hot coals, a more luxurious version of which would include the scraped flesh of young coconuts. The taste of that almost elemental broth will never leave me, evoking balmy equatorial evenings, conjuring images of sepia-toned beaches and wood-stoked fires.

As with the other groups in Borneo, preserved fish (and meat) figures heavily in the cuisine of the Kadazandusun. Smoked or dried fish may be used in *pinaranas*, while salted fish may be used to give body to rice gruels, with a particularly scintillating rendition including tidy handfuls of bosky *kuhat*, common split-gills. Salted *sulit* in particular is sublime with *tarap* or unripe jackfruit, in a chest-stroking braise whitened with coconut found along Sabah's northern coastline. Salted *sulit* is also delectable cooked over barbecue, turning it into *tinunuvan pindang*.

The fish preserve most commonly associated with the Kadazandusun is surely *bosou sada*, sometimes called *tinamba* or, as it is here in Papar, *sinamo*. Any fish can aspire to be *bosou*. Little ones, like anchovies, will be left whole, while medium to large fish will have to be butterflied or cut up. They are then cleaned and massaged with salt, cooked rice and the crushed black viscera of cured *pangi* (*Pangium edule*), believed to relieve the ferment of foul odours. The party is then directed into Tupperwares or glass jars and stowed in a dark, cool place for at least a week. In the past, a vessel known as *balenei*, first glossed with beeswax, or *kalanan*, small clay jars, would be called upon. Once adequately funky, the *bosou sada* will be either fried with oil and aromatics, such as onion, ginger and garlic, or consumed raw – certainly not an option for the faint of heart.

There are a handful of variations on the idea. Vegetables and fruit, such as slices of unripe jackfruit and *polod* shoots are welcome to join the fray. The Dusun of Tambunan are fond of adding cool slices of succulent banana pith. The fish may be omitted entirely, the resulting vegetarian ferment branded *bosou sayur*, or replaced with cow skin, pork or shrimp. Prepared without the cooked rice, *bosou* may be called *pinongian*.

SPIRIT SATISFACTION

We continue to hover around the marble-top table in William's porch, chatting, waiting for teatime to descend. Gleaming with satisfaction, though nowhere near stultified, we soon end up nibbling on boiled *kamansi* seeds, which taste of macadamias and freshly baked bread. (It is of little wonder that the fruit of *Artocarpus camansi* is indeed called the breadnut.)

Tapioca and other root crops, such as sweet potato, yams and squash, are staples, eaten boiled or steamed, at breakfast or teatime, dripped with local honey and grated coconut. These same crops may be cooked with glutinous rice and coconut milk into the gruel that is *dinimpulan*. William's eyes sparkle at the mention of a wine derived from tapioca. "Some of the most excellent wines come from palm trees", he says, highlighting milky *paha*, collected from the flowers of the *sawit* palm before they fruit. Fresh from the tree, it is sweet, ambrosial even, and requires the addition of a cinnamon-like bark to aid fermentation.

For all their love for sweet, starchy roots, rice is the chief, most beloved, carbohydrate of the Kadazandusun, as it was in ancient times. The Kadazandusun have traditions based on rice agriculture, growing wet paddy in the coastal plains and valleys and dry paddy inland, on the slopes of hills. As it was once their sole source of livelihood, the success of each crop was paramount. Every crop cycle, local farmers would do their utmost to appease and satisfy the *bambarayon*, rice spirits, engaging in a series of rituals, culminating in what is the most well-known, the joyous Tadau Kaamatan or Harvest Festival. This usually falls at the end of May and it is during this time that the toothsome *hinabakan do mata* may be enjoyed, a delicacy of unripe glutinous rice, sweetened with sugar and eaten with scraped young coconut.

Today, short and medium grains in shades white, red and purple are grown and eaten by the Kadazandusun, simply boiled and consumed as is, sometimes receiving chunks of taro yam or squash as extenders. The cooked grains may be enveloped in the generous leaves of the *doringin* tree (*Dillenia suffruticosa*), thereby producing *linapot*, though those of *tarap*, *wangian*, *wonihan* (*Macaranga bancana*) and *tintap* (*Neonauclea gigantea*) are regarded with equal fervour. Besides being biodegradable, portable and, well, beautiful, these parcels are believed to prolong the shelf-life of their cargo, sometimes even up to a week.

Besides being fermented with crushed yeast (*ragi*) into *tapuy*, glutinous rice is usually reserved for snacks and sweets, such as the *hinapot*, cakes of ground glutinous rice in banana leaf wrappers. I tend to identify them as *hinompuka*, which is what they are known as in Penampang. When made with banana, usually *kepok*, or tapioca, they become *tinapong*.

Hendretha and her helper arrive at our table bearing a portable stove, a large wok, a tray of ingredients, several mugs and a pot of freshly brewed coffee. Hendretha lights the stove and places the wok on it. Once sufficiently hot, she sprinkles over grated coconut, languidly stirring the snow as it warms up. In goes a heady amount of sugar and damp sago flour (*sagu basah*) and everything is flung around until a modicum of stickiness is acquired. The mixture is then gathered in the middle of the cooking vessel, before getting cajoled into a plump disc. While she cleans up, William takes over the stove, watching the flames like a hawk and occasionally running his frying slice around the edges of the disc. The aromas of singed flesh and burnt sugar fill the air.

Five minutes in, the disc, though set at its edges, still looks worryingly fragile. William, however, is certain it is ready. Without uttering so much as a prayer, he shoves his frying slice beneath the disc and flips it without a moment's hesitation. It miraculously lands on its other side, unscathed, its fuzzy surface burnished, blackened in parts. The *pinumpol* is left to cook for a couple more minutes before being cut into wedges, rather like a pizza, and cautiously applied to face. Smoky, sweet and pleasantly chewy, I cannot help but feel I am eating something from an ancient time.

Tea is not over though, and the next item feels and tastes older still. Also conjured from sago, coconut and sugar, *hininggazang* receives further enrichment from banana, *pelangan*, to be exact. The sago-coconut rubble is cooked in the same way as for *pinumpol*, but with coins of the banana half-heartedly buried in its centre, allowing them to steam into fragrant butteriness. Unlike *pinumpol*, *hininggazang* does not emerge from the wok all that neatly, its finished form a veritable mess, like a tart that had to be salvaged from the kitchen floor. But it is just as toothsome as its neater kin, especially in between sips of biting coffee, and that is all that counts.

This is sometimes spelled as *hinata*, which is the Lotud name for *hinava*.

There are likely as many versions as there are cooks, made with all kinds of fish as well as the flesh of buffalo, wild boar, chicken and snails. This particular *hinava*, containing the grated heart of the *bambangan* (*badu*) and ridged crescents of bittergourd, is usually linked to the Dusun community in Penampang. They may add slices of torch ginger fruit if luck is on their side.

Some minor preliminary prep is in order: the *badu* needs to be washed and dried for 2 days before using. This will still be delicious in its absence, so do not worry if you cannot find it.

HINAVA SADA TONGII

SERVES 4-6

1 *bambangan* seed, prepared as above
250g Spanish mackerel fillet, skinned
  and boned
4 tbsp calamansi lime juice
125g bittergourd, deseeded and
  thinly sliced
4 shallots, peeled and cut into thin
  half-moons
2cm ginger, peeled and cut into thin slivers
3 red bird's eye chillies, finely sliced
¼ tsp salt, plus more to taste
Pinch of sugar
Freshly ground black pepper

1 Finely grate the dried bambangan seed and place this in a bowl. Cut the Spanish mackerel fillet into thin slivers. Add to the bowl, then mix in the calamansi juice. Leave for a couple of minutes, or until the fish just crosses over to opacity.

2 Mix in the remaining ingredients and plate up. Taste and adjust seasoning with salt and black pepper.

In Borneo, dried *Acetes*, like coral-coloured filings, are blanched and then dried or smoked (in other words, roasted over very gentle heat over woodfire). Similarly preserved *Acetes* can be bought from Thai and Japanese grocers. Usually, these are washed and added straight into the dish, but I prefer to dry roast them very slightly, not to crisp them up, but to awaken their senses.

HINAVA GIPAN

SERVES 4

4 tbsp dried *Acetes*, washed
20g turmeric, peeled and finely grated
100ml calamansi lime juice
250g medium shrimps, peeled weight, halved lengthwise
4 shallots, peeled and cut into thin half-moons
4 red bird's eye chillies, finely sliced
¼ tsp salt, plus more to taste
Pinch of sugar
Freshly ground black pepper

1 Lightly wash the dried *Acetes*. Squeeze to remove excess liquid, then toast in a frying pan over low heat until faintly aromatic. You want to catch the whiff of hot beaches without a tan.

2 Combine the grated turmeric with the calamansi lime juice. Leave to sit for 5 minutes then strain, extracting as much juice from the turmeric as possible. Pour this golden liquid over the halved shrimp in a bowl. Leave to stand for 5 minutes, or until opaque, before mixing in the remaining ingredients.

This is somewhere in between a salad and a relish, something to add zing and oomph to a meal. I like it just with some piping hot rice and, for more umami, a glug of good fish sauce or soy.

LINOMBUR BUBUK OM TULOD-ULOD

SERVES 4

50g dried *Acetes*, washed
6 bilimbi, sliced into rounds
¼ tsp salt, plus more to taste
2 red bird's eye chillies, finely sliced
100g cucumber, peeled and cut
    into thin slices
2 tbsp lime juice
Pinch of sugar

1 Lightly wash the dried *Acetes*. Squeeze well to remove excess liquid, then tip into a bowl. Add the bilimbi, salt and chillies and, with the aid of a spoon, lightly bruise. Mix in the remaining ingredients and taste and adjust seasoning with salt.

This is punchy and unyielding, and not just in terms of saltiness. To call the *bambangan* odoriferous would be understating things. The brown-skinned, unprepossessing fruit has a scent reminiscent of curry leaves and pesticide, emitting an energy so pervasive that even the most secure Renoma luggage would have issues containing it. I adore its churlish personality. Hotels in Borneo, I have found, do not.

This is sublime with hot rice, red bird's eye chillies and crisp-fried fish.

NOONSOM BAMBANGAN

MAKES APPROX. 500G

6 *bambangan*, each approx. 200g
50g sea salt flakes

1 Run a sharp knife vertically around one *bambangan* and strip off its hide. This takes a modicum of effort and is seldom a neat job. Make grid-like incisions all over its fibre-fraught flesh. Run your knife parallel to the stone, taking off as much flesh as possible, collecting them in a bowl. Prepare all the *bambangan* this way, reserving 2 stones.

2 Finely grate these reserved stones over the flesh, then mix in the sea salt. Pack into a sterilised 750g Kilner jar and keep in a cool place for at least 1 week before eating.

Tuhau, *Etlingera coccinea*, has bags of personality, each cane laced with the combined perfume of torch ginger and Vietnamese mint, kept on its toes with a rusty blade.

Rinalau is the Dusun term for *sambal*, and you may up the quantities of salt and chilli, making this properly fiery. I remember using one such *sambal* to colour a bowl of pig offal noodles one rainy afternoon in Penampang. It was divine.

RINALAU TUHAU

SERVES 4

6 stalks *Etlingera coccinea*
½ tsp salt
4 red bird's eye chillies

1 Run a knife down a stalk of *Etlingera coccinea*. Strip off its tough, outer layer. Continue until you arrive at a crisp white, slightly malleable, marrow. Prepare all the *tuhau* this way. Slice thinly, disregarding the sticky, slimy threads. Place in a bowl.

2 Crush the salt and red bird's eye chillies into a paste and mix into the *Etlingera coccinea*. Serve as an accompaniment to a meal.

As mentioned, I encountered this wonderful preserve at the Koposizon Homestay in Papar. I was so besotted by them that I had to ask for the recipe, which they generously provided.

I steep my bilimbi in brine for a shorter period than William, who soaks his overnight. I have found that while this works a treat for fruit straight from the tree, which he had, in all their taut, crisp glory, those of us with less fine fruit will be saddled with limp, soggy pickles.

You may of course have these as a snack, but they are wonderful as part of a meal. I love these with steamed rice, fried fish, slices of unripe mango and a punchy *sambal*.

ONSOM TONDUGUAN

MAKES 1KG

2kg bilimbi
100g sea salt
1 litre water
1kg granulated sugar

1 Wash the bilimbi. Combine the sea salt and water in a bowl and stir to dissolve. Add the bilimbi, cover with teacloth and set aside in a cool place for 4 hours.

2 Drain the fruit, dry them well. Pack them into a 1½ litre sterilised Kilner jar. Inundate with the granulated sugar. Shake well to disperse the crystals among the fruit and stow in a cool, dark place for at least 2 months. The sugar crystals will dissolve, forming a syrup tinted by the juices released by the now shrivelled, dimmed fruit. At some point, the bilimbi will be in disconcerting, lifeless, suspension, but worry not: the sugar does take some time to creep into their veins, and when that happens, the fruits will sink, arranging themselves to fill up the jar quite beautifully.

Many kinds of river fish (*ikan sungai*) may be used in *bosou ikan*, also known by certain groups as *sinamo* or *noonsom*. Some of the more common ones include Malaysian mahseer (*pelian*), tilapia (*talapia*) and, as in this case, *sarawi*. Although it is true that small fish are best, do not worry if you can only get big ones: cut them up into medium-sized chunks and remove any lethal bones.

Any self-respecting Kadazandusun cook will tell you *nasi kondinga*, a species of hillside rice, makes the best *bosou*, cooking into robust grains. I use regular jasmine rice and it works alright.

Many lace their ferment with garlic, shallots, ginger, torch ginger, *tuhau*, black pepper and small white chillies (*lada topurak*). This one uses just shallots, white chillies and ginger, but features the inky flesh of *pangi, Pangium edule*. In Sabah, this can be easily gleaned in plastic pouches from markets. In Singapore, I can only get the seeds, sold boiled, fermented and dried; they are poisonous raw. Upon purchase, I wash them in several changes of water and soak them in a bowl of fresh water for anywhere between 2-5 days, so they soften slightly. I crack them open on a chopping board with a pestle and gouge out their flesh. I then pound the collected flesh in a mortar into a crumbly paste. For this recipe, 10 *pangi* seeds should more than suffice.

BOSOU IKAN SARAWI

MAKES 750G

200g jasmine rice
400ml water
2 tbsp sea salt flakes
2 shallots, peeled and finely sliced
8 small white chillies
20g ginger, peeled and slivered
2 tbsp *pangi* flesh (see above)
300g *ikan sarawi*, no longer than
        10cm, cleaned

1 Wash the rice three times or until the water runs clear. Place the washed grains and 400ml water in a saucepan. Bring to a boil over medium heat, then cover, reduce the heat to its lowest and cook until the rice is soft but not too mushy. Tip out into a large mixing bowl and cool completely.

2 Into the cooled rice, massage 4 tsp of the sea salt flakes, shallots, white chillies, ginger and *pangi* flesh until well combined. The *pangi* should speckle the rice as Oreo crumbs would a tub of Cookies and Cream ice-cream. Rub the cleaned fish with the remaining sea salt, then add it to the seasoned rice. Give it a good mix, then pack into a sterilised 1 litre Kilner jar. Seal and keep in a cool, dark place for at least a week.

3 To cook (though some people do eat it raw), add the desired quantity of *bosou* to a pan of shallots and ginger sizzling in a shallow pond of vegetable oil. Fry, stirring, until the fish is on the verge of collapse, the oil separating from the starchy mass.

Pinasakan involves cooking fish in a liquid honed with acidic fruit, be it unripe mango or *bambangan*, tamarind or, in this case, *takob akob*, until the liquid has mostly evaporated. For the photograph, I used silver catfish no larger than marker pens, as that is what I had. This species seems unavailable in Sabah but is, I have been assured, a decent substitute; the Kadazandusun make this with almost any freshwater fish. I add chillies too, as I like it a bit spicy.

Fish cooked this way seems tastier the following day and I take a leaf out of William's book when upcycling them. After removing the fish from the fridge, I arrange them on a tray lined with kitchen towel to absorb excess moisture and discard the fibrous aromatics. I heat 2cm of vegetable oil in a large wok (or deep frying pan) over medium heat, then introduce the fish, basting them in the bubbling fat. I lower the heat slightly and fry for 10-12 minutes until deepest gold, then drain them on fresh kitchen towel. You may have to do this in batches depending on the capacity of your vessel. You want them ravaged by oil, crisp all the way through, poised for uninterrupted bodily consumption. They will look unspeakable. Hideous. But boy, will they be tasty. Serve with rice, a bright and fresh *sambal cili merah*, essentially *sambal belacan* (page 495) sans fermented product but a touch more salt and sugar, shredded semi-ripe mango and *ulam rajah*. Food of the Gods.

PINASAKAN SADA

SERVES 6-8

40g ginger, sliced
15g turmeric, sliced
4 red bird's eye chillies
3 lemongrass stalks, tender
  portions only
400g small silver catfish, cleaned
  (see above)
1 tsp salt
150ml water
8 dried *Garcinia forbesii*

1 Using a pestle and mortar, pound the ginger, turmeric and bird's eye chillies into a *very* rough paste. Add the lemongrass stalks and give them a few light bashings, just to bruise them. Tip this fragrant mixture, along with the remaining ingredients, into a deep frying pan or casserole, spreading them out evenly over the base.

2 Place the fish-laden vessel over medium heat. Once the liquid bubbles, half-cover and simmer until most of the liquid has evaporated and the fish is cooked through. This usually takes no more than 5 minutes.

Clams simmered in broths to varying degrees of dryness, with the shoots of palms or taro yams, is standard fare for the Kadazandusun. Their bivalves of choice would be mangrove clams (*kokogis*, *lokan*; *Polymesoda expansa*) or Javanese razor shells (*seput pahat*; *Pharella javanica*). I use Asiatic hard clams, *Meretrix meretrix*, that folks in Sabah either call *dalus* or *kunau*. Of course, any clam will work.

The instructions beneath include the peeling of taro shoots, although I get mine from a Philippine grocer already peeled and cut into sections. Shoots as thick as crayons are best, but even those as fat as leeks are not an issue, as they tend to cook into succulent slipperiness in about the same time; you need not cut them. In the absence of these glorious shoots, I recommend yardlong beans.

The addition of fried taro is thoroughly my own — I love how the chunks imbibe the briny liquid, thickening it slightly and infusing it with their own bready sweetness.

DALUS NONSOK MIAMPAI SUNSULAG

SERVES 4

500g Asiatic hard clams
300g young taro shoots
250g taro, peeled and cut into 1cm slices
2 garlic cloves, peeled and crushed
4 shallots, peeled and sliced
2cm ginger, peeled and crushed
500ml light chicken stock
Vegetable oil, for frying
Salt

1 Rinse the clams several times, then place them in a bowl and cover with cold water. Peel the taro shoots, exposing their softly corrugated, pale green interiors. Cut these into 8cm sections.

2 Heat 2cm of vegetable oil in a deep medium-sized saucepan or wok over medium heat. Once hot, fry the taro slices in batches until lightly crusted and pale gold. They should be very slightly undercooked, tender but hesitant. Remove these to a plate and discard all but 2 tbsp of the oil.

3 Over medium heat, fry the garlic, shallots and ginger in the reserved oil until lightly coloured and fragrant. Stir in the young taro shoots and chicken stock. Once the liquid bubbles, cover and simmer for 10 minutes or until the taro shoots are just tender.

4 Return the fried taro to the saucepan. Drain the clams and add them as well. Cover and leave to bubble steadily for 3-5 minutes, or until the clams have sprung open and released their briny juices. By this time, the fried taro should have cooked to perfection, their crusts melting into the shallow pool of broth, their edges blurred, breaking in parts. Taste and adjust seasoning with salt.

The name means "soup, bamboo shoot, pork".

For the photograph, I used 1 tablespoon of the small, bullet-like, torch ginger buds described on page 140, instead of slices of an entire regular one stipulated beneath.

INANGSAK HOBONG VOGOK

SERVES 8

A small fresh bamboo shoot,
  approx. 400g
2 tbsp vegetable oil
75g pork skin, cut into thin slivers
6 garlic cloves, peeled and bruised
8 small white chillies
1cm turmeric, bruised
1 torch ginger bud, finely sliced
200g pork shoulder, thickly slivered
½ tsp salt
1 litre light chicken stock
8 dried *Garcinia forbesii*

1 First, prepare the bamboo shoot. With a sharp knife, peel off as much of its skin as possible. Halve it lengthwise and boil it in a medium saucepan of lightly salted water until just tender. Drain, cut into thin slivers, then cook briefly in water again. Drain and set aside.

2 Heat the vegetable oil in a deep saucepan or casserole over medium heat, then add the pork skin. Fry until pale gold and most of its fat has rendered down.

3 Add the garlic cloves, white chillies, turmeric and torch ginger. Fry for 2 minutes, until fragrant, then add the pork shoulder and fry just to seal.

4 Add the salt, chicken stock and *Garcinia forbesii*. Bring to a boil, then cover, lower the heat and simmer for 20 minutes. Add the prepared bamboo shoots, cover and continue simmering for another 20 minutes or until both meat and bamboo shoot are tender. Taste and adjust seasoning with salt.

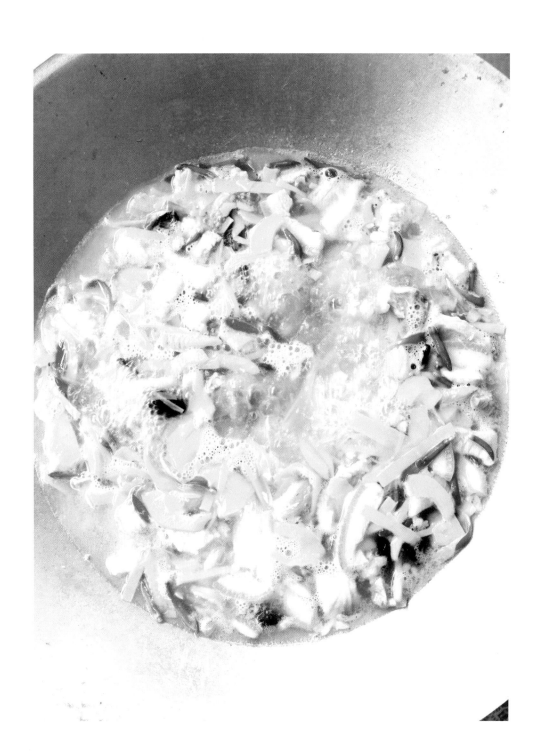

The stipulated amount of ginger is not an error. You want its presence to be especially muscular to combat the *lihing*, sweet yellow rice wine, which has to be as sweet as Sauternes. This is quite simple to make at home. Steam 1.2kg glutinous rice, first washed until the water runs clear, then mix in crushed wine tablets as per their packet's instructions. Chinese grocers and medicine shops sell two kinds of wine tablets, sweet or spicy. In this case, plump for the former. Then pack into a sterilised 2 litre Kilner jar and keep in a cool, dark place for 21-24 days, shaking the bottle occasionally. Now all you need to do is strain the fermented grains with muslin and bottle the wine. You should get approx. 1 litre.

In the accompanying photograph, *manuk lihing* is served with purple rice, *noonsom bambangan* (page 156) and a bright and fresh *sambal cili merah*, essentially *sambal belacan* (page 495) sans fermented product.

MANUK LIHING

SERVES 8

350g young ginger
2 tbsp oil
8 garlic cloves, peeled and crushed
1½kg free-range chicken, jointed
    into eighths
1 tsp salt, plus more to taste
1 litre sweet yellow rice wine

1 Roughly slice the young ginger and lightly crush in a pestle and mortar.

2 Heat the oil in a deep saucepan or casserole over medium-high heat, then add the garlic. Once fragrant and faintly coloured, add the crushed ginger. Once the ginger has released its aromas, add the chicken and salt. Stir, cover, lower the heat and allow the chicken to steam in the pot for 10 minutes.

3 Stir in the yellow rice wine. Cover and continue simmering gently for 45 minutes, or until the chicken is tender. Taste and adjust seasoning with salt.

In Sabah and Sarawak, it is common to find packets of damp sago flour, *sagu basah*, in markets. I soak my flour in a little water overnight instead.

Traditionally a wok is called for, but I use a frying pan here. What demands some sleight-of-hand is not so much the flipping but the uniting of coconut, sago flour and sugar on hot metal. This has to be done quickly for the *pinumpol* to be light; leave these ingredients to their own devices or give in to that nagging temptation to overmix and they will merge to form a coaster. *Pinumpol* is a textural sensation, a thick disc of coconut snow bound by sago, that results in a faintly jelly-like interior and a light, crisp exterior.

For *hininggazang*, make the *pinumpol* in a large frying pan, approximately 21cm in diameter. At step 3, add *all* the coconut, then *half* of both sago and sugar. Cover the lumpy-bumpy surface with coins of banana. I cannot get the *pelangan* William used and so use *raja*. It is hard to give a precise measurement; you want enough fruit to cover the snow. Sprinkle over the remaining sago and sugar, lightly press the mess down, compacting it slightly. Once the underside is a light brown, about 2-3 minutes, flip the pancake in sections, breaking it up, and cook for another 2-3 minutes. If it looks like a car crash, you are probably doing the right thing.

PINUMPOL

MAKES 2; SERVES 8

300g sago flour
175ml water
200g grated coconut
50g caster sugar

1 Place the sago flour in a bowl and stir in the water. You will get a phase-defying substance, a white batter somewhere between liquid and solid. Cover and leave overnight.

2 The next day, you should find that most of the water has been absorbed by the flour. Give it a stir, to break up the now-solid mass, and go in with your fingers to produce a crumble-like rubble. Set aside.

3 Put an 18cm frying pan over medium-high heat. Once hot, but not smoking, sprinkle in half the grated coconut. Lightly fry, stirring always, just to dry it out. Sprinkle over half the sago, stir it in quickly, and finally, half the sugar. Lightly press the mixture down on the frying pan, compacting it slightly. Once the underside is lightly scorched, flip it over and cook for another 2-3 minutes.

4 Make the remaining pancake this way, too. Cool for the briefest of moments, then cut into wedges and eat with coffee.

Although the concept of dessert is alien to traditional meal structures in Sabah (and indeed much of Asia), I think little bowlfuls of *nanggiu*, short noodles of sago flour cooked in a creamy, not-too-sweet coconut soup, is an excellent way to conclude a meal.

NANGGIU

SERVES 4-6

FOR THE NOODLES
300g sago flour, plus more for dusting
200ml freshly boiled water

FOR THE SAUCE
400ml coconut milk
   (second extract; page 521)
500ml water
1 pandan leaf, knotted
250ml coconut cream
125g sugar
½ tsp salt

1 Place the sago flour in a large mixing bowl. Pour over the freshly boiled water and stir with a wooden spoon or a pair of chopsticks, then go in with your hands to form a smooth, bouncy dough. (The dough loses heat quite fast.) Add a spot more sago flour or regular water if necessary.

2 Roll out the pastry into a large rectangle, approx. 3mm thick, on a work surface dusted with sago flour. Cut the pastry into thin strips, each roughly ½cm wide and 3cm long. Lightly dust these strips with more sago flour to keep them separate, then spread them over a tray lined with muslin. Leave in a cool place to dry out for 2 hours. I usually do this overnight.

3 Place the coconut milk and water for the sauce in a large saucepan. Bring to a boil over medium heat. Drop in the pandan leaf, followed by the pasta. It will appear as if the water is insufficient, but worry not, just breathe and stir very gently to prevent sticking and simmer until cooked, approx. 3-4 minutes. (If your pot is indeed in need of water, add a modest splash.) The pasta will not look crystalline just yet, but foamy and faintly slimy, filled with tiny bubbles. The milky liquid should have thickened slightly in the process. Add the sugar, salt and coconut cream. Simmer for a final 2-3 minutes. You can serve this hot, but I prefer leaving it to settle for 10 minutes or so.

While in Sabah this would be made with the flour derived from glutinous varieties of *todugan*, I use black glutinous rice flour from an organic grocer. Although the name *todugan* points to a particular species of purple (or black, to most of us) upland rice, in Sabah any kind of purple rice tends to be blithely labelled *todugan*.

Grated coconut may be added to the batter for more texture. Leftover *hinompuka* is quite good snipped up and fried in a lightly oiled pan, eaten promptly with a sprinkling of sugar or a drizzle of honey.

HINOMPUKA

MAKES 8

250g glutinous rice flour
25g black glutinous rice flour
½ tsp salt
60g coconut sugar, shaved (page 524)
75g caster sugar
275ml water
Eight 20x20cm banana leaf squares,
    softened (page 520)
Vegetable oil, for brushing

1 Combine the two glutinous rice flours and salt in a large mixing bowl. Stir to combine.

2 Place the coconut sugar, caster sugar and 100ml water in a small saucepan. Bring to a boil over medium heat, stirring so the sugars dissolve, then strain into the flour mixture. Stir with a wooden spoon until a claggy mixture is obtained, then pour in the remaining 175ml water to get a thick batter. Cover and set aside for 1 hour.

3 Prepare your steamer and lightly lubricate the sheets of banana leaf with oil. Divide the batter among these, approximately 3 tbsp per sheet, and fold into thin, rectangular parcels. Arrange them snugly in the perforated compartment and steam for 30 minutes over medium heat. Cool slightly before defrocking.

Kombos is traditionally cooked in young coconut kernels plunged into smouldering charcoal. This recipe has been tailored to suit the modern kitchen.

You will require three young coconuts to yield the stipulated quantity of flesh. This may leave you with surplus coconut water. Do not whinge; just drink.

I do not sweeten *kombos*; the whole point lies in its neutrality, which is what makes it so soothing. You may serve a saucer of sugar alongside, so that eaters can adjust the sweetness to their liking.

KOMBOS

SERVES 6

125g glutinous rice, thrice washed
    and soaked in water overnight
450ml coconut water
300g scraped young coconut flesh
Pinch of salt
Sugar, to serve

1 Drain the glutinous rice and place in a saucepan with the coconut water. Over medium heat, bring it to a boil. Lower the heat, cover and simmer for 15-20 minutes, or until the grains are sticky and tender, forming a loose-textured gruel. You may add a touch of water (or extra coconut water if you have it), if necessary.

2 Add the young coconut flesh and a pinch of salt. Simmer for just 3-5 minutes, to warm the curls of soft white flesh. Divide among 4-6 bowls and serve with a saucer of sugar.

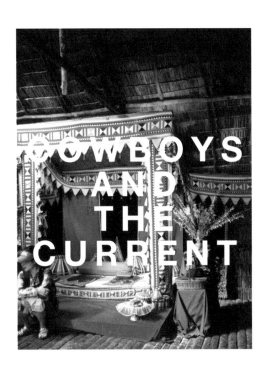

COWBOYS AND THE CURRENT

At just seven in the morning, the seams of the *kedai kopi* are on the cusp of splitting. Patrons on the waiting list are hovering around its entrance in clots, while most of those who managed to get squeezed in have had to share tables. The configuration of stools around many a faux marble countertop echoes that of a choker pearled to the point of buckling.

Pison and I were fortunate to be granted a table solely for ourselves, with an extra stool to boot, gratefully occupied by a bag bearing the fruits of a wickedly early jaunt to the *tamu* at Tamparuli. Leaving it in the truck may have been the more sensible thing to do, but after the hour-long ride at cake chiller temperatures, I reckoned some fresh air would do its contents a world of good.

We managed to get some good things. A pair of *bambangan* and a sheaf of *tuhau*. A paper bag exploding with *engkalak* (*Litsea garciae*), like the bulbous knobs of vintage cabinet doors, their delicate Percy Pig skins concealing flesh with the mild taste of soap and texture of avocado. A bouquet of *daun jipun*, sometimes called *garing* in Sabah and *ensabi* in Sarawak, perhaps for the biting, wasabi-like qualities it possesses. The Dusun love these blanched and dressed with lime juice and chilli.

I wish I had more time to fiddle and play. I would have helped myself to the bundles of *molopou* leaves that the Dusun add to broths of rice and river snails, and some *tayahan*. "Heard those are rare", I bleat, taking a swig of *kopi*. Also known as *kaakatung*, *Sagittaria sagittifolia* is most often found in paddy fields and only harvested during planting season. The Dusun apparently turn their arrow-shaped leaves into salads, lightly bruised and mixed with lime juice and shallots. They are also added to soups and stir-fries. "Always a next time," Pison says, sagely, as a pair of ceramic bowls, plumed with steam, descend on the table before us. We lower our dimpled mugs and place them to one side. The malevolent brews can take a backseat for now.

Mee sup is one of Kota Belud's most beloved dishes, a box that even the most casual, most fleeting, traversers feel compelled to tick. It is unfussy, as is much of the best food. A tangle of wiry egg noodles, the colour of hay, a handful of sliced tender chicken and a broth whose limpidity belies a savouriness that reverberates, like a succulent bass line, through its aqueous being. The heat of the broth restores whatever senses the caffeine neglected. Its taste returns comfort to our bones.

As we eat, I notice a pair of *tudung*-clad women at an adjacent table, locked in animated conversation, cedar-hued tea in one hand, *pinjaram* in the other, the flying saucer fritters dyed lizard green. I have only ever encountered them plain and white or brown with *gula merah*, coconut or palm sugar. "Those have pandan in them," Pison says, noticing my curiosity. "A recent thing. The Bajau vendors across the road make good ones."

Pinjaram or *panjaram* plays a vital role in many festive occasions, from weddings and birthdays to Hari Raya, believing to bring good fortune and prosperity. This does not apply only to the Bajau, but the other ethnic groups who predominantly subscribe to Islam, like the Suluk, Iranun, Kagayan, Banguingui and Ubian; pockets of animists continue to exist among their number. The *pinjaram* seldom grace such occasions alone, often in the company of other sweet things. *Penganan*, fried knotted biscuits of ground roasted corn. *Panggi-panggi* or *koling-koling*, thick, fried whorls of rice batter. *Wajit*, a delectably chewy cake of glutinous rice, bronzed and plump with coconut sugar. *Gerigit*, baked biscuits of flour and coconut. And perhaps the fiddliest and most highly coveted of all, *jaa*, golden nets intricately fashioned from a paint of ground rice and sugar, shaped into half-moon purses or tight cylinders during their final moments in hot fat.

SEA CHANGE

The word Bajau is an exonym for the groups of Sama who live in Sabah. The West Coast Bajau are the ones who are based here, in Kota Belud, as well as towns such as Kota Marudu, Kudat, Sandakan, Petagas and Papar. Their East Coast counterparts are concentrated in the areas of Semporna and Lahad Datu. Although most historians seem to agree they are not indigenous to this part of Borneo, their origins remain mired in mystery, as is the cause for their movement. The most widespread theory is that they had beginnings in the Sulu Archipelago, a cluster of small islands situated off Borneo's northeastern coast, and have always led a littoral existence, the salty waters coursing through their veins since time immemorial.

It is said that they migrated southwards (as well as northwards to Mindanao) around 10-11th century, setting up settlements along the northwestern and southeastern coasts of Sabah for trade, where preserved fish, dried and salted, served as currency.

Another theory, based on linguistic similarities among other things, claims their true origins to be Johor on the Malaysian Peninsula. Yet another concludes that they likely came from the South Barito area of South Kalimantan, with beginnings as river and delta dwellers, acquiring sea shipbuilding and navigation technology skills and nous from the Malays.

What most seem to agree on, however, is the Sama's splintered, ever-shifting nature as a people, who until 19th century were emergent, yet to assume proper political form. Even today, confusion clouds their identity. The Sama are comprised of numerous small groups who have decided to mostly distinguish themselves by the name of an island, island clusters, or region, usually either their place of birth or principal area of settlement. For example, the title Sama Simunul describes those from Sinumul, while Sama Ubian points to those from South Ubian, Sama Banguingui those from Banguingui. The last two groups exist in Sabah as the Ubian and Banguingui.

While the vast majority of the East Coast Bajau continue to make a living off the sea, the West Coast Bajau, especially those living further inland, have managed to develop a material culture removed from their chiefly maritime history. Many have assumed roles in industries ranging from agriculture to politics and business, although it is true many continue to work as fishermen and artisans. In the not-so-distant past, the West Coast Bajau reared cattle and horses. "When I was younger, the chiefs would ride their steeds around Kota Belud," Pison shares, as we wrap up breakfast. Hence their title: Cowboys of the East.

Another ethnic group found on Sabah's western coast are the Kagayan (or Cagayan). They are the Jama Mapun of the Philippines, occupants of Turtle Island and Mapun, also known as Cagayan de Sulu. In his book, *The Sulu Zone 1768 – 1898*, James Francis Warren states that they traded with North Borneo and Palawan in coconut oil and mats woven with pandan leaves, although it remains to be seen if trade impelled the first Jama Mapun to venture southwards about 400 years ago. Trade does, however, most likely account for the presence of the Suluk people in Sabah. Known as Tausug in the Philippines, the "People of the Current" began migrating to North Borneo around 18th century, during the era of the Sultanate of Sulu, setting up posts in Balambangan, an island off the coast of Kudat, and in Paitan, Sugut, Labuk and Kinabatangan, trading with the Chinese, Indians, Arabs and Europeans in various exotics. Pearls and mother of pearl from Sulu. Clove, pepper and betel from Mindanao. Camphor, beeswax, edible nests and *tripang*, sea cucumber, from Borneo.

Besides containing a sizeable Bajau (and Dusun) community, Kota Belud is also home to many Iranun. The name derives from *Il-lanaw-en*, a Maguindanaoan word meaning "People from the Lake". Indeed, it has been suggested by some researchers that they began as the Maranao, who lived in settlements around Lake Lanao in Mindanao. In *A Voyage to New Guinea and the Moluccas, from Balambangan*, Scottish navigator Thomas Forrest shares, through an account of his 1774 voyage, that it was a natural catastrophe, an enormous volcano eruption around 1765, that sent the Maranao dispersing, with a few reaching the northeast coast of Borneo. Other possible reasons cited included the pressures of a living in a highly stratified society and the general desire for greener pastures, an especially feasible option for merchant clans.

In the days of the Sulu Sultanate, the Iranun were notorious for terrorising trading posts and slave raiding. Today, they have a reputation for being skillful fishermen and cultivators of crops, such as paddy, sweet potato and sugarcane. They are also heavily involved in the manufacturing and selling of *gula tebu*, an unrefined sugar derived from the gradual reduction of sugarcane juice.

The Iranun are also held in high regard for their fish preserving techniques, each one deserving of a specific term. *Tiapa* refers to fish that are harpooned, usually with thick bamboo skewers, stood upright, near glowing embers, so they softly smoke. *Seda'a inagag* are fish that are dried immediately after slicing. *Seda'a tiampik* are fish, usually some form of mackerel, that are thinly sliced and dried. *Seda'a tinimusan* are fish that are sliced, salted, then dried. *Seda'a liking* refers to split and lightly dried *ikan talang* (queenfish; *Scomberoides commersonnianus*), locally known as *sampantiyau*, possibly a distortion of its Chinese name, *shan ban tiao*. In the market here in Kota Belud, one will find, spread out across newspaper-lined counters, *liking berlada*, for which their exposed flesh is rubbed with salt and chilli powder. "Those are good fried and eaten with *sambal*", Pison says, persuading me to get some before we leave the city.

Of course, the Iranuns are not the only people who continue to preserve fish. Indeed, for many coastal Bajau, Ubian and Kagayan, dried fish or *ikan kering* puts rice on the plate in more ways than one. Some of the most common types include *anjang-anjang* or *sulig* (fusilier; *Caesionidae*), *todak* (swordfish) and *udang gagau* (*Acetes*). The Bajau in particular are known for excellent *udang salai*, smoked shrimp, which are sun-dried after being slowly cooked over fire. *Ikan salai*, smoked fish, exists in the Bajau dictionary, but is, somewhat perplexingly, synonymous with *ikan panggang*, grilled or barbecued fish, typically skipjack tuna (known variously as *lengkunis*, *bakulan* and *kayu*, based on pigmentation) or similar *Scombrids*.

On our way back to the truck, I ask Pison about the probability of getting some Bajau food in the area. The sobering reality is that unless I am lucky enough to receive an invitation to a Bajau home, I will have to wait for my return to Kota Kinabalu, or perhaps pay a visit to Sandakan or Semporna. In these cities, broadstroke Chinese and Malay dishes notwithstanding, the food of the Bajau is the most easily accessed local cuisine, found in myriad markets and roadside eateries. The shimmering quality and wide array of sea creatures that lie at the heart of the cuisine is one reason for this phenomenon. Another reason, I surmise, is that for many there is an inherent joy, a primordial satisfaction, that comes with the consumption of marine harvests, a point of convergence of the quotidian and luxurious, familiar and alien.

My introduction to Bajau food happened several years ago, one afternoon on the fringes of Sabah's capital, comprising boiled *saba* bananas and two seaweed salads. One was of *agar-agar* (*Eucheuma cottonii*), the gummy green strands seasoned with lime and pounded roasted coconut. Another was *lato*, sea grapes (*Caulerpa lentillifera*), spiked with shallots, tomatoes and green mango. It was simple, more like a snack, but it felt like a total treat.

The years the followed brought more gems to my plate and palate. *Tehe-tehe*, that sees *Tripnuestes*, a genus of sea urchin, filled with rice – regular, sometimes glutinous – and boiled with lemongrass. The cooked husks, once shattered, reveal rice cakes imprinted with fossilised gonads. The vermillion gonads of another sea urchin, *tayum*, genus *Diadema*, are slurped raw or fried with garlic, ginger and lemongrass and eaten as a viand. *Lawar*, acid-seared fish, usually Spanish mackerel, spruced up with shallots and green mangoes. *Tinunu*, cleaned and scored fish rubbed with crushed chillies and turmeric and grilled over smouldering coconut husk.

Delectable as these are, they are not responsible for the attention that this cuisine has recently received. There are three seafood dishes for which the Bajau are justifiably famous. At the top of the list is *sagol*, poached-then-flaked fish, usually *yu* (shark), *pari* (stingray) or *buntal* (pufferfish), fried with onions, garlic, lemongrass, turmeric and chilli, made to varying degrees of juiciness. The key ingredient, rather unusually, is the liver of the starring fish, which gets cut up and crushed into sizzling oil in the nascent stages of its being. The second is *ampap*, a quick braise most commonly prepared with *basung* (sardine), febrile with lemongrass and turmeric, and lip puckering with tamarind. The third is *loho*, a fish stew, its aromatic base echoing that of *ampap*, but ruddy with tomatoes and heady with lemon basil. It is also spared any souring agent – unless of course one counts the tomatoes.

Loho may also be prepared with chicken or beef, but this is commonly reserved for special occasions – meat does not figure hugely in the Bajau diet. When it does grace the table, it is often in dishes that spring from a generic Malay register. In my interviews with Bajau cooks, the most common local meat and poultry dishes in their households seemed to be *kari ayam*, a chicken curry laced with coconut milk and some form of curry powder and *daging sapi masak hitam*, sliced beef fried with sweet soy sauce. There is one meat dish, however, that seems unique to the Bajau on this side of Sabah, one that has been swept away by the winds of time: *daging masak kaliah*, beef braised with coconut milk, tamarind and, the real clincher, *rempah buwas*, a spice blend with toasted rice as its key ingredient. It was not just meat that benefited from the sun-lit tones and sultry raspiness of this powder: it was apparently also added to vegetable dishes.

The Bajau do cook with the milk of *Cocos nucifera* but perhaps not as lavishly as one would think. They add it sometimes to the odd meat dish, such as the mentioned *kaliah*, but mostly to braises of fruit and vegetable, such as those built around unripe bananas, jackfruit and breadfruit, with clams, shrimp or salted fish added for necessary oomph. The Bajau do not seem to have a name for this dish that is entirely theirs, adopting a Bajau-Malay one, *rapa mapi lemak*, "vegetables cooked with coconut milk". The default description for any Bajau dish awash with coconut milk may just be *masak lemak*.

And then there is the ever important subject of energy-giving carbohydrate. Common as it has become for the Bajau to eat rice, boiled or in the form of *ketupat*, for which the grains are encased in woven hearts of nipa palm blades, their traditional starch is tapioca, favoured for its hardiness and ability to quickly stultify. Brought over from South America, likely by explorers in the 15th century, the Bajau magic this root crop into plump, pasta-like beads, *eggang*; steamed blond patties, *putu*; or boiled, fat logs, *biyanban*, first mummified in coconut blade.

SO SIMILAR SO DIFFERENT

Given the proximity of their provenances, and similar resources and histories, it would be reasonable to expect the cuisines of the Kagayan and Ubian to be similar to that of the West Coast Bajau, and they are, strikingly so, with the odd difference in nomenclature. For instance, the Kagayan refer to the Bajau *sagol* as *labug*, *eggang* as *kinuha*. The Ubian recognise *eggang* as *solleng*.

It would be similarly reasonable to suppose the Kagayan and Ubian have their own specialities, and indeed they do, born from the same clutch of ingredients. The Kagayan can speak of *pinosak*, for which taro, sweet potato, tapioca and *saba* bananas are boiled in coconut milk and mashed, and *kebombong*, chunks of sun-dried tapioca cooked in coconut milk and sugar. The Ubian can boast of *gattak*, a soupy coconut braise, best prepared with unripe papaya and shrimp, and *kullia*, a stew made with all manners of seafood, sweetly clouded with coconut milk and dimmed with burnt coconut paste, *pamapa itum*. This ingredient plays an important role in the cuisine of the Suluk. Their version of *sagol*, spelled *siyagul*, dispenses with the liver, and exalts in this black substance, as does their signature beef soup, *tiyula itum*, and *piyaksak*, a dry preparation of cow liver.

As with the Kagayan and Ubian, the Iranun and the Bajau share many common food interests. They adore grilled fish. They have their version of fish salads, *rawar*, although these may also be concocted with unripe bananas or papaya or ripe pineapple. They swirl coconut milk into vegetable braises, also fleshed out with shrimp or salted or dried fish, but never smoked fish – the marriage between *tiapa* and *gata* is a forbidden one for this community. Unlike the Bajau, the Iranun have a word for such dishes: *giata'an*.

The similarities do not end there. They cook *loho*, which in the Iranun tongue is *'lo* or *sawau*, in itself a variety of *lasu*. The word *lasu* is used to describe any dish that involves cooking with a considerable amount of liquid, often with aromatics such as onion, lemongrass, turmeric and ginger. They also make *sagol*, that they call *siager*, but with one fascinating and unique addition: *palapa* or the grated flesh of coconut. It is this ingredient that sets Iranun cuisine apart from its Muslim counterparts.

There are two kinds of *palapa*. *Palapa' a mailau*, or fresh grated coconut, and *palapa' a sinindag*, dry-fried or pan-roasted grated coconut. Which to use is up to the cook's discernment. *Pialapaan* is meat, fish or vegetables cooked with spices and aromatics, such as shallots, the local spring onion, lemongrass and chillies, and sometimes salted fish. *Piaren* is similar, the main difference being a healthy lick of coconut milk. The Iranun *kulia*, unlike the one prepared by the Ubian, may also be similarly described, except that it tends to contain ground roasted spices, like cumin, coriander and fennel seed.

There is one difference between Iranun and Bajau eating habits, though it is a slight one. Unlike the Bajau, the staple carbohydrate of the Iranun has for a long time been rice, not tapioca. In the savoury realm, the edible tuber may on occasion be enlisted for their version of *eggang*, called *limping a ubi*, but is otherwise used as an extender for rice when the grains are in short supply. Cooked together in a pot, with shards of dried fish added at the end to warm through, the finished dish is known as *tabidak*. Most of the time, however, the tapioca is viewed as snack food, boiled in water or coconut milk, or in hearty griddle cakes called *tumpi*, analogues of which are found all across Borneo.

While the Iranun I have met harbour relatively tepid sentiments for *Manihot esculenta*, they seem to have more charitable views on the sweet potato, known variously as *ubi rapa'*, "creeping yam"; *ubi manis*, "sweet yam"; *ubi keledek*; and *ubi rambat*. Besides being boiled, these are much loved sliced, battered and deep-fried into *kui a ubi'*. The Iranun also possess some affection for corn and sago, both of which may be united with coconut milk and sugar and transformed into a sweet, comforting gruel known as *betul*.

The *saba* bananas have to be green-skinned. I once used ones on the verge of yellowness, and despite not disintegrating into mush – it takes a lot for them to – the banana pieces imbibed so much of the gravy, thickening the little that was left, that the cooked dish looked like it was meant to be draped over waffles.

The Kagayan use the raw, quivering pads of *kima*, giant clams, cutting them into small pieces, and adding them to the sauce. I devised the method below, which involves pre-cooking the shellfish, as it is impossible to get raw clam meat where I am. I use Angel Venus or Lettered Venus clams. Use whatever is available to you. This is also stunning prepared with blood cockles.

SAGING PINAT'TIAN NIUG

SERVES 6

FOR THE SPICE PASTE
2 garlic cloves, peeled
4 shallots, peeled and sliced
4cm ginger, peeled and sliced
4cm turmeric, peeled and sliced

TO COOK
1½kg clams (see above)
300ml water
3 tbsp vegetable oil
3 lemongrass stalks, bruised
½ tsp salt
300g unripe *saba* bananas,
    peeled weight
100ml coconut cream

1 With a pestle and mortar, crush the spice paste ingredients into a rough mixture. Set aside.

2 Place the clams and water in a saucepan over medium-high heat. Cover and allow to come to a bubble. Once the shellfish have sprung open, immediately remove the pan from the heat. Strain the liquor into a large measuring jug and allow the clams to cool slightly before harvesting their flesh and discarding their shells. This takes far less time than you might think, about 5-7 minutes. Set aside.

3 Heat the oil in a large saucepan over medium heat. Once hot, add the paste, fry for a minute. Lower the heat and drop in the lemongrass stalks. Pour in 350ml of the clam liquor and salt. Bring to a boil, cover and simmer for 5 minutes.

4 Meanwhile, quarter each *saba* banana lengthwise and cut each baton into chips roughly 2mm in thickness. Stir these into the pot. Cover and continue puttering away for 10-15 minutes or until tender.

5 Stir in the coconut cream and clam flesh. Simmer, uncovered, for just 2 minutes. Taste and adjust seasoning with salt.

As with the previous recipe, the bananas for this have to be green-skinned. These are often camel-humped, shaped in coconut husks. I use a pair of lightly moistened hands and shape them into thick patties.

You can eat these with many things, such as the *kullia* on page 199 or the *gattak* on page 197. It is especially wonderful partnered with barbecued fish, especially tuna. Crush 2 garlic cloves, 2cm turmeric root and 2 sliced red chillies into a fine paste. Mix in ½ tsp each salt and sugar and 2 tsp of tamarind water (page 524). Score both sides of a cleaned young mackerel tuna, about 500-600g in weight. Slap over the paste and massage it very thoroughly with gloved hands. Leave for an hour and cook over burning charcoal. Alternatively, cook on a lightly oiled roasting tray, on the second highest shelf of an oven preheated to its highest setting, for 12-15 minutes, turning over midway. I sometimes turn on the grill towards the end if it needs a hit of blackness. I concede, however, that you will never get the wonderful smokiness that hot coals or wood provides.

To unite *daeng tinunu* and *pisang tinapah*, I recommend a simple sauce, beginning with 1 garlic clove, 2 shallots and bird's eye chillies and 1 medium tomato. You chop these, put them in a bowl, and mix in 2 tbsp each soy sauce, *kecap manis* and water, and a good hit of calamansi juice. Taste, tweak, serve.

PISANG TINAPAH

SERVES 6

1kg unripe *saba* bananas, unpeeled
250g grated coconut
½ tsp salt

1 Place the *saba*, unpeeled, in a snug saucepan and cover with water. Put over high heat and bring to a boil. Cover, lower the heat, and cook for 35-45 minutes, or until the bananas are cooked through.

2 Drain the bananas and leave them to cool, just until they are manageably warm. Then peel and cut them into 1cm coins.

3 Pound the cut banana flesh with a pestle and mortar until you get a stiff paste. This is not difficult, but may take a few minutes. The odd lump is welcome. Add the grated coconut and salt, and continue pounding until the white snow is dispersed throughout the banana mash. With lightly moistened hands, shape the *pisang tinapah* into 6 bulging discs. You may use whatever moulds you fancy.

Spicy, salty and lip-smackingly tart, *ampap* is easily the most popular way to treat fish among the Muslim communities who live along Sabah's craggy coastline. It is regarded as their take on the Kadazandusun *pinasakan*. The Rungus make it too and call it *tinopuru*.

The most common fish used are oleaginous *basung* (sardine) and meaty *kayu* (skipjack tuna). I tend to go with chub mackerel (*luma'an*).

At its most whittled down, shallots, turmeric and lemongrass are the only spices and aromatics involved and no oil gets anywhere near it. This version, then, is *ampap* with additional complexities and layers of narrative.

If the turmeric leaf eludes you, you may omit it.

LUMA'AN MASAK AMPAP

SERVES 8

FOR THE SPICE PASTE
4 garlic cloves, peeled
2 shallots, peeled and thinly sliced
2cm ginger, peeled and sliced
2cm turmeric, peeled and sliced
5 red bird's eye chillies

TO COOK
4 tbsp vegetable oil
3 lemongrass stalks, bruised
1 tsp salt
Pinch of sugar
500ml water
600g chub mackerel, cleaned
4 tbsp tamarind water (page 524)
1 turmeric leaf, roughly shredded

1 With a pestle and mortar, crush the ingredients for the spice paste until smooth.

2 Heat the oil in a large saucepan over medium heat. Once hot, add the paste, stir for a minute. Lower the heat and fry, stirring constantly, until it deepens in colour and becomes fragrant.

3 Stir in the lemongrass stalks, salt, sugar, water and bring to a boil. Lower the heat, cover and simmer for 10 minutes.

4 Slip in the fish, tamarind water and turmeric leaf. Give the pan a shake and baste the fish in the hot liquid. Cover and cook for 5-7 minutes. Taste and adjust seasoning with more salt, sugar and tamarind water if necessary. Serve with plenty of rice.

I thank Mr Mabulmaddin bin Shaiddin for leading me to this deliciousness. While skipjack tuna and barramundi make top candidates, I tend to use chub mackerel instead. And while some Iranun cooks insist on the fruit of the elusive *bangutan*, "tree garlic", *Scorodacarpus borneensis*, for the spice paste, I omit it and use regular garlic.

PIALAPA'AN A LUMA'AN

SERVES 6-8

FOR THE FISH
500g chub mackerel, cleaned
1 tsp cumin seeds
2 tsp coriander seeds
2 tsp fennel seeds
1 tsp salt
½ tsp sugar

FOR THE SPICE PASTE
3 garlic cloves, peeled
5 shallots, peeled and sliced
25g ginger, peeled and sliced
10g turmeric, peeled
2 lemongrass stalks,
    tender portion only

TO COOK
60g grated coconut
6 tbsp vegetable oil
1 yellow onion, peeled and
    cut into thin half-moons
6 red bird's eye chillies,
    split lengthwise
A handful of lemon basil leaves
4 tbsp water

1 Score the cleaned chub mackerel several times on both sides at regular intervals. Place these in a shallow bowl.

2 Toast the cumin, coriander and fennel seeds in a large, deep, oil-free frying pan over medium heat until aromatic and faintly coloured, then tip into a pestle and mortar, cool slightly, then pound into a powder. Sprinkle this, as well as the salt and sugar, over the scored fish. Give them a thorough massage, then cover and set aside for 1 hour.

3 Meanwhile, return the frying pan to medium-low heat, then sprinkle in the grated coconut. Toast until crisp and golden, stirring constantly to ensure an even colour. Tip these filings into a mortar, cool slightly, then pound into a fine rubble. Decant into a bowl and set aside. Give the pestle, mortar and frying pan a brief wipe.

4 Use the mortar and pestle one last time to pound the spice paste ingredients into a smooth balm. Cover with a plate and set it aside. Do not bother scraping it out.

5 After the fish has had its hour marinating, return the frying pan yet again to medium heat and pour in the vegetable oil. Once hot, scrape in the spice paste, fry for a minute, stirring, then lower the heat and continue frying until it is fragrant, has deepened in colour and has begun to split from the fat.

6 Add the fish and stir in the pounded coconut, yellow onion, bird's eye chillies, lemon basil and water. Reduce the heat slightly, cover and let the fish steam for 5-7 minutes, turning them over midway. By this time, the fish should be cooked, the sauce thickly clinging to their bodies as they sizzle softly in hot fat.

I am indebted to the President of the Ubian Committee, Mr Liasin bin Kaloh, for sharing this beauty of a recipe with me. He described it as being mellow, milky and soupy, like a suntlit *tom kha gai* in appearance, but you may cut back on the liquid and make it more viscous and rich if you prefer.

While slicing the papaya into matchsticks is the regular thing to do, I prefer courting a crinkle-edged vegetable peeler, as the coarse shreds it produces, identical to those in Thai papaya salads, are less brittle, packing greater bite.

GATTAK

SERVES 4-6

250g unripe papaya, peeled and
 seeded weight
2 tbsp vegetable oil
3 garlic cloves, peeled and crushed
2 shallots, peeled and finely sliced
2cm ginger, peeled and pounded
2cm turmeric, peeled and pounded
100g small shrimp, unpeeled
650ml coconut milk
½ tsp salt
2 red chillies, sliced on a diagonal

1 With a crinkle-edged vegetable peeler, turn the unripe papaya into thin shreds, approximately 4cm in length.

2 Heat the vegetable oil in a medium saucepan over medium heat. Once hot, add the garlic and shallots and fry until fragrant. Stir in the ginger, turmeric and the small shrimp. Reduce the heat slightly and fry until the shrimp turn pale gold, stirring constantly to prevent the aromatics from catching.

3 Add the coconut milk and salt. Let the mixture come to a boil. Stir in the papaya shreds, cover and simmer for 5-7 minutes or until just tender. Uncover, add the chillies and cook without a lid for 2-3 minutes or until they soften. Taste and adjust seasoning with salt.

I first learned of this in Semporna, where it was described as "black tom yum", its menacing hue supplied by burnt coconut paste (*siyunog lahing* in Sinug), the recipe for which lies on page 521. Typically, this is first made into a spice paste, *pamapa itum*, by pounding it with aromatics, but as this recipe already begins with a bold, charismatic blend, I have skipped this step.

The template for this recipe was supplied by an Ubian friend, Liasin bin Kaloh. Various seafood may used here; I happen to love the combination of shrimp and octopus.

KULLIA

SERVES 6

TO COOK
400g baby octopus, cleaned
600ml water
3 lemongrass stalks, bruised
4 tbsp vegetable oil
3 tbsp burnt coconut paste
  (page 521)
4 makrut lime leaves, torn
½ tsp salt
½ tsp sugar
300g medium shrimp, peeled
  weight
75ml coconut cream
4 tbsp lemon basil leaves, torn

FOR THE SPICE PASTE
4 garlic cloves, peeled
4 shallots, peeled and sliced
4cm ginger, peeled and sliced
4cm galangal, peeled and sliced
2cm turmeric, peeled and sliced
4 red bird's eye chillies, sliced

1 Place the octopus and water in a medium saucepan with 1 bruised stalk of lemongrass. Bring to a boil over medium heat, cover, and simmer for 45-60 minutes, or until the octopus is tender.

2 Meanwhile, with a pestle and mortar, roughly crush the spice paste ingredients. Set aside.

3 Drain the cooked octopus, reserving 600ml of its purplish cooking liquor. Cool the octopus slightly before slicing into bite-sized pieces.

4 Give the saucepan a wipe. Add the oil and warm it over medium heat. Once hot, add the spice paste and fry for just 3-4 minutes, stirring, until it is fragrant and has deepened in colour slightly. Stir in the *siyunog lahing*, the remaining bruised lemongrass stalks and the octopus liquor. Bring to a boil, cover, lower the heat and simmer for 15 minutes.

5 Add the cut octopus to the pan, along with the torn lime leaves, salt and sugar. Continue simmering for another 10 minutes. Add the shrimp and coconut cream and simmer uncovered for 3-4 minutes, or until the shrimp are cooked. Add the lemon basil, then taste and adjust seasoning with salt. Remove from the heat and eat with rice.

While *loho* prepared with fish is diurnal fare, those made with chicken and beef seem to only emerge during grand occasions. The unusual addition of torch ginger was recommended to me by Hj. Mohd Anuar, President of the Kagayan committee, and I enjoy how it sends its piercing perfume into the already exuberantly spiced, brightly lit, liquid. The addition of basil is worthy of contemplation, though this herb tends to be reserved for piscine renditions.

Hj. Anuar also shared with me that despite it being uncommon, vegetables may be added, in particular yardlong beans.

MANUK NI LOHOAN

SERVES 6-8

5 garlic cloves, peeled
3cm ginger, peeled and sliced
2cm galangal, peeled and sliced
2cm turmeric, peeled and sliced
4 red bird's eye chillies
3 tbsp vegetable oil
4 medium tomatoes
2 medium red onions, peeled and sliced
1½kg free-range chicken, skinned, cut
    into ten portions
1 tsp salt
3 lemongrass stalks, bruised
1 torch ginger bud, halved
1 litre light chicken stock

1 With a pestle and mortar, crush the garlic, ginger, galangal, turmeric and chillies into a rough paste.

2 Heat the oil in a large saucepan over medium heat. Once hot, add the paste, stir for 30 seconds, lower the heat slightly and fry until lightly coloured and fragrant.

3 Roughly slice 2 of the tomatoes and add them, with the red onions, to the pot. Once they have softened into the aromatics, add the chicken and salt. Stir to seal, then drop in the lemongrass stalks and torch ginger. Cover, reduce the heat to its lowest and steam for 10 minutes.

4 Pour in the chicken stock. Raise the heat, summon it to a boil, then cover, reduce the heat again, and simmer for 40 minutes, or until the chicken is very tender.

5 Cut the remaining tomatoes into quarters and add them to the pot. Once they soften slightly, but without losing their form, the *loho* is done.

I first came across this recipe in the book *Traditional Cuisines of Sabah*. It seems on the verge of extinction; only a handful of elderly cooks in West Sabah have heard of it. Even fewer have tasted it. Incidentally, I have met Maranao cooks in their seventies, in Mindanao, Philippines, who recall thickening and perfuming their *rendang* with crushed roasted rice, not coconut.

While most spice blends are at their apogee on the very day of preparation, this *rempah* seems to blossom a day or so after, its sandy hue and husky breath intensifying.

REMPAH BUWAS

MAKES APPROX. 150G

200g raw jasmine rice
20g turmeric, finely sliced
20g ginger, finely sliced
4 lemongrass stalks, peeled and
    finely sliced
4 red bird's eye chillies

1 Wash the jasmine rice until the water runs clear. Drain well in a sieve.

2 Heat a large wok or frying pan over medium-high heat. When hot but not smoking, sprinkle in the drained rice and stir. Once whitely opaque, turn the heat down to its lowest setting, then add the remaining ingredients. Stir leisurely, until the rice is golden and the spices and aromatics have dried and turned brown. This can take 25-35 minutes. Leave to cool slightly, then reduce to a powder with a pestle and mortar, grinder or bullet blender. Store in an airtight jar and stow in a cool, dark place, where it will last for a month or so.

As with its starring *rempah*, this recipe is based on one from *Traditional Cuisines of Sabah*. I have taken several liberties, adding galangal and dry spices, which local cooks add to dishes as they fancy, and frying the paste of fresh spices and aromatics in heat-split coconut cream, the derived oil once the preferred fat for cooking.

The Bajau would have this with *buwas lemah kuning*, glutinous grains laden with cultural significance, a ritualistic food prepared and offered to ancestors to express gratitude for the blessings of the previous year and hope for prosperity, security, protection and contentment in the next, as symbolised by turmeric-derived yellow. The recipe for this lies on page 47 under the title *pulut kuning*.

DAGING MASAK KALIAH

SERVES 6-8

FOR THE SPICE POWDER
1 tsp cumin seeds
1 tsp coriander seeds
1 tsp fennel seeds
6 cardamom pods

FOR THE SPICE PASTE
20g garlic cloves
25g shallots, peeled
15g ginger, peeled and sliced
15g galangal, peeled and sliced
10g turmeric, peeled
25g red chillies, sliced

TO COOK
500g chuck tender, thinly sliced
250ml coconut cream
2 lemongrass stalks, bruised
1 tsp salt
600ml coconut milk
    (second extract; page 521)
4 tbsp *rempah buwas* (page 201)
1 tbsp coconut sugar, shaved
    (page 524)
2 tbsp tamarind water (page 524)

1 In a dry frying pan over medium heat, warm the cumin, coriander and fennel seeds and cardamom pods until very aromatic. Tip into a pestle and mortar, crush to a fine powder and sprinkle over the sliced chuck tender. Give the meat a thorough massage and set aside for at least 30 minutes.

2 Meanwhile, with a pestle and mortar, crush the spice paste ingredients until fine. Alternatively, use a cosy blender, adding a little water if need be.

3 Heat the coconut cream in a large saucepan or wok over medium heat. Allow it to fry and separate, pushing it around until it splits into soft curds. Add the spice paste and bruised lemongrass. Lower the heat and fry until the paste is deep red and fragrant. Stir in the meat and salt. Cover and leave to steam for 10 minutes.

4 Uncover, pour in the coconut milk. Return the lid and simmer for 45 minutes, or until the meat is just tender.

5 Stir in the *rempah buwas*, coconut sugar and tamarind water. Cover and simmer for another 10 minutes, then uncover and simmer for another 10, by which time the meat should be tender, the sauce thick and clinging to it, glossed with a thin film of oil. Taste and adjust seasoning with salt.

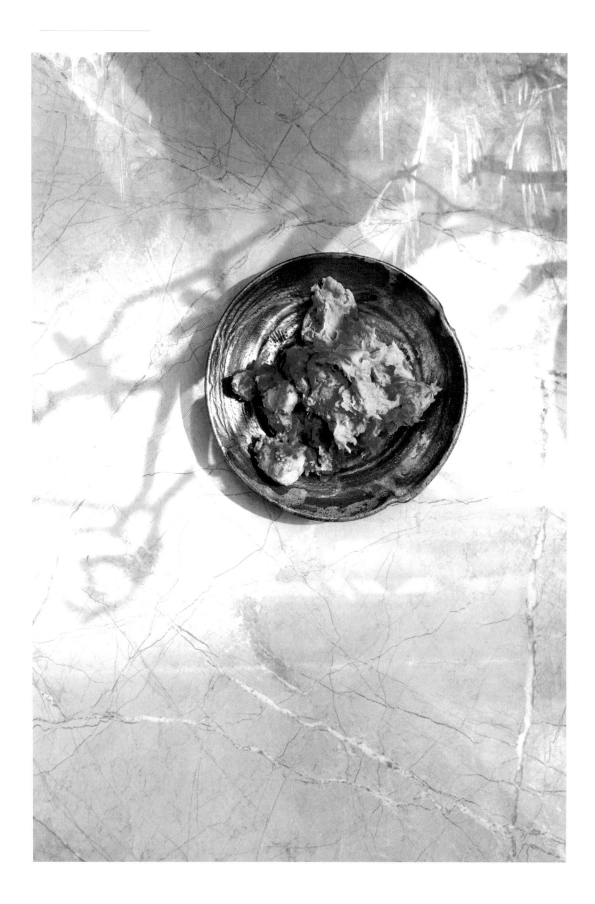

I am grateful to Hj. Mohd Anuar, President of the Kagayan committee, for telling me about this comforting dish, which he recommends eating with *sagol* (page 273) and a strong black coffee for breakfast.

Most of the time, all the ingredients are congregated in a pot, cooked into a starchy mess, then merrily pummelled into oblivion. My approach is a little fussier: I introduce them to the vessel in a sequence dictated by their cooking times.

Whatever sweet potato you pick, ensure that it cooks dry and starchy. I love the purple ones from Vietnam. I was instructed to go easy on the tapioca, as too much tends to make the *pinosak* too thick, too fibrous. I would not recommend omitting it altogether, however, as it seems to impart an airiness and ineffable breadiness that lighten the dish, keeping it out of pudding territory (although some cooks like it sweet and pile on the sugar.) I approach the *saba* with similar restraint, but for a different reason: going overboard turns what ought to be a touch of tropical twang into a slick of suggestive astringency.

PINOSAK

SERVES 6

150g tapioca, peeled weight
250g sweet potatoes, peeled weight
250g taro yam, peeled weight
200g *saba* bananas, peeled weight
Approx. 500ml water
150ml coconut cream
3 tbsp sugar
½ tsp salt
1 pandan blade, knotted

1 Cut the tapioca, sweet potatoes and taro into approximately 2cm pieces, the *saba* banana into 2cm sections.

2 In a medium saucepan, add the water, coconut cream, sugar, salt and pandan blade and put over medium heat. Once it boils, add the tapioca, cover and cook for 5 minutes, then add the sweet potatoes and taro. Cover, lower the heat and cook for 10 minutes or so, until they are all on the edge of tenderness. Add a little water if the pot is getting thirsty.

3 Uncover, add the bananas and simmer, without a lid, for 5 minutes, until tender. At this point, the cooked items should be fuzzy-edged, some on the verge of crumbling, sitting in a shallow pool of thick liquid, which will continue to thicken as it rests.

4 Cover and leave for 10 minutes, then whip up with an electric handwhisk or crush with a potato masher. I consult a large wooden pestle and mortar that I got from a Thai grocer.

Some cooks bang on about whisking the batter furiously, even insisting on a free-standing mixer, believing this will help the *pinjaram* swell in the pan and give it its requisite honeycomb interior. I am not so sure.

You want the fat hot enough for the batter to swell gracefully, but if it is smoking, it will burn before this can happen. Recklessness will reward you with a cinder coaster.

In Mindanao, the Tausug who make this believe that rapping the sides of the pan as the *pinjaram* fries helps to achieve a frilly rim. I usually just push it around the pan and baste it in hot oil.

PINJARAM

MAKES 10-12

125g coconut sugar, shaved
   (page 524)
30g caster sugar
200ml water
100g plain flour
100g rice flour
   (*tepung beras*, page 523)
½ tsp salt
Canola oil, for deep-frying

1 Place the coconut and caster sugars and water in a small saucepan. Cook over medium heat, just until the sugars have dissolved. Strain into a measuring jug. You should have 200ml, so top up with a little water if necessary. Leave to cool completely.

2 Sift the plain and rice flours and salt into a large bowl. Whisk in the cooled syrup thoroughly. You need to achieve the consistency of pouring custard, so add a touch more water if necessary.

3 Heat 1½ cm of canola oil in a small wok, with an approx. 18cm wide mouth, over medium heat. Once hot but not smoking, give the batter a stir and ladle in approximately 3 tbsp worth. The formed disc should swell along its rim, curving inwards, rather like a lily pad. Gently push the *pinjaram* around, basting it in hot fat. Its middle should bulge slightly in the process. Once the bottom is golden, flip it and fry for a couple more minutes. Make them all this way. Drain on kitchen towel and cool slightly before eating.

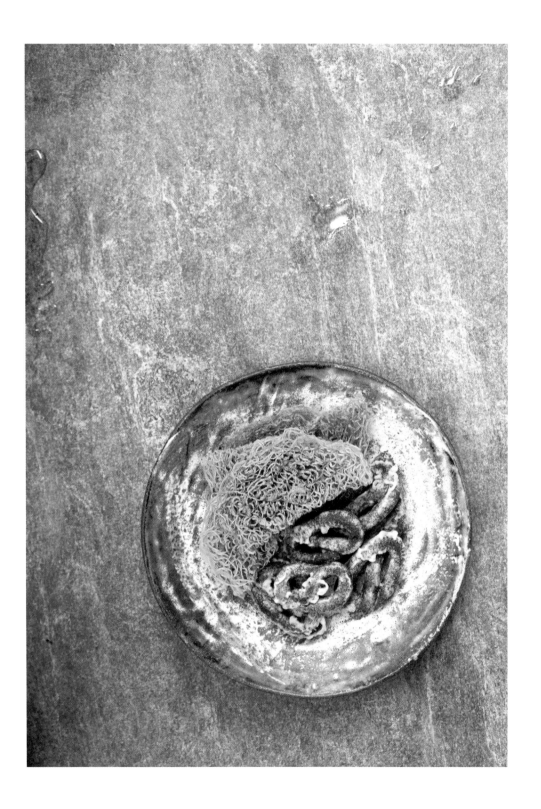

Penganan or *panganan* is a fried biscuit of ground roasted corn, vaguely shaped like a figure "8", vain enough to demand its frock of batter be gossamer, so that its voluptuous, chocolaty body may be admired.

Traditionally, the corn used is waxy, robust and firm, the kind that is sunned and ground into meal. I have tweaked the recipe to accommodate the more common sweetcorn.

PENGANAN

MAKES 16

FOR THE DOUGH
6 sweetcorn cobs (see above)
90g golden caster sugar
¼ tsp salt
75g plain flour
50g rice flour
   (*tepung beras*, page 523)
Approx. 150ml water
Canola oil, for deep-frying

FOR THE BATTER
60g rice flour
   (*tepung beras*; page 523)
60ml water
Pinch of salt

1 Shave the sweetcorn kernels off the cobs. You should get approx. 600g. Spread them over a tray (or winnowing basket) lined with kitchen towel and sun for 2-3 days or until shrivelled into chipped teeth. (I leave them next to an open window.)

2 Heat a large, oil-free wok or frying pan over medium-high heat. When hot, but not smoking, sprinkle in the corn kernels and push them around for a few seconds. Lower the heat, then continue roasting them until they are brown. The odd glimmer of yellow is innocuous. Tip the corn out onto a tray and cool slightly before blending to a fine, coffee-coloured, dust, in a cosy grinder.

3 Tip the flour into a bowl and cool completely. (You should get approx. 125g.) Then, stir in the sugar, salt, plain and rice flours, and just enough water to produce a soft, cohesive dough. There should be a hint of stickiness. Cover and set aside for 30 minutes.

4 Divide the dough into 16 balls. On a dry work surface, roll a ball into a thin sausage, about 20cm in length. (I recommend lightly moistening your hands with water. Also, avoid dusting the surface with flour, as this seems to make the sausages of dough crack.) Then quickly fashion this sausage into a "figure 8", gently pressing where tip meets body. Make all the *penganan* this way.

5 Make the batter simply by mixing the ingredients in a bowl into a thin cream. Heat about 4cm of canola oil in a large saucepan over medium heat. Once the oil is hot but not smoking, introduce 3-4 of the *penganan* to the batter. Shake off excess and drop them into the hot fat. Fry for 3-4 minutes, turning them over midway and regulating the heat to prevent burning. Their batter should turn into a gauzy, off-white carapace, light gold at the most. Drain on kitchen towel. Make the rest of them this way.

This is one of those recipes where the amount of instruction dispensed is inversely proportional to its actual helpfulness. All I will say is practice makes perfect. Even if your fritters look clunkier than they should, they will still taste great.

The traditional cooking implement for sending the batter out in squiggles is a perforated coconut husk, attached to a wooden handle. You may use a *jala* maker or a plastic squeeze bottle, those used for squirting ketchup over hotdogs, but with a cap bearing 3-5 fine nozzles, each about 2mm wide. Apply force to the bottle gently and steadily, and do not stop until an adequately sized raft has been woven into the hot fat. Just as pauses equate to commas in sentences, so any interruptions will put knots in your nets.

JAA

MAKES 7-8

200g rice flour
   (*tepung beras*, page 523)
90g caster sugar
¼ tsp salt
Approx. 200ml water
Canola oil, for deep-frying

1 Combine the rice flour, caster sugar and salt in a bowl. Stir to mix, then add just enough water to produce a batter thick as paint. Cover and set aside for 30 minutes.

2 In a medium-sized wok, pour enough canola oil to get a pool that is approximately 20cm in diameter and 4cm in depth. Place the oil-bearing wok over medium heat to warm up while you fill your squeeze bottle with the rested batter.

3 Test the heat of the oil by dropping in a few squiggles of batter. They should not brown instantly but make their way there at a serene, steady pace. Remove these golden squiggles with a slotted spoon and discard them; they have done their work.

4 With as much confidence as you can muster, steadily squeeze the batter into the centre of the pan, moving outwardly in a concentric, clockwise, fashion, then back to the centre again. Repeat this in-out process 2-3 times, until you get a raft of fine noodles, softly sizzling in the hot fat. This raft should be very well-knitted, with hardly any noticeable gaps at its centre.

5 Once its underside appears to have set, but without actually having acquired colour, fold one side of the raft over with a pair of chopsticks, creating a half-moon. Continue flipping the raft with the chopsticks, exchanging them for a pair of tongs once the *jaa* is firm and begins to look closer to the lacy net you were promised. Press the fritter against the sides of the pan, thereby compacting it. Once your net is golden, remove it to a kitchen towel, where it will crisp up further and deepen in colour. Take a deep breath, then continue with your good work until all the batter has been used up.

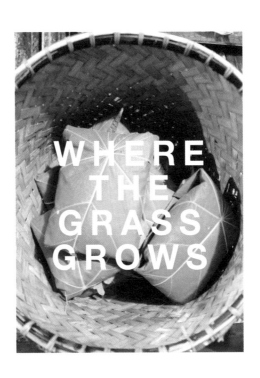

The *sinalau bilis* are as long as matchsticks. Fresh out of their newspaper wrapper, they looked riveting, each dainty talisman dipped in a silver as piercing as hope. Much of their metallic sheen was lost, however, when they were pushed around a dry pan, over diffident flames, until they rustled like spirits along a dim corridor. Shattered into crisp splinters over a salmon basin filled with green mango, cucumber, *lompodos* (lemon basil) and chillies, they assumed a different kind of beauty.

Evening is making its inevitable descent over Kampung Bavanggazo, a village neatly tucked into the heart of Kudat province. The hills surrounding the property, recently awash in shades of olive and lime, have been subdued, now mere silhouettes against a greyish sky. In an hour so, they will vanish into the ink of night.

Kudat is the hub for Sabah's community of Rungus, recognised as a sub-group of the Kadazandusun. For the past couple of days, I have been in the tenderest care of Susan Angkung, recognised for her knowledge on local culinary traditions and exquisite cooking. As we are to depart the following day, she has decided to make our final meal thoroughly Rungus and thoroughly memorable.

Fish, vegetables and fruit form the bulk of the Rungus diet, conjured into dishes through grilling and braising, the two arrows in their quiver of traditional cooking techniques, though steaming and frying have also become popular in recent decades, a situation that applies to all ethnic groups native to Borneo. And while traditional recipes seldom involve more than a single step in cooking, it is gradually becoming acceptable for two or more methods to be enlisted, resulting in more dimensions of flavour, more layers of narrative. It would not be unreasonable for a modern rendition of *tinopuru sada*, an all-in-one dish of braised fish, to begin with the gentle frying of shallots, lemongrass, ginger and white chillies. Nor would it be deemed peculiar to fry grilled-then-flayed aubergines with a little garlic and lightly beaten eggs for *linugu soguntung*.

Collective attitudes towards the use of pungent aromatics seem to be shifting as well. In the not-so-distant past, foods were seasoned with little else other than salt and sparingly perfumed with *lompodos* and ginger. Onion, garlic and turmeric seldom ever received invitations, then deemed too brash for any party. It may seem the Rungus have an exception to this rule, in the shape of *tinutu longkuas*, but this is regarded as a condiment, a highly scented, almost medicinal, floss of pounded galangal – its literal translation – granted savoury life by dried anchovies.

With a snap of a switch, several fluorescent bulbs above us flicker to life, and all focus falls on the array of plates, bowls and utensils cluttering the glass-protected bamboo table before us. Susan adds bold squirts of lime to the *kinohut sangub inunsul*, gives it a final toss and proclaims it complete. *Kinohut sangub* means "scraped cucumber", which is exactly how the cooling fruit was prepared, an invasive tablespoon running along the length of its pale jade interiors. *Inunsul* refers to the salad itself, said to be an invention of farmers in need of a quick fix while out in the paddy fields. Char-grilled aubergines are often prepared in the same way, the finished dish christened *tinunuvan soguntung*.

Green mango has also been employed in another item at the table, thought of as an instant *sinamo* (*jeruk* or ferment). It also contains unripe papayas, unpeeled, and *sinamo bilis*, fresh anchovies fermented in salt until subfusc and muddy. A proper *sinamo* demands the sliced fruit be massaged with salt, raw freshwater fish, perhaps some cooked rice, then left to sit and fizz for at least a week. The finished product is bracing on the palate to say the least, packing a fetid punch in which the Rungus revel and glory. So passionate is their love for *sinamo bilis*, that an ideal way for them to spend late nights is eating spoonfuls, straight from the jar, in between sips of beer, or perhaps *tinonggilan*, a sparkling maize-based liquor that is usually reserved for festive occasions. In such instances, the *jeruk* fulfils its duty as *pusas* – bar chow.

Also at the table is a plate of *ondoruzo*, like *ensabi*, and another bearing *sobilikan*, the astringent, sour leaves of *Embelia philippinensis*, slashed into ribbons and mixed with pounded dried shrimp. There is also a large plate of *ayam masak hitam*, chicken breast, thinly slivered, fried with garlic, chilli and *kecap manis*. The star for tonight's dinner, however, is *taduk linunson*, a braise of assorted vegetables, typically involving fruits from the river for the umami they so effortlessly supply. There are several recommended combinations. Banana heart and shrimp. Unripe *tarap* and river clams. Unripe jackfruit with *sinalau sada*, basically smoked fish, which is a real treat during the dry season. Today's version features bamboo shoot, pea aubergines, each sphere halved to reveal their sanctum of tiny seeds, *tultul* (river snails) and chocolaty, spindly crabs, no bigger than an infant's palm. Some cooks sluice coconut milk into it, turning the thin gravy creamy and comforting, making a dish they would not consider part of their culinary heritage: the coconut is not a traditional Rungus ingredient.

As with all dishes with genteel, palate-neutral flavour profiles, nuance is key, so respect must be given, attention paid, to the ingredients comprising it. The Rungus tend to use only two kinds of bamboo shoots (*soko*). Today, the one Susan used for her *taduk linunson* is known as *poring*, which has thick skin. The other shoot, *tivong*, is young and thin-skinned, with sweet and tender chartreuse flesh, and tends to be preferred. The pea aubergines, *binterung*, were plucked from shrubs right outside the kitchen, as were the generous, furry leaves of *longkobuhan*, recently converted into neat, corpulent purses for hot *ginazawu* – rice.

Susan has speckled her white rice with several spoons of black grains. The white grains may be combined and cooked with corn kernels (*darai*), first ground to golden granules (*wagas darai*), or glutinous rice, though the latter tends to be reserved for *bintanok*, boiled cakes in jackets of banana leaf. *Bintanok* may be made from corn, but with fresh kernels, grated into a pulp and enveloped in their corrugated, hay-coloured, husks.

Besides rice, sweet potatoes (*ubi manis*) and tapioca (*ubi*) are other sources of energy for the Rungus, most commonly boiled and eaten as they are. Tapioca, however, can be grated, mixed with coconut and turned into pancakes called *tinopis runti*. It was once common for these hefty, ragged-edged discs to be eaten for breakfast. These days, however, wheat flour usually stands in for the tuber, producing something less leaden and more malleable, though at the expense of personality.

The closest thing I could get to the silvery blue anchovies Susan used were from a Japanese supermarket. I get the ones that are about 3cm long. They seldom need washing or gutting.

She also used the striped cucumber found all over Southeast Asia, the Straight 8. This, thankfully, is the easiest cucumber for me to procure, so I follow suit.

KINOHUT SANGUB INUNSUL

SERVES 6

100g dried anchovies (see above)
2 cucumbers, approx. 600g
1 small green mango, approx. 150g,
    unskinned, cut into slivers
2 red bird's eye chillies, finely sliced
3 tbsp calamansi lime juice
½ tsp salt, plus more to taste
½ tsp freshly ground black pepper
Pinch of sugar
Handful of lemon basil leaves

1 Lightly toast the anchovies in a dry frying pan over medium-low heat. You want them to crisp up slightly without going brown. Tip into a pestle and mortar and lightly crush into splinters. Set aside.

2 Halve the cucumber lengthwise and gouge out the interiors – seeds and flesh – in fat, rough curls, going as close as possible to their skins. Place these in a bowl, discard their skins. Mix in the crushed dried anchovies and the remaining ingredients. Taste and adjust seasoning with salt. Plate up and serve.

This version of *taduk linunson* includes bamboo shoots, unripe jackfruit, pea aubergines and mud creepers (*Cerithidea obtusa*) or *seput sidut* in Malay, harvested along coastal areas. You may replace them with small clams or shrimp.

TADUK LINUNSON

SERVES 6-8

400g mud creepers
1 fresh bamboo shoot, approx. 600g
2 tbsp vegetable oil
2 garlic cloves, peeled and chopped
1 medium red onion, peeled and sliced
2cm ginger, peeled and chopped
1 lemongrass stalk, bruised
250g unripe jackfruit, peeled weight,
    cut into thin pieces
750ml dried anchovy stock (page 520)
100g pea aubergines, halved
A large fistful lemon basil
Salt, to taste

1 With a sharp knife, hack the pointy tips off the mud creepers. Place them in a large bowl and wash several times until the water runs clear, relatively free from dirt and grit. Cover with water and leave to sit for 2 hours, changing the water if it becomes murky.

2 Bring a large saucepan of water to a boil over medium heat. Meanwhile, use a paring knife to relieve the bamboo shoot of its tough skin. Give it a rinse, then continue running your knife along its length, producing thin shavings.

3 Once the water is boiling, drop in the bamboo shoot shavings and blanch for 5-7 minutes or until tender. Rinse under a cold tap and squeeze well. Taste a piece. It should not be bitter. If it is, repeat the blanching process once more. Otherwise, put them in a bowl and set aside.

4 Heat the oil in a saucepan over medium heat. Once hot, add the garlic, onion and ginger and fry until aromatic. A touch of colour is alright. Add the lemongrass stalk, then the unripe jackfruit. Stir, then pour in the anchovy stock. Bring to a bubble, lower the heat, cover and simmer until the jackfruit is tender.

5 Add the blanched bamboo shoot, pea aubergines and prepared snails. Cook for 5 minutes, by which time the pea aubergines should have softened a little. Sprinkle in the lemon basil. Once the leaves wilt, the dish is done. Season to taste with salt.

Not all cooks include grated coconut, but I love the texture, aroma and flavour it imparts.

Some like their *bintanok* firm and solid, others tender and creamy. I am with the latter camp. Some make them large and secure them with butcher's string or ribbons of corn husk, while I prefer leveraging on the husk's natural curves to keep the parcels intact.

BINTANOK DARAI

MAKES 10

6 sweetcorn cobs, husks on
150g grated coconut
75g cake flour
4 tbsp coconut cream
150g caster sugar
½ tsp salt

1 Gently strip the husks off the corn cobs, reserving 10 of the largest, best-looking, pieces – you will be using these to wrap the dumplings. Wash and set aside.

2 Grate the corn cobs into a large bowl, you should get 550-600g of broken kernels. Mix in the grated coconut, flour, coconut cream, sugar and salt. The resultant mixture should be thick, but loose and juicy. Not dense or stiff. (Add a little more coconut cream if need be.)

3 Prepare your steamer. Load half a corn husk with about 4 tbsp of the corn mixture. Pat it down, so that it occupies about 10cm of the husk. Fold the unoccupied half of the husk over to conceal, then curl around the loaded portion. The result should be a flattish, tapering pouch. Make all the *bintanok* this way and arrange them in the steamer compartment. Any leakages, as long as they are minimal, may be disregarded. Steam for 30 minutes. Allow them to cool slightly before eating.

MOUTH
OF SALT

A two hour-drive down a southerly serpentine road takes vehicles from Sandakan to Kinabatangan, the gateway to the wildlife sanctuaries for which Borneo is so famous. *Batangan* is Dusun for "long river", which points to Sungei Kinabatangan, the second longest in Malaysia. *Kina*, in several local dialects, refers to the Chinese merchants who lived in settlements near the river's mouth, in the face of the Sulu Sea, from as early as 7th century. For silks and ceramics, these merchants traded in exotics, such as beeswax, rattan, ivory and the edible – and still pricey – nests of *Aerodramus fuciphagus*, a species of swiftlet.

Kinabatangan is also the hub for the Orang Sungei, an ethnic group who have inhabited the banks of the Sungei Kinabatangan for hundreds of years. The name began as an exonym in 1881, during an expedition launched by William Burgess Pryer, the first British resident in Sandakan, to Kampung Imbok, a village situated along the river. There, he discovered a collection of civilised people who, apart from having red skin and long hair, also possessed commendable farming skills and know-how. Ill-equipped for proper communication, he branded them "River People", a title that continued to be used during the reign of the British North Borneo Chartered Company (BNBCC) and evolved to become an umbrella term for the indigenous folk who resided not just along the Kinabatangan River, but others in the area, such as Bengkoka, Labuk, Sugut, Paitan and Segama.

With their numbers beneath two thousand, the Orang Sungei are considered a minority, albeit with at least thirty ethnic subgroups, with the Sukang, Melian and Makiang being three of the more prominent ones. Every subgroup has its own dialect of the *Bahasa Melayu* that unites them.

Many Orang Sungei are of mixed ancestry, a result of intermarriages with Dusun, Tausug, Bugis, Chinese and Bajau families. The predominant religion is Islam, although many subscribe to Christianity and animism, the last being especially true for communities located in the more secluded parts of the dense, green basin. Although it may have been once normal for the inhabitants of a village to be dedicated to a single belief system, it has become common for individuals of different faiths to cohabit. For some, Islam and animism have become intertwined, producing a new faith.

As expected of their name, much of the Orang Sungei diet, even in present times, revolves around the river, giver of life, supplier of hope. Its sweet waters are teeming with myriad species of finned beauties. Some of the more lucrative catches are *lampan* (tinfoil barb), *lais* (glass catfish), *limpata* (*lais besar*, "big glass catfish"), *pelian* (Malaysian mahseer), *baung* (*Mystus*), *patin* (iridescent shark) and *tapah* (wallago). There is also tilapia, but these are usually plucked from oxbow lakes.

The fish with the shiniest scales and reddest gills are treated with due respect, rubbed with tamarind, turmeric and pepper, cloaked in banana leaves and popped over smouldering coconut coir. They may also be introduced to shimmering ponds of coconut milk, sulphurously enhanced with crushed turmeric.

Before the advent of refrigeration, locals had to devise a way to preserve their excess catch. The most common solution was to clean, salt and dry them under a baking sun. The desiccated bodies would then be fried to a bronzed turn and eaten with rice, hammered into *sambals* or slipped into vegetable braises for a desirable hit of pleasantly putrid savouriness. One particular fish does not benefit from this treatment and that is *patin*. Its high fat content seems to produce something more suited to carpentry.

Another solution involved the route of fermentation. While many, if not most, ethnic groups in Borneo use salt and rice, the Orang Sungei use salt and boiled sweet potatoes. After being mixed, concealed and stowed in a cool, dark place for up to a week, the *jeruk ikan* will be consumed as is or sweated in oil with garlic and onions, perhaps a crushed knob of ginger.

The lack of proper storage also predisposed fishermen to the habit of leaving their catches in nets and only taking what they required for a meal. It was thus common to find some fish, several days after the haul, sliding towards decadence, on the cusp of inedibility. At a time when food was scarce, these were not to be dismissed. Instead, these victims of unintentional neglect would be converted into *gensus*, fried in oil and aromatics until their bodies disintegrated into a heady balm. Unlike *jeruk ikan*, *gensus* is a culinary tradition that is slowly fading, mostly prepared by elderly cooks.

The rivers also offer several kinds of freshwater shrimp, collectively known as *udang galah*. The largest specimens, with their electric blue claws, are best boiled or grilled. Glassy medium-sized ones tend to be fried in relatively Chinese fashions, with garlic, onions and oyster sauce, or slipped into soups laced with ginger, chilli and tamarind. The smallest ones, being the most richly flavoured, are added to braises mellow with coconut milk. Slices of semi-ripe papaya may be added, their jade interiors cruising towards sunset, as may slivers of *umbut kelapa*, the tender shoots of the coconut palm. Sought out with equal fervour are the shoots of the *sawit* palm, chiefly grown for their glossy vermillion baubles from which an especially lucrative and extremely controversial liquid is derived.

Shrimp in their dried state also play a sizeable role in the food of the Orang Sungei. These come not from rivers but the briny waters of the Sulu Sea up north. Together with chillies, lime juice, shallots and coconut, they bring depth and fullness to the salads (*kerabu*) of which the river folk are so fond. The best are prepared with greens that grow wild and rampant. There is *patinong*; *pucuk pakis*, fiddleheads of the vegetable fern *Diplazium esculentum*; *togkat langit*, the herbaceous *Helminthostachys zeylanica*; and *ulam raja*, *Cosmos caudatus*, whose leaves explode with citrus and green mango. A simpler way to consume these greens would be to blanch them in boiling water and anoint them with *sambal*, ideally one violent with chillies and throaty with *belacan* (fermented shrimp paste). Other *sambals* of the local repertoire, like those of green mangoes and white chillies, would not be turned down.

Curiously, the dish for which the Orang Sungei are most well-known comes not from the water but the forests: *marang* or red durian. Cooks combine its flesh with salt and leave it to ferment for several days for the local *tempoyak*. Tubs of these are easily procured from markets in and around Kinabatangan, though at a notably high price, as the spiky fruits now come from small farms; deforestation has unfortunately thinned the population of wild trees. To enjoy *tempoyak marang*, all one has to do is dollop some into a hot pan with crushed onions, ginger and chillies, and cook it until it melts into a hot, thick sauce. This unfussy treatment may be applied to unfermented durian flesh, too. An individual may opt to eat the flesh straight from the husk, when it is so fatly sticky that it clings to the roof of one's mouth, together with salt and rice, for a proper meal.

Despite being active cultivators of hard crops, like sweet potatoes, potatoes, corn and tapioca, it is rice that serves as the chief carbohydrate of the Orange Sungei, the grains brought in from Sandakan, Kota Kinabalu and Kota Belud. This is not to suggest that the Orange Sungei do not grow paddy in any capacity: they do, especially those upstream, but more as a hobby than for actual sustenance. The reason behind this, allegedly, is the outlawing of hunting, with the unfettered numbers of pestilential animals impeding the success of this demanding and temperamental crop.

The cessation of hunting has also prevented *payau*, sambar deer, from trotting their way onto the plates of many. Besides hewing them into thin slices and grilling them over woodfire, the Orang Sungei used to dry or smoke their ruby flesh. This preserved meat comes into its own when braised with ginger, galangal, turmeric and, in many modern homes, ground cumin and fennel. Neither chicken nor beef seems to be similarly pampered. In fact, these meats receive comparatively prosaic treatments, made into soups and curries.

Another indigenous ethnic group occupying the northernmost areas of Sabah is the Tombonuo, also spelled Tambanwa. Although a decent number have recently taken residence in the state's bustling capital, many continue to lead quieter existences in areas such as Beluran, Kota Marudu, Kanibongan, Paitan and Pitas.

Considered by many to be a subgroup of the Orang Sungei, the Tombonuo have been traditionally linked to forms of primary agriculture, such as the growing of paddy, and fishing. As with the Orang Sungei, their food has received hardly any documentation beyond the thresholds of their community. The little I know is the result of a short series of conversations with Juans Bin Tikuson, a Tombonuo gentleman based in Pitas.

The first food item to crop up during our discourse was *tamba*, for which river or sea fish gets fermented with boiled tapioca and slices of green-skinned unripe papaya. It struck me immediately as being related to *bosou* and *pekasam*, with the tuber and fruit standing in for rice. When I asked if they would ever add the black flesh of *Pangium edule* to their ferment, Juans dryly remarked, "No, we don't need it for ours to taste good".

Other dishes revealed themselves gradually over the course of the next few conversations, most of them painted with a natural flavour palate, as had been expected. *Tiwak polod linampan* is a braised dish marrying the shoots of fishtail palms (*Caryota sp.*) with chicken or mangrove clams (*lokan*; *Polymesoda expansa*). "When we prepare this with *lokan*, we add coconut milk" he elaborated, also urging me to try cooking the large bivalves with slices of *lumbu*, Calabash gourd.

There was mention of *piuh sinontanan*, essentially a Malay-style chicken curry with coconut milk, curry powder and curry leaves; a swathe of simple fish soups immaculate with ginger and lemon basil (*bawing*); and *impopaat* (*pucuk daun meranti*; *Solanum nigrum*) and *lomiding* (*midin*; *Stenochlaena palustris*), both usually chased around a searing wok with garlic and a little salted fish or fermented shrimp paste (*belacan*).

When it comes to carbohydrate, rice is the Tombonuo choice. Tapioca is eaten with great relish simply boiled, as is corn, but more as a snack. Regular rice is boiled and wrapped in the generous blades of *tarap*, *rungin* or *lingkobung* plants, the resultant purses known as *linuput*. Glutinous rice is also part of the local diet, but usually in sweet things, the grains kept whole or ground into flour. Such treats include the ubiquitous *wajik* and *pinyaram*. Unripe glutinous rice is also eaten, pounded into flakes, known as *sinondau*, or *emping padi* in Malay. To eat, all one has to do is massage with sugar and shredded coconut. Very much a seasonal indulgence during harvest time.

This recipe will work with the durians we normally eat. To elevate it into a dish that may be served as part of a meal, heat 2 tbsp vegetable oil in a small pan over medium heat. Add a chopped garlic clove and a sliced shallot and fry until fragrant. Dollop in 100g *marang tempoyak* and continue cooking, until it splits. With rice and a main dish, like a curry or grilled fish, this amount should be sufficient for 4 – it is fiesty.

MARANG TEMPOYAK

MAKES APPROX. 250G

250g red durian flesh
2 tsp sea salt flakes

1 Crush the red durian flesh in a bowl, then mix in the salt. Pack into a sterilised 250ml Kilner jar and keep in a cool, dark place for 5-7 days or until it begins to smell tangy. At this point, it is ready for use. Because of the heat and humidity levels of my country of residence, I tend to keep it in the fridge from this point on. If you happen to enjoy less harsh conditions, you could just continue to keep it outside.

Although I specify *ubi manis* with yellow flesh, the important thing is that it produces starchy, crumbly flesh when cooked. Those that yield watery flesh are good for pies, cakes and breads, but not this (nor any other recipe in this book). I use a freshwater iridescent shark (*patin*) here, as would all Orang Sungei. Any clean-tasting, white or whitish-fleshed fish will work. Unlike *marang tempoyak*, this fish pickle is to be consumed as is, further spiked with sliced red bird's eye chillies and squirts of calamansi lime.

JERUK IKAN

MAKES APPROX. 250G

1 medium yellow-fleshed sweet
   potato, approx. 150g, peeled
1 tbsp sea salt flakes
200g iridescent catfish, skinned and
   boned weight, cut into thin slices

1 Boil the sweet potatoes in a small saucepan of water until cooked. Drain, leave to cool, then crush into small, ragged nuggets.

2 Mix in the salt, then the sliced fish. Pack into a sterilised 500ml Kilner jar and keep in a cool, dark place for 5-7 days. It should smell tangy but not decadent. The fish would also have stiffened and turned faintly opaque. At this point, it is ready. As per the previous recipe, due to the heat and humidity levels where I live, I keep it in the fridge from this point on. If you enjoy less harsh weather conditions, by all means continue to keep it outside.

The Murut also use this name to refer to a similar ferment of theirs, though it appears closer to the *bosou* of the Kadazandusun. The boiled tapioca in *tamba* results in a milky balm. It also imparts a pleasing, sweetish, fragrance, that foils the invasive pong of the fermented fish quite beautifully.

I use *sepat* (three-spotted gourami; *Trichopodus trichopterus*) for this *tamba*, as that is what is available to me, but by all means use whatever fish you can get, freshwater or otherwise, hewing large specimens into smaller chunks. The Tombonuo are fond of enlisting the flesh of telescope shells harvested from brackish waters along the northern coast.

TAMBA

MAKES APPROX. 650G

150g small freshwater fish, cleaned
1 tbsp sea salt flakes
300g tapioca, peeled weight
200g unripe papaya, unpeeled

1 Rinse and dry the fish, then put them in a clean bowl and mix in 1 tsp of the sea salt flakes. Cover and refrigerate for at least 8 hours or overnight.

2 The following day, remove the cured fish from the refrigerator and place them in a cool part of your kitchen (or home). Cut the tapioca into 4cm chunks and cook in a small saucepan of boiling water until tender. This should take approx. 20 minutes. Drain, allow to cool completely, then crush into small, starchy nuggets, removing tough fibres as you go along. Contain these in a large mixing bowl.

3 Thinly slice the unripe papaya and add to the cooked tapioca nuggets. Mix in the remaining quantity of salt, followed by the lightly cured fish, which by now should have lost most of its chill. Pack the mixture into a sterilised 750ml Kilner jar and keep in a cool, dark place for 5-7 days. It should smell tangy, but not decadent. The fish would also have stiffened and turned faintly opaque. At this point, it is ready. As per the previous two recipes, due to the heat and humidity levels where I live, I keep it in the fridge from this point on. If you enjoy kinder weather conditions, by all means continue to keep it outside.

It feels as if I have entered a time warp.

Since getting decimated during the Second World War, Sandakan has struggled to rebuild itself, though never quite attaining the prosperity it enjoyed during its time as the active commercial and trading centre of North Borneo, a role bestowed upon it by the British North Borneo Chartered Company (BNBCC).

The word Sandakan is apparently Suluk for "the place that was pawned". For some time, the British referred to it as Elopura, "beautiful town", due to its natural harbour, as did its Japanese occupants during the war. It was and continues to be endearingly called "Little Hong Kong", as many merchants from Hong Kong eventually settled here, having been encouraged by the British to migrate over to improve the economy. A recently constructed mall and hotel close to the harbour are thought to pay homage to this moniker, as are the clusters of stilted wooden shacks along the coast, once the residences of said Chinese merchants. Now most of them are restaurants specialising in live seafood.

Present-day Sandakan attracts visitors for two reasons. The first is wildlife, sun bears and orangutans in nearby nature reserves, and sea turtles. The second is its food. I know people who would catch a plane to have a bowlful of seafood *bak kut teh*, the teak-deep broth infused with spring onions and ginger, a plate of *tan kung mien*, hand-pulled noodles, or perhaps a box of UFO tarts, more like dainty sponges topped with a very yellow custard and a puffy halo of boiled icing. The last, as one may surmise, is a fairly recent innovation.

Odd as it may sound, it is the food of the Bugis that has summoned me to these parts. If anything, Tawau, situated further down Sabah's eastern coast, boasting a heftier Bugis community, would have been a much better place to drink in the cuisine and hospitality. However, it is here, in a terrace house within walking distance from Sandakan airport, that the chance to dine and cook with a Bugis family has arisen. Such opportunities are only turned down by fools.

There are five of us on site this afternoon: my friend Ken, our host and cook Nora, supported by her mother and sister. While Nora puts the finishing touches to a salad (*kerabu*) of unripe mango and bittergourd, the rest of us sit cross-legged on the cool, ecru tiles of the cyan-walled living room, around a sealed aluminium pot, as if waiting for spirits to be summoned.

Nora emerges from the kitchen bearing a tray burdened with bowls. She places these on the floor, beside the pot, for our perusal. There are as many bowls as there are eaters, the contents of each speaking for themselves. A dry, almost crumbly, *sambal* livid with chillies. Wedges of *limau kapas*, the name literally meaning "cotton lime". Crisp, bronze-fried shallots and a massacre of Chinese celery. A ramshackle pile of *perkedel jagung*, corn fritters, fat nuggets of old gold. All of these, I quickly learn, are designed to accompany the contents of the pot, which is soon revealed to be *barobbo*, a gruel of rice, corn and greens. Nora hunches over the vessel and uncovers it, soft plumes of steam dancing upwards to greet her. With a large ladle, she disturbs its contents, the consistency of a suggestive *risotto*, before doling out portions into bowls and distributing these among our number.

Closer inspection reveals the greens to be water convolvulus and bayam spinach. "These are the only two leaves we use", Nora highlights, as she returns the lid to the pot and joins us on the cool floor. There also appears to be sections of yardlong beans, chunks of chicken thigh and specks of ground black pepper.

We are unnecessarily encouraged to embellish with condiments as we feel fit. I go blistering with everything, especially the chilli and *perkedel*, deliberately devoting all attention to my well-decorated helping to avoid any scalding looks of reproach. Spoons are sent around and we soon find ourselves slipping into the plushest cocoons of appreciative silence.

The greens and beans enlisted for the *barabbo* also happen to be crucial in *kapurung*, the Bugis take on *ambuyat*. "You can add banana heart, too," Nora's mother, Rasmi adds. Unlike *ambuyat* which is simply ladled into bowls, with some sourish broth waiting alongside, *kapurung* is shaped into corpulent globules with a pair of chopsticks, or spoons, in the same way one would fashion quenelles, and left to sit in a basin of cold water until it is time to eat. They are then divided among serving bowls and shocked with a hot broth, typically made with either tinned sardines or chicken. "I can make some of the broth for you to try," Rasmi offers, in a fine demonstration of typical Bugis hospitality. I decline, out of fear of imposing, and in the knowledge that this repast is far from over.

The components of the first course are soon replaced with fresh ones. A pot of boiled rice is the first to land, followed sharply by another bearing *sayur bening*, a clear soup of vegetables, in this instance yardlong beans, bayam spinach and aubergines, reticently scented with lemon basil and receiving no seasoning save a smack of salt. Next is the salad of green mango and bittergourd that Nora was overseeing earlier, perked up with dried *Acetes* and calamansi juice, and a chilli-red *sambal*, bulked up with the flaked flesh of several fried salted *ikan gelama* (*Nibea soldado*).

Then arrives a mounded platter of twice-fried bananas, namely *pisang kepok*, flattened into thick, ragged-edged sheets in between oil sessions. Nora says these are best had with a *sambal* of tomatoes and fermented shrimp paste, and this soon magically appears on the floor, in a vessel as large as a soup tureen.

The recipes for these wonderful dishes were bequeathed to Nora by Rasmi, who comes from Pinrang in Southern Sulawesi. She migrated to Sabah with her father, who is from Boné, for work. The remaining Bugis subgroups, such as the Enrekang, Sinjai, Makassar, Toraja and Rappang are also represented in Sandakan.

It is unfortunate that one will only encounter difficulty finding a Bugis eatery in Sabah; the cuisine does not seem to appeal to the present-day palates of the paying public. Many Bugis dishes are time consuming, making them a rare occurrence in the modern Bugis household. It took Nora over a solid hour and much elbow grease to conjure up the *barobbo* – boiling the rice, shaving the corn and picking the leaves – as well as its accompaniments. As a result, simple curries and stir-fries, instant noodles, deep-fried chicken and boiled seafood dishes have prevailed.

The best times to try Bugis dishes are special occasions, such as wedding banquets or Hari Raya feasts at home. *Barobbo* and *kapurung* will likely be present. There will also be *lawa*, a salad of acid-cooked fish that the Bugis share with the Bajau; *nasu likku,* chicken braised with controversial quantities of galangal; *nasu baleh*, fish braised with dried green mango or tomato; *ikan pari masak lemak*, barbecued stingray simmered in a turmeric-gilded coconut sauce; and *bura* or *burasak*, banana leaf parcels of glutinous rice, sumptuous with coconut milk. No celebration will be complete without a meat dish of sorts, usually a generic beef curry, or *konro*, a soup of beef ribs, dimmed with the inky flesh of *Pangium edule* and perfumed with galangal, lemongrass, clove, coriander and nutmeg. Red meat does not feature hugely in Bugis cuisine, seldom making an appearance at the table on a regular day.

Suffice it to say, there will be sweet things. Plenty, usually an entire table's worth. "The only other thing the Bugis love more than chilli is sugar," Nora says brightly as she clears the polished dishes, before listing some favourites. *Sawella*, deep-fried fingers of glutinous rice pastry, made irresistible with coconut sugar. *Ketiri sala* or *katisala*, a coconut milk custard, also sweetened with coconut sugar, steamed atop a futon of glutinous rice. *Kue susu*, steamed crème caramel, and its rather remarkable tropical sister, *sikapor*, made with coconut milk and set in two tiers, one lime green, the other an aching mustard. It is precisely this luridly tinted concoction that we will be having for dessert, presently enjoying its final moments in damp heat.

Sanggarak (or *sanggara* or *sanggar*) means "fried bananas", *pappe* (or *peppe*) "flattened". The best bananas for the job are semi-ripe *pisang kepok*, still hard with pale green skins. Ripe ones will fry alright, but you will not obtain a fluffy, floury interior or all that crisp an exterior.

SANGGARAK PAPPE

SERVES 6

FOR THE SAMBAL
5 tbsp vegetable oil
1 medium red onion, approx. 50g, peeled
4 garlic cloves, approx. 15g, peeled
50g red chillies
15g bird's eye chillies
2 tomatoes, approx. 150g total
10g fermented shrimp paste, grilled (page 522)
Salt, sugar
Calamansi lime juice

FOR THE BANANAS
8 semi-ripe *saba* bananas, each approx. 100g, peeled
Canola oil, for deep-frying

1 Warm 2 tbsp vegetable oil in a frying pan over medium-high heat. Add the red onion, garlic and chillies. Lower the heat slightly and cook until fragrant, tender and blistered in parts. Tip into a mortar. Add the tomatoes to the pan whole and fry until they soften and their skins are blistered and browned in parts. Add to the mortar with the grilled fermented shrimp paste and crush into a pulp with a pestle.

2 Add the remaining 3 tbsp oil to the frying pan. Place over medium heat. Once hot, scrape in the pounded paste. Fry for several seconds, then reduce the heat and cook for 5 minutes, stirring, until it begins to split from the oil. Taste and adjust seasoning with salt, sugar and calamansi juice.

3 Heat 2cm canola oil in a deep frying pan over medium heat. Once hot, add the bananas whole and fry for 4 minutes, turning them over midway. You want them half-cooked. Remove them to a plate, but do not discard the oil or the pan yet.

4 Cool the bananas for several minutes, then crush them between two plates. This is easier than you might think. It is also frightfully satisfying. You should get ragged-edged sheets, roughly ½ cm thick.

5 Reheat the oil in the pan over medium-high heat. Once hot, slip in the flattened bananas and fry until light gold and crisp. Drain on kitchen towel. Cool slightly and serve with the *sambal*.

Slicing and drying the green mango beforehand is the only bit that requires some effort. The dried slivers may be stored in an airtight container and tucked away in a cool, dark place for up to 6 months.

In *Bahasa Bugis*, *nasu baleh* refers to fish that is stewed or braised. For some cooks, this means whacking everything together in a pot and putting flames under it. I prefer to fry the aromatics in a little oil, which rounds and fattens the dish's flavour profile somewhat.

NASU BALEH

SERVES 8

2 small green mangoes, each
   approx. 150g
2 tbsp vegetable oil
4 garlic cloves, peeled and chopped
1 tsp turmeric powder
700g milkfish, cut into 2cm steaks
1 tsp salt
½ tsp sugar
200ml water or fish stock
2 red chillies, finely sliced

1 Peel the green mangoes and cut their flesh into slivers. Arrange these on a muslin-lined tray and leave in a dry, sunny place for 10-14 days, until they shrivel and oxidise into hard, brownish shards. I usually leave the tray near a grille-protected window.

2 Heat the vegetable oil in a medium saucepan over medium heat. Once hot, add the garlic. Fry until fragrant, then add the turmeric. Fry for a minute or so, to expel any rawness. Add the milkfish steaks, salt and sugar and cook for 2 minutes. Pour in the water or stock, bring to a boil, then drop in the chillies and dried mango slivers. Cover, lower the heat and simmer for 5 minutes, or until the fish is cooked. Taste and adjust seasoning with salt.

My idea of heaven is a pot of this, a plate of *perkedel jagung* (page 248) and a bowl of *sambal belacan* (page 495).

BAROBBO

SERVES 6-8

FOR THE SPICE POUCH
4 cardamom pods
1 tsp cumin seeds
1 tsp fennel seeds
1 tsp coriander seeds
1 star anise
2cm cinnamon stick
3 cloves
2 tsp white peppercorns

FOR THE PORRIDGE
1½ litres water
4 chicken thighs, skinned and halved
125g jasmine rice, washed and drained
Kernels from 2 sweetcorn cobs, approx. 200g
100g water convolvulus greens, cut into 4cm sections
100g amaranth greens, cut into 4cm sections
1½ tsp salt, plus more to taste

1 Place the whole spices in a little pouch of muslin cloth. Tie to secure.

2 Bring the water to a boil in a large saucepan over medium-high heat. Add the chicken thighs, the spice pouch and drained rice. Once it returns to the boil, cover, lower the heat and simmer for 40 minutes, or until the grains have swollen and are on the cusp of mushiness.

3 Add the corn kernels and simmer for 15 minutes. Add the water convolvulus, amaranth greens and salt. Once the vegetables are tender, the porridge is done.

4 Remove the spice pouch. Add a touch of hot water if the *barobbo* needs loosening. Taste and adjust seasoning with salt.

Frozen or tinned corn kernels may replace their fresh counterpart, but only if you have no other option. You will, however, need to boost the quantity of flour to cope with the increased moisture.

PERKEDEL JAGUNG

MAKES 20-22

3 sweetcorn cobs, peeled
2 red onions, peeled and finely sliced
4 garlic cloves, peeled and finely chopped
75g white cabbage, roughly sliced
4 tbsp Chinese celery, roughly chopped
1¼ tsp salt
½ tsp freshly ground black pepper
1 egg, lightly beaten
Approx. 100g plain flour
Canola oil, for deep-frying

1 Grate the sweetcorn cobs into a large mixing bowl. You need about 300g of grated kernels. (Any surfeit should be added to the *barobbo*, which you ought to be making to go with these.)

2 Mix in the red onion, garlic, white cabbage, Chinese celery, salt, black pepper and the beaten egg. Fold in just enough flour to get a thick, but not stiff, batter. You want the ingredients to just cohere so the fritters do not fragment in the oil later.

3 Heat 2cm canola oil in a deep frying pan over medium heat. Once hot, drop in large tablespoonfuls, careful not to overcrowd the pan. Fry for 3-4 minutes, turning over midway, until golden. Drain on kitchen towel and eat.

The tinned sardines may sound dubious but work a dream here. Frankly, every Bugis cook I have spoken to uses them, promptly dismissing any suggestion of fresh fish.

Nora, who so generously shared with me her recipe, recommended adding common split-gills, which I happened to have when I made this for its photoshoot. Because they were dried, they had to be rinsed several times to rid them of debris, soaked in water overnight and rinsed again.

KAPURUNG

SERVES 8

FOR THE DUMPLINGS
400g sago flour
900ml water

FOR THE SOUP
75g raw peanuts, unskinned
1¼ litres water, plus 100ml
Kernels from 2 sweetcorn cobs
125g yardlong beans, cut into
  4cm sections
150g water convolvulus, cut into
  4cm sections

150g amaranth greens, cut into
  4cm sections
2 medium banana hearts, each
  approx. 400g
2 tbsp vegetable oil
6 garlic cloves, peeled and
  chopped
6 shallots, peeled and sliced
2 x 155g tins sardines in tomato
  sauce
2 tsp salt, plus more to taste
¼ tsp sugar
Freshly ground black pepper

1 Place the sago flour in a large bowl and stir in 500ml water. Leave to rest for 2 hours.

2 Meanwhile, make the soup. Preheat the oven to 170°C. Scatter the peanuts on a roasting tray and let the oven turn them brown and aromatic. Let them cool slightly before blending to a paste with the 100ml water. Scrape this paste out into a bowl and set aside.

3 Prepare the corn, yardlong beans and leafy vegetables as described above. As for the banana hearts, strip off their purplish bracts, stopping once you arrive at yellowish territory. Slice these peeled hearts into 1cm rounds, immersing them immediately in a large bowl of acidulated water.

4 Bring a large saucepan of water to a boil over medium heat. Drain the banana heart slices and add them to the pot. Cook until tender, about 15 minutes. Drain and rinse under a running tap, then squeeze to remove excess liquid. Set aside.

5 Give the saucepan a wipe and set it over medium heat again. Pour in the oil. Once hot, add the garlic and shallots and fry until fragrant. Add the sardines and their tomato sauce, crushing them into the oil and aromatics. Pour in the 1¼ litres water. Once it boils, cover, lower the heat and simmer for 10 minutes.

6 Stir in the peanut paste, corn kernels, salt and sugar. Simmer for 5 minutes, then add the prepared banana heart and yardlong beans. Cook for another 5 minutes.

7 Add the water convolvulus and amaranth greens. The soup is ready once they wilt. Turn off the heat. Taste and adjust with salt and black pepper.

8 Now, for the fun bit: cooking and shaping the *kapurung*. Bring the remaining 400ml water for the dumplings to a boil in another large saucepan over medium heat. The sago batter would have separated, so give it a stir with a wooden spoon, then stream it into the boiling water, stirring constantly to prevent lumps (there will be several anyway, but worry not.) Lower the heat and cook for 5-7 minutes, beating away until a thick, stubborn and translucent mass is obtained. Not a single streak of white should be seen. Remove the pan from the heat.

9 Fill a large bowl with cold water. Have a chopstick ready in each hand. Dip one chopstick into the translucent mass. Raise it, then spin the seized portion of cooked sago starch around the tip of the other chopstick, forming a jelly-like globule. Push this globule off the chopsticks by scraping them against one another, allowing it to drop into the bowl of cold water. Make all the *kapurung* this way. The other way to make them is to use a pair of tablespoons, which is as effective but not quite as fun.

10 With a slotted spoon, retrieve the *kapurung* and divide them among 8 serving bowls. Bring the soup to a rolling boil and pour several ladles over each portion, drowning the translucent dumplings. Serve with calamansi limes and your *sambal* of choice. Mine would be the truly versatile *sambal belacan*, found on page 495.

My phone says it is 0503 hrs. Already there is pale morning light filtering through the curtained windows. I rise, a trifle imbalanced, manage a sip of water and return to the hallowed space beneath the covers, praying for sleep to take me. I do have a swelling suspicion, however, that by the end of the next few hours, my retinas and the darkened ceiling would have established a highly intimate relationship.

It could not have been the rum. It might have been of notorious make, but I have survived rougher stuff. It was likely the searing heat and my own failure to hydrate. I wonder how my friends would react to me being indisposed from an afternoon of island hopping, when most emerge renewed, wreathed in auras of indigo.

Regular visitors to the Tun Sakaran Marine Park claim the beauty of Sipadan to be unsurpassed, a statement fiercely corroborated by a fellow traveller I had the pleasure of meeting. My heart plummeted when the gentleman mentioned losing his business partner to kidnappers a decade ago, in the waters swirling off Sabah's eastern coast. Based in Peninsular Malaysia, he travels there at least once a year, refusing to yield to fear, visiting the other islands and cays the Celebes has to offer.

I might have spent the boat ride from Sibuan back to Semporna with my head lolling about like a half-inflated balloon, back sunburnt and lips salt-rimmed, but the memory of those waters, unabashedly turquoise and sapphire beneath a meekly feathered sky, remain untarnished. Those outrageous hues will remain with me forever. Judging from the burgeoning numbers of diving centres, hotels and restaurants catering to Chinese tourists, all that is blue must surely be gold.

SEA ON THE AIR

The next time I inspect my phone it is several minutes past nine. Vestiges of grogginess continue to linger. It is to my great benefit then, that we are on the verge of entering the city's main market, for indeed there is nothing quite like mayhem and the whiff of fish in the morning to jolt one to life.

A stone's throw from the jetty, Semporna's market is a loose collection of counters and stalls littering a relatively small area, its boundaries influenced by the ebb and flow of human traffic through and around them. Locals can set up shop where they please and sell whatever they want, whenever they want. There will be no need for demarcations and structures until licences are made mandatory. Today, I feel blessed to be in the company of Kaka Rukiah and Teacher Zulianah, for the drama and theatrics in this space are heady, teetering on the comedic.

We pass a couple of men wrangling rusty old bicycles with sausage-shaped banana leaf parcels suspended from their handles. Kaka Rukiah identifies them as *petulakan*, steamed cylinders of ground rice and coconut milk, usually served as part of a meal. She proceeds to direct my attention to a long wooden counter groaning beneath compact, cream-coloured wheels and wedges wrapped in clingfilm. These, it turns out, are made of grated tapioca, already relieved of excess moisture. Tapioca, especially in this form, is the main source of carbohydrate for the Bajau, though these days rice is gleefully consumed. Kaka Rukiah purchases the largest wedge she can find. All she will have to do later is shatter it into crumbs and cook it as she pleases.

We find a stall selling various species of stingray, or *pahi*, as the Bajaus call them. There are small ones with rhombic bodies which may be barbecued or gutted and dried, the fossil-like result known as *kihampau*. *Kihampau* is usually either deep-fried or clobbered into floss (*serunding*). There are also immense ones, the size of coffee table tops, presently being hewn into steaks by cleaver-armed, singlet-clad men. These, Teacher Zulianah says, is what we will be requiring for lunch later, proceeding to get a pound's worth, together with a ruby chunk of *ati* – their liver.

The two women guide me towards a cluster of stalls close to the water's edge, selling what one could easily mistake for aquarium decorations. Their wares, as it transpires, form an important part of the Bajau diet. Teacher Zulianah gives me a run-through while making some very necessary purchases.

There is *kima*, a name applied to all species of giant clam, and *kahanga*, spider conches, their extracted flesh sold on melamine plates for purchasers to appraise and prod. There are plates offering fat bunches of *lato* (*Caulerpa lentillifera*), widely known as sea caviar, and bags bursting with gardens of green and white *agal-agal*, *Eucheuma cottonii*, the gummy seaweed from which gelatine is derived. Seaweeds are collectively known in Malay as *rumpai laut*.

Held captive in plastic pouches are the secretions of sea cucumbers, the dark green strands reminiscent of Korean buckwheat noodles, that make a fine *kilaw*, squirted with lime and dressed with sliced shallots, ginger and chilli. Sea cucumbers, *tripang* in Malay and *bat* in Sinama (the Sama language), are seldom consumed by locals, who much prefer drying and selling them to Chinese tourists for a solid buck.

There are soda bottles packed with the gonads of *tayum*, one of the two species of sea urchins the Bajau consume, the other being *tehe-tehe*. It is easy to distinguish the two. *Tayum* (*Diadema*) is known for having a small husk and a fierce armour of long, black spikes. Its gonads are enjoyed raw, as *kilaw*, but may be also fried until brown and crisp, enlivened with shallots, ginger and chilli, and eaten with rice or fried noodles. This practice may sound wanton, but when one is inundated with something on a diurnal basis, it surely makes sense to find as many uses for it as possible.

In contrast, *tehe-tehe* (*Tripnuestes*) has a larger [body], with short, almost bristle-like, salt and pepper spikes, radially striping its teal, [nodu]lle-dotted body. These are always sold whole; useful as their gonads are, cons[ume]d in the same way as *tayum*, their husks also have some culinary purpose. Afte[r ren]dering them bald, Bajau cooks would gouge out their mouths, eviscerate and st[uff th]em with rice, plug them with blades of lemongrass or pandan, and boil them [in w]ater. In the heat, the rice expands within them, forming compact cakes that one a[cce]sses by cracking their calcium casings. This delicacy, known after the starrin[g se]a urchin, is eaten together with viands as one would rice.

At the foot of the counters of one p[artic]ular stall, we find a collection of basins brimming with water, occupied by s[ome] rather mysterious creatures. Like a mass of entrails of some alien lifeform, it s[eem]s utterly impossible to tell where one ends and another begins. These, Zulianah [eni]ghtens, is *bobohan*, a kind of anemone harvested from rocks during high tide. Sh[e pl]unges a hand into a large blue basin and swishes it about, before somehow extrac[ting] five green-tinged specimens. Apparently, the rest of their number, vaunting purp[le a]nd blueish highlights, can gift their consumers with a fiendish itch. Yet, he[re th]ey are, up for sale, their vendors silent on the hazards they pose. In these parts, [the] responsibility to discern rests solely on the shoulders of the buyer.

EAST COAST BUSINESS

An hour later, we arrive at the res[iden]ce of Puan Rukiah, where an immaculate, airy kitchen welcomes us, poised [for] some serious action. Teacher Zulianah passes our bags of purchases to the kit[chen] assistant, Norma, who immediately begins preparations. The cake of grate[d ta]pioca is the first to be tackled, chucked into a large bowl and swiftly broken i[nto] crumbs, like moistened sawdust, to prevent it from souring. An array of ceramic p[lat]ters emerges from a cabinet and are subsequently dressed with the anemone, c[or]n, agar-agar seaweed, sea caviar, stingray steaks and liver. A wicker basket of lem[on]grass, ginger, shallots, red chillies and fresh turmeric is brought out from an unde[rco]unter cabinet.

As Norma begins [stri]pping the papery, puce skins off the shallots, the rest of us gather around the kit[che]n table and share a pot of freshly brewed tea and a plate of *kue*, namely *bamban g[and]um*, crushed, sweetened corn steamed in the husks that once protected them; a[nd w]ajik, a cake of glutinous rice sweetened with *gula merah* or coconut sugar. In betw[ee]n sips of the hot, teak-coloured infusion, I nibble gratefully but cautiously, quite [aw]are of the magnitude of the lunch that beckons us.

Hajah Zulianah hails from Look Sisarah, an island off the coast of Semporna. Much of the Bajau food she cooks is typical of the area, often conceived, perhaps erroneously, as being "purer" than its West Coast counterpart. People have the tendency to think of Semporna as the origins of the Bajau within Sabah – including the Bajau themselves, as it is here that they have remained the predominant ethnic group. As highlighted in a previous chapter, the Bajau are the Sama, a diverse ethnolinguistic group inhabiting the Sulu Archipelago and islands off the southwestern coast of Mindanao. The term Sama Dilaut, "Sama of the Sea", refers to the group often called sea gypsies, Badjao or Bajo, named for how they spend most, if not all, of their lives in or on water, their disproportionately large spleens – courtesy of natural selection – enabling them to dive deep and long.

As with their West Coast counterparts, their cuisine mostly comprises *makanan laut* or seafood, prepared in the simplest of fashions, with meat, such as chicken and beef, being the occasional indulgence. All of the food here can be found in West Coast Bajau homes, although the converse is not necessarily true. Having interacted with other ethnic groups, like the Kadazandusun, Brunei, Bugis and Malays, the West Coast Bajau have roped foreign ingredients and techniques into their cuisine. Those in Petagas, for instance, ferment *tebadak* with salt, simmer the fruit and leaves of the *angan-angan* plant with salted fish, and make salads with *kembang tuli* leaves and *akar buras*. These dishes are virtually unknown here in the east.

In Bajau cuisine, shallots, white onions, lemongrass, ginger, chillies and turmeric form the foundation for many dishes, the last mostly used fresh, seldom powdered. Garlic is hardly used and although coconut milk is splashed liberally into sweet things, it tends to be added to savoury dishes with great restraint. Having said that, Puan Rukiah shares that one of her favourite Bajau dishes is a braise of unripe *saba* bananas with coconut milk as its liquid medium, bejewelled with purplish pieces of dried octopus (*kurita*). Squash is also excellent prepared this way, but will instead get its umami jab from dried bluespot mullet (*ikan belanak*).

Half an hour later, with our pot of tea declared empty, Hajah Zulianah has decided it time to begin, soon urging me towards the stove where a wok has begun making itself comfortable over a ring of large flames. She takes a plate bearing the *bobohan* and, without any ceremony whatsoever, plops them straight into the pan, where they hiss vehemently, defiantly. "They need no water," she says, coolly. "They have enough in them".

True to her word, after a couple of minutes, the anemones begin exuding a clear greenish liquid that seems to be getting murkier by the second. She leaves them to their devices, prodding them occasionally, and after a solid quarter-hour, they are

shrunken, frilly-edged and opaque, swimming in a pool of foamy liquid that is now as heady as bile. It is a spectacle to behold, worthy of a sci-fi flick. The cooked *bobohan* are drained, washed, chopped up and then blanched briefly in a saucepan filled with water. These two steps are crucial in relieving the anemone of *hanyir* – fishiness.

The clean anemone pieces are then fried with sliced ginger, shallots and chillies, pounded fresh turmeric and lemongrass, salt and a trickle of water that is then bubbled down to a rich, mustard-toned syrup. Once conveyed to a plate, she quickly works on the *kima*, which is cooked in pretty much the same way, but with an additional fillip of shredded turmeric leaves.

The stingray steaks have been magically transformed into a collection of boiled flakes, their liver cut into chunks. Unbeknownst to me, Norma was quietly preparing them the entire time I was observing Teacher Zulianah. She also managed to blanch the *agal-agal* and conch meat. The *agal-agal* now sit in a capacious basin of water, while the conch has been cut into slivers. These two items are to collide in a salad, with onions, green mangoes, tomatoes, crushed roasted coconut (*kerisik*) and a healthy squeeze of calamansi juice. Norma intimates that it is crucial to give the *agal-agal* a proper cleaning to remove the *lindir*, the mucus-like substance coating their stalks.

Teacher Zulianah snappily calls me towards her smoking wok in which she has begun to fry several stalks of bruised lemongrass. She pushes in the stingray liver and fries it, crushing it into the fat so that it cooks into a crumbly, chocolate-brown paste, a process that she says will afford the dish body and depth. In go the usual aromatics, a little salt, the flaked stingray, a slurp of water and finally several spring onions, snipped into small sections. This particular dish, called *sagol*, which means "to mix many things together", is also popularly prepared with *ikan buntal* (pufferfish) or *yu*, dogfish or shark.

For the third time, the assiduous lady cleans her wok and whacks it on the stove, this time over a timid heat. It is kissed with oil, then fed with the crumbled tapioca. "You can add grated coconut if you want," she tells me, flinging around the cream-coloured snow with great vigour until it swells into fat beads, also turning slightly jaundiced and translucent in the process. Grated tapioca combined with coconut can be fried into scorched discs, *tompe*, or steamed into *putu*, commonly sold in sausage shapes cloaked in plastic.

Contrary to my own preconceptions, the *putu* only assume this form after getting cooked, not before. The grated tapioca are first steamed in a *temburong*, a bowl fashioned from coconut husk, bearing several perforations. The loaded *temburong* is popped onto the mouth of a suitably sized *belanga*, a pot-bellied vessel filled with water, which is then put over high heat, so that its cargo may cook. Only after being freed from its mould in a bulging hemispherical patty is it promptly coaxed into a cylinder with spatulas, sometimes asbestos hands, and then swaddled in clingfilm.

Norma tidies up the kitchen and plates the food, sending them dancing out onto the dining table in an adjacent room. Rukiah, a portrait of satisfaction, says even in Semporna, the so-called heartland of the Bajau, such dishes are seldom eaten at home. These days, households prefer applying themselves to generic Malay dishes, such as braised or grilled fish, chicken curry, fried rice and noodles. It is only during festive occasions, like weddings and Hari Raya, that they grace dining tables, and even then they will be cushioned with all-time favourites like *rendang*, *ayam masak merah* and *ketupat*.

As we sit down to the feast, Teacher Zulianah brings out one final item, a plate of sea caviar, their emerald beads glistening in the artificial light, accompanied by a solitary saucer carrying an effortless ointment of lime juice, salt and several crushed bullets of bird's eye chilli. "*Lato* is believed to cure tuberculosis and goitre", Puan Rukia shares, before nudging us towards the plates and imminent stultification.

This salad may be made with white or green *Eucheuma cottonii*. In Indonesia, it is possible to purchase this gummy seaweed dehydrated in nifty little packets. The fresh stuff remains far superior.

AGAL-AGAL

SERVES 6

100g grated coconut
300g fresh *Eucheuma cottonii*
2 medium tomatoes, cut into
   thin half-moons
2 small green mangoes, peeled and cut into
   thin slivers
½ tsp salt, plus more to taste
Calamansi limes

1 Heat a frying pan over medium heat. Once hot, add the grated coconut. Stir for a minute or so, then lower the heat and fry until it turns deep gold. Remove from the heat and crush with a pestle and mortar into a fine rubble.

2 Blanch the *Eucheuma* in a large saucepan of boiling water over medium heat, until tender, about 5-10 minutes, depending on the thickness of the stalks. Drain, rinse under a cold tap and put in a bowl with a little water. Massage the seaweed to remove the slime from the stalks, what the Bajau call *lindir*. Wash one more time, drain and return to the bowl.

3 Snip the cleaned seaweed into 6-8cm sections. Mix in the tomatoes, green mangoes, crushed toasted coconut and salt. Taste and adjust seasoning. Serve with calamansi limes.

I was initially hesitant about including this recipe, provided by Teacher Zulianah, as several species of *Tridacna* have become endangered due to overfishing, be it for their flesh or decorative shells. My decision to put it here anyway was motivated by the urgent need to document the dish's preparation. It is recipes like this, simple, mid-toned and nuanced, that are being lost as our appetites for the complex and fulsome continue to swell.

I urge you to try it instead using clams or mussels, adding about 600g, with their shells on, to the pot in place of the *kima*, and using 200ml coconut cream instead of the stipulated amount of coconut milk, as the juices exuded by the shellfish will only lead to its dilution.

KIMA

SERVES 6

Flesh of 3 giant clams, total weight
    approx. 250g, washed
6 shallots, peeled and sliced
4cm ginger, peeled and sliced
2cm turmeric, peeled and sliced
2 lemongrass stalks, tender portions only,
    finely sliced
3 tbsp vegetable oil
4 red bird's eye chillies, sliced
½ tsp salt, plus more to taste
250ml coconut milk
1 white onion, peeled and cut into
    thin half-moons
1 small turmeric leaf, thinly shredded

1 Cut the clam flesh into 1½cm pieces. Set aside.

2 In a pestle and mortar, crush the shallots, ginger, turmeric and lemongrass into a rough paste.

3 Heat the oil in a large frying pan or wok over medium-high heat. Add the spice paste and red bird's eye chillies and fry for 30 seconds. Then lower the heat and continue to cook until soft and fragrant, stirring.

4 Add the prepared *kima*, salt, coconut milk, white onion and turmeric leaf. Simmer for just 3-5 minutes, so the clam cooks and absorbs all the flavours and the coconut milk reduces to a light, syrupy sauce. Taste and adjust seasoning with salt.

The preliminary preparation of the *bobohan* does take time but is crucial as it expels the *hanyir* or fishiness. This, however, comes at a price: the anemone toughens up somewhat, treating your jaw muscles to a nice little workout. This is not a terrible thing: the more you chew, the closer you feel to the sea, the rockpools and ozone. You will also be treated to a lurid action sequence from a sci-fi flick as it cooks and splutters in its pan.

BOBOHAN

SERVES 6

4 *bobohan*, total weight
   approx. 600g, washed
6 shallots, peeled and sliced
4cm ginger, peeled and sliced
2cm turmeric, peeled and sliced
4 tbsp vegetable oil
4 lemongrass stalks, tender portions only,
   cut into 4cm sections and bruised
4 red bird's eye chillies, sliced
200ml dried anchovy stock (page 520)
½ tsp salt

1 Place the *bobohan* in a large frying pan over medium heat. Once they sizzle, turn opaque and exude liquid, reduce the heat and cover. Grant them some privacy, checking once in a while, until they have shrunk and are swimming in a primordial pool of greenish juices. This process takes 15-20 minutes.

2 Drain, rinse under a cold tap, then blanch in a saucepan of water over medium heat, for 5 minutes, to remove any residual fishiness. Drain, wash once more, then cut into 1½cm pieces.

3 In a pestle and mortar, crush the shallots, ginger and turmeric into a rough spice paste. Heat the oil in a large frying pan or wok over medium-high heat. Add the lemongrass. Fry for just a minute, then add the spice paste and red bird's eye chillies.

4 Lower the heat, fry until soft and fragrant, then add the prepared *bobohan*, stock and salt. Simmer for 5 minutes, so the anemone absorbs all the flavours and the stock reduces to a light, flavoursome syrup. Taste and adjust seasoning.

The sea urchin for the job here is *Tripnuestes*. On some islands, this is prepared with glutinous rice.

If you cannot find lemongrass stalks with the requisite leafage, use softened-and-knotted strips of banana leaf as stoppers instead. I would still recommend dropping several sections of bruised lemongrass into the pot for fragrance, however.

TEHE-TEHE

SERVES 6

6 sea urchins (see above)
About 4 lemongrass stalks, with leafage
75g jasmine rice, washed and soaked
   in water for at least 4 hours
Water

1 Begin by denuding the sea urchins. There are several ways to do this, including abrasing them against a knife sharpener, but the most effective, though inelegant, method is to hold one in each (gloved) hand and aggresively rub them against one another beneath a running tap.

2 Give the bald sea urchins a brief rinse. Incise out the mouth of one with a small knife, hold it under a lenient tap so the water just trickles into its husk, and gently persuade out its black innards with your fingers. Do take care not to damage the precious gonads. Clean all the sea urchins this way.

3 Assess your lemongrass stalks. You want the section of their leafage that is still rigid to serve as stoppers. So cut these portions out and snip these into 4cm lengths. You need 12 such lengths. Do not discard any other part of the lemongrass yet, though.

4 Drain the rice and feed about 2 tbsp into each husk. It is impossible to be precise here, as it is likely that your husks will vary in capacity. Essentially, you want them about a third full. Into the mouth of each husk, insert a pair of lemongrass blade lengths perpendicular to another, thereby producing a cross, mostly concealing the orifice.

5 Place the prepared sea urchins in a cosy saucepan and cover generously with water. Drop in whatever lemongrass you have left and bring to a boil over high heat. Turn the heat down to its lowest, cover and boil for 1 hour.

6 Remove the cooked *tehe-tehe* from the pot. Leave them to cool and compose themselves for 15-20 minutes. There are two ways of serving them: cut them into halves or quarters with a sharp knife or strike them repeatedly all over with a pestle or hammer and peel, as you would hardboiled eggs.

I have been talking about this dish since page 187. Now, finally, the recipe has come. Do not skip the stingray liver. It is a crucial component. If you want your *sagol* juicier, simply add more fish stock.

SAGOL PARI

SERVES 6-8

1kg stingray, cut into large steaks
1 tsp salt, plus more to taste
6 shallots, peeled and sliced
4cm ginger, peeled and sliced
2cm turmeric, peeled and sliced
4 red bird's eye chillies, sliced
5 tbsp vegetable oil
4 lemongrass stalks, tender portions only,
   cut into 4cm sections, bruised
200g stingray liver, cut into 2cm cubes
200ml fish stock (page 520)
4 spring onions, cut into 2cm sections

1 Bring a large saucepan of water to a boil over medium heat. Add the stingray and salt. Lower the heat and simmer for 5 minutes or until the ray is just cooked. Drain, cool slightly, then break into large flakes.

2 In a pestle and mortar, crush the shallots, ginger, turmeric and bird's eye chillies into a rough spice paste.

3 Heat the oil in a large saucepan over medium heat, then add the bruised lemongrass. Fry for 2 minutes, until fragrant, then add the stingray liver. Lower the heat slightly and fry, crushing the liver into the hot oil, until you get a dryish chocolaty paste.

4 Add the spice paste and fry until soft and fragrant, stirring. Add the stingray flakes and stock. Simmer for 3-5 minutes, so the fish absorbs all the flavours and the liquid reduces to a light, flavoursome syrup. Taste and adjust seasoning with more salt. Toss in the spring onions. Once these soften, the dish is done.

The reddish gonads of *Diadema* are the ones to use here. I understand that for many, sea urchin gonads are considered a true extravagance and to put them through such a treatment may seem like the greatest sin. But the spicing here adds interest while being subtle, and if the Italians can toss *ricci di mare* into mounds of pasta, I see no reason why this cannot have a place at the table when the opportunity presents itself.

TAYUM

SERVES 4

75g sea urchin gonads
2 garlic cloves, peeled
4 shallots, peeled and sliced
2cm ginger, peeled
2cm turmeric, peeled
2 lemongrass stalks, tender portions only,
   thinly sliced
1 red chilli, sliced
2 tbsp vegetable oil
1 large tomato, deseeded
   and finely diced
4 green bird's eye chillies, slit
Salt

1 Prepare your steamer. Haphazardly arrange the sea urchin gonads over a medium-sized heatproof plate. Steam for 5 minutes, just until the gonads solidify slightly. They would also have shrunk in the process. Leave to cool a little.

2 Meanwhile, crush the garlic, shallots, ginger, turmeric, lemongrass and red chilli into a rough spice paste.

3 Heat the oil in a medium-sized frying pan over medium heat, then stir in the spice paste. Fry for a few seconds, then lower the heat slightly and continue frying until soft, fragrant and a deeper orange.

4 Gently push in the cooled sea urchin, tomato and green bird's eye chillies. Fry for just 1-2 minutes, lightly tossing them into the aromatics. Season lightly with salt. Serve with rice and calamansi limes.

Dried stingray, *kihampau*, is essential for this recipe. Fresh stingray, poached and flaked, may be used, though to slightly different effect – the result tends to be heavier.

Just so you know, hydrated *kihampau* is also delicious fried and eaten with *sambal*.

SERUNDING KIHAMPAU

SERVES 6

250g dried stingray
3 garlic cloves, peeled
25g shallots, peeled and sliced
10g ginger, peeled and sliced
20g galangal, peeled and sliced
10g turmeric, peeled and sliced
3 dried red chillies, softened (page 520)
30g red chillies, sliced
5 tbsp vegetable oil
1 tbsp vinegar
1 tbsp sugar
1 tsp salt, plus more to taste

1 Soak the dried stingray in water overnight. Drain, rinse and strip off the flesh in long, fine, shreds. (Skinning them is inessential.) Set aside.

2 Pound the garlic, shallots, ginger, galangal, turmeric, dried chillies and red chillies into a fine paste. Alternatively, blend them in a cosy blender, adding a little water if necessary.

3 Heat the oil in a wok over medium heat. Add the spice paste and fry for a minute. Lower the heat and fry until the paste has split in the oil and has turned fragrant and a deeper red.

4 Add the shredded stingray, vinegar, sugar and salt. Stir well, turning the stingray shreds in the paste, so that every shred is coated, albeit scantily. Continue cooking, stirring always, until these are crisp and redly bronzed and there is no liquid left in the pan. This process should take 15-20 minutes. Taste and adjust seasoning with salt. This should be emphatically seasoned, so be generous.

Known variously as *solleng*, *kinuha* and *siyanglag* by the Ubian, Kagayan and Suluk on Sabah's west coast, this is a Bajau staple that is eaten with almost any dish.

EGGANG

SERVES 4-6

1kg tapioca, peeled weight
200g grated coconut
½ tsp salt

1 Finely grate the tapioca. Squeeze with muslin, in batches, to extract as much liquid as possible.

2 Place the grated tapioca on a wide tray lined with more muslin. Using your fingers, break it up into small lumps, like crumble topping. Leave in a cool place to dry slightly, for about 3-4 hours. They should not feel damp when touched.

3 Place a large wok over medium heat. Once hot, add the tapioca rubble and fry, stirring constantly, until it begins to turn translucent. Add the grated coconut and salt, lower the heat and continue frying and stirring until the beads of tapioca are plump and tender and the coconut is slightly toasted and aromatic. Serve as quickly as you can.

COALS
FOR
BONTANG

No sooner than our bodies leave the car do my ears catch the flick of a BIC. Hefni, designated driver, is at it again. While Yudha and Arul tend to their cellphones, I survey the area. We are alone, but for how long, goodness knows. There is no time to waste. I scurry towards one side of the asphalt, an ever-growing cluster of thought balloons trailing sharply behind. The biggest and loudest reads 'so this is what dogging must feel like.'

While I have always felt at ease at the stove, it takes a lot of time and effort to stave off brittleness whenever I have an eye pressed against the viewfinder. It was not passion that drove me towards photography, but the dull ache of necessity: a professional was out of my fiscal orbit. Familiarising myself with the camera, allowing it to hang pendulously, bossily, around my neck, and letting it teach me how to capture images that matched those of my dreams, has been a veritable process, to say the least. Ten years on, I am far from *au fait* and still get my nerves into pretzels at the notion of shutter speeds and aperture stops.

It is axiomatic that scale, angle, lighting, juxtaposition and composition are important factors for any kind of photography. When shooting food in a studio, one has the luxury of being able to adjust these components to one's liking. When shooting landscapes however, the photographer has little, or no, control over the subject or its physical environment, which makes the task of shooting very straight forward, sometimes extremely painful. Quite often, success boils down to the simple business of being in the right places at the right times so that the right accidents can occur. For the Baitul Muttaqin Mosque, the jewel of Samarinda, on what is an unexpectedly baking February morning, we have selected an unfinished highway on the opposite side of the Mahakam River, encroaching the hemline of the city. With the majestic building placed against a quilt of uninspiring low-rise architecture, waterway thickly oozing at the forefront, the view from here exudes what Yudha has dubbed an "Istanbul vibe".

The capital of East Kalimantan, Samarinda earned its name from the way the Bugis houses that once occupied the area were designed and constructed so that neither was significantly taller or shorter than the other – *samarenda* means "equal in height" – as a form of social symbolism. The Bugis arrived in Kalimantan during the 17th century, having fled Dutch-invaded Sulawesi, which was then under the leadership of one Lamoheng Daeng Mangkona. They were welcomed by the Kutai sultan at the time who allowed them to settle in Kampung Melantai, modern day Selili, a district in Samarinda, and, actually, not very far from the highway we are on.

All credit goes to Hefni for the exquisite location. As I thank him for blithely disregarding the row of cautionary signboards and barricades, he lights his eighth stick for the day and nods in acknowledgement. "*Sama…*", he sings, teeth clenched around a smouldering Malboro. Hemorrhaging with the coolness of a rock star fresh from a successful gig, he struts towards the guardrail where I am, anxiously nourishing my lenses before we can get accosted. This happens not five minutes later, and not by construction officials, but the weather.

A sunshower has come to relieve Samarinda of heat-induced torpor. Just as Baitul Muttaqin and its seven minarets begin to fade into a blur behind a sparkling veil of tears, several quarry-like cargoes of coal sidle into view. We watch them from beneath a pair of freshly sprung parasols. Monstrous hillocks, dark and malevolent as a million ill wishes, gracefully inching their way across crêpe paper waters on the backs of freighters, untroubled by the sky's sudden change of heart. I let my camera take several more sips just before the ships begin taking turns obstructing the mosque. "Time to go", Yudha chimes, turning his back and returning to the vehicle with Hefni and Arul. I follow suit.

East Kalimantan shares its borders with Sabah and the remaining four provinces of Kalimantan. West, South and North Kalimantan get especially lavish helpings of these notional boundaries. The waters that cling to East Kalimantan's coastline are supplied by the Celebes Sea and Makassar Strait, the two bodies separated by the protuberant Mangkalihat Peninsula.

The population of the province is a heady blend of peoples – Banjarese, Buginese, Chinese, Dayak, Javanese and Kutai, with the foreigners taking an especially thick wedge of the pie. The same applies to North Kalimantan, occupied by the Javanese, Chinese, Tidung, Bulungan, Suluk, Banjarese, Murut, Lun Bawang, Lundayeh and other Dayaks. The strong Javanese presence here, and the rest of Kalimantan, can mostly be ascribed to *transmigrasi*, the transmigration program initiated by the Dutch colonial government (and continued by the Indonesian government) in an attempt to alleviate overpopulation woes on Javanese soil. For the Chinese, it was commerce that brought them to this part of Borneo during the 14th century, the chief natural resources of allure at the time being rattan and resin. These days, East Kalimantan is synonymous with mining, oil, timbre and liquefied natural gas, even though production in these sectors has witnessed a decline for several years now. Most of the province's coal mines are located in the vicinity of Tenggarong, the capital of Kutai Kartanegara Regency.

KING AND SWING

The word Kutai can create confusion as it can refer to several things. Besides being a geographical location, it is an ethnic group and the name of an ancient kingdom, located in the district of Muara Kaman, dating back to the 4th century.

Little is spoken of the Kutai Kingdom. Indeed, not much is known about it at all. Even its true name remains a bit of a mystery: it is called Kutai because that is the place where seven *yūpa* or plinths were discovered, salient for the Sanskrit and Pallava inscriptions they bore, which shed light on certain cultural, social and political aspects of life at the time. It is from these *yūpa* that we know the kingdom's founder, Kudungga, his son Aswawarman, and grandson Mulawarman. It was during Mulawarman's reign that the kingdom seemed to be especially prosperous. They also state the existence of Brahmins and a group of knights comprising the king and his close relatives, thereby indicating the presence of some form of caste and establishing the emergence of an Indianised kingdom in Indonesia.

Despite lasting from 4th–17th century, the Kutai era was occupied by two kingdoms. The first is the one mentioned above, more specifically known as the Kingdom of Kutai Martadipura. The second is the Kingdom of Kutai Kartanegara, which emerged many years later, during the 13th century, in an area called Tepian Batu or Kutai Lama. Both kingdoms were situated around the Mahakam River. Years of rivalry culminated in battle in the 16th century, with the Kutai Martadipura eventually being absorbed into the triumphant Kutai Kartanegara. This new kingdom, Kutai Kartanegara Kingdom Ing Martadipura, is known in Javanese literature as Negarakertagama.

The 17th century brought with it the arrival of Islam, which was welcomed by the rajah at the time. As the Kutai Kingdom began to embrace this new religion, the title rajah was replaced by sultan and the kingdom became a sultanate. Kutai Kartanegara Sultanate Ing Martadipura remained intact until 1947, when it entered the Federation of East Kalimantan, along with other sultanate regions. It joined the United Republic of Indonesia in 1949.

Given how little is known about this kingdom's history, it should come as no surprise to discover that even less is known about the food of this period. It does take some rooting around to uncover dishes that exhibit connections to East Kalimantan's monarchical past, or least *appear* to. One is the suitably titled *sambal raja*, "sambal for the king", that gathers fried yardlong beans, shallots and aubergines and hardboiled eggs on a single platter and lavishes them with a spice paste, livid with chillies and pungent with *terasi* (fermented shrimp paste). Another is what *sambal raja* often chaperones, a rice dish known as *nasi bekepor*.

Nasi bekepor begins life as a mess of grains, water, several blades of *daun salam* (Indonesian bay; *Syzygium polyanthum*), in a pot-bellied vessel known as a *kenceng*. Although present-day *kenceng* are made from flimsy aluminium and spend most of their working hours atop lit stoves, in the past they would have been made of bronze, suspended by their loop handles above wood-stoked fires, and oscillated until the rice was evenly and properly cooked – *bekepor*, in the Kutai language, means "swing". Salted *ikan gabus* (snakehead murrel) will then be rinsed, fried, flaked and stirred in, together with several bird's eye chillies, a squirt of calamansi and a handful of *daun kemangi* (lemon basil), the tender leaves purring their uplifting scent into the pot of warm, starchy grains.

We had these two dishes for lunch on our first day in Samarinda, in the interiors of a restaurant whose walls dripped with the unforgettable hues of overcooked salmon. All that mattered was the food, which did not disappoint, representative of the Kutai people, their population dispersed over Kutai Tenggara, West Kutai, Kutai Kartanegara, the last province frequently going by the portmanteau kukar.

THE KUTAI TABLE

The majority of Kutai folk reside in rural areas and eke out livelihoods as fishermen, hunters and farmers as they have for centuries. This shines through in their food, the cuisine at the heart of East Kalimantan, a repertoire of soups, grilled meats and river fish and *sambals* of forest fruit, with a talent for stretching the little they have, a talent that is shared by the Dayaks further inland, in the lush interiors of the state. We repasted on *gence ruan*, a fried, butterflied mudfish daubed with a tomato-based *sambal* – *gence* is *sambal*, *ruan* mudfish, in Kutai – and a gorgeously sour *sayur asem*, a warming braise of vegetables, in our case water convolvulus, banana heart and taro shoots, bolstered with handsome steaks of *ikan patin* (iridescent shark). Its traditional souring agent is *terong asem*, but these days many cooks reach for slices of *asam sunti*, dried bilimbi, an ingredient which features prominently in Sumatran cooking.

Sayur in Indonesian is the term for any dish of cooked vegetables, like stir-fries and braises. In Kalimantan, the latter category tends to be more commonly referred to as *gangan*. Therefore, the abovementioned *sayur asem* from Kukar would be more commonly referred to as *gangan asem kukar*. *Gangan manok* points to a soup of bittergourd, amaranth greens and chicken meatballs, *gangan waluh* a coconut-white broth bearing chunks of squash.

Together with *sambal* and fried salted fish, *gangan* moistens many a plate of *nasi subut* in North Kalimantan. A dish of the Tidong people, *nasi subut* involves cooking rice with cubes of sweet potato or tapioca, sometimes shaved kernels of corn; *subut* in Tidong means "to mix" or "mixed". Although it would be natural in this day and age to think of such additions as enhancements, their main purpose was to

stretch the grains in times of scarcity. It is said that Tidong families make it a point to dedicate one meal to *nasi subut* every month, as a reminder of humble beginnings, of strife and uncertainty.

Suffice it to say, in this age of greater comfort, *nasi subut* is consumed with a wide array of dishes, as befits any rice dish. It has become exceedingly popular to partner it with grilled skewers or *sate*, in particular ones of *pari* (stingray), *tudai* (blood cockles), *temburung* (telescope shells) and *payau*, the now endangered sambar deer. At the home of a friend one night in Tarakan several years ago, dinner involved a *nasi subut*, studded with the most absurdly purple sweet potatoes; *lawar gamai*, a salad of *laut putih* (white *Eucheuma cottonii*) and toasted coconut; and *ayam cincane*, for which a spatchcocked chicken is braised to tenderness in a violently red, hauntingly spiced, sauce, then turned over hot coals so it develops a crust. Throughout its flame-licked sojourn, it receives bastings of its sauce, which the heat turns into the most delicious callouses, a technique that reminds me greatly of the *ayam percik* of Kelantan. Though it can be found all over East and North Kalimantan – the latter was part of the former up till 2012 – *ayam cincane* is recognised as one of Samarinda's culinary gems. And as our vehicle departs its concrete sprawl and heads into the ruralities of Kutai Kartanegara, my only regret is not eating more of it.

On the fringes of Kotabangun, in disturbing proximity to a timber yard, the car is brought to a halt on the side of the road. After gaily lubricating ourselves with several litres of water, payment is now in order. Gingerly, we make our way through the wild foliage towards a comfortable-looking spot near a bereft noni. From here, we see the river in its full glory, and, in the distance, spot the same coal-loaded freighters that we saw earlier. Hefni, who has predictably made a chimney of himself several metres from me, says they are destined for Bontang, home to the offices of coal mining corporations. From there, the coals will be exported to Japan, Korea and Taiwan. Such industry is the main reason for the small city having a disproportionately large expatriate community. For a few friends who have visited Bontang, it was only reason. None intimated particularly fond memories or expressed the remotest keenness in returning. Not even a sizzling plate of the city's famous *gami* will change their minds.

Less jagged opinions were dispensed on Balikpapan and the reasons are plain to see. The city is, after all, the gateway to East, North and South Kalimantan. The architecture is more modern, the streets are slightly wider. There are several large shopping malls and decent hotels, not to mention a staggering variety of eating options.

There is no single dish utterly unique to Balikpapan. Even its famous *bingka kentang*, an eggy coconut cake creamy with chunks of boiled potato, and *pisang gapit*, grilled-then-flattened *saba* bananas, draped in a thick, sweet coconut sauce, can be found all over this side of Borneo. Ask any hotel concierge where to eat and you will likely be directed to one of its many seafood restaurants, offering local catches cooked in a variety of ways available throughout Indonesia, and perhaps Southeast Asia. There, one will find *trakulu* (pompano) rubbed with *sambal* and grilled, *kakap* (barramundi) steamed and dressed in a tangy sauce made from fresh limes, *udang* (shrimp) fried and flung into thick golden ponds of salted egg yolk sauce. But of all the fruits of the seas, river and swamps, it is the mudcrab (*kepiting*) that Balikpapan has decided to make its mascot. Many seafood-centric establishments have massive plastic crabs festooning their entrances. It is an indication of serious business and eating.

The mudcrabs are harvested from all over the province at a cheap price and brought into the city, where they are sorted, distributed among eating establishments, converted into an array of delicacies and sold for a pretty penny. I have had mudcrab in several styles in Balikpapan but have especially fond memories of *pepes kepiting*, a banana leaf parcel bearing petals of crab flesh spiced with chilli, ginger and galangal and perfumed with lemon basil. Even in grocery shops, the power of the crab can be felt, with shelves lined with bottles of *sambal* and *abon* (floss) and packets of *amplang* (puffy crackers) and coraline *peyek* (wafers).

Gami, in Bontang, refers to what most would call *sambal*, making its usual title on *restoran* menus, *sambal gami*, a tautology. The one with which Bontang is synonymous is red with chillies, both bird's eye (*cabe rawit*) and crinkly, pencil-thin ones (*cabe keriting*), and tomatoes and served on a sizzling clay *cobek*. As stated in the glossary pages, *cabe merah keriting* may in their absence be substituted with regular red chillies, with an extra bird's eye throw in to make up for the slight loss in heat.

Gami typically plays host to *cumi* (squid), which I use here, *tudai* (blood cockles), *udang* (prawns) and various fish, especially *bawis* (*Siganus*). The waters off the Bontang coast are apparently teeming with *bawis*.

You prepare the baby squid as you would regular ones, except there is no need to skin them. Tug out the legs, trim off everything above the eyes. Then incise out the eyes and remove the ink sac and beak. As for the body, expel the gladius and slice the remaining tube into ½cm pieces.

The *gami* I had in Bontang were bejewelled with the tiniest shallots, like magenta sapphires, and also contained margarine that mellowed and enriched it at the same time. I suspect this to be a fairly recent tradition. This recipe uses butter.

GAMI CUMI

SERVES 6

FOR THE SPICE PASTE
50g red onion, peeled and
  chopped
15g garlic cloves, peeled
2 red bird's eye chillies
60g *cabe merah keriting*
  (page 520)
½ tsp fermented shrimp paste,
  grilled (page 522)

TO FINISH
5 tbsp vegetable oil
2 medium tomatoes, chopped
75g small shallots, peeled and
  halved
500g baby squid, prepared as
  above
¼ tsp salt
1 tbsp unsalted butter

1 Crush the spice paste ingredients in a pestle and mortar into a fine pulp. Alternatively, grind them in cosy blender, adding a little water if necessary.

2 Heat the oil in a *cobek* or frying pan over medium heat. Once hot, but not smoking, add the spice paste. Fry for a minute, then lower the heat and cook, stirring until it splits, deepens in redness and is aromatic, 7-10 minutes.

3 Add the tomatoes and shallots, cook for just 2 minutes, to soften them slightly, then add the squid. The squid will exude some liquid, but just keep cooking until most of it has evaporated, approximately 2-3 minutes. Stir in the salt and butter. Have a quick taste and take it to the table. Serve with rice.

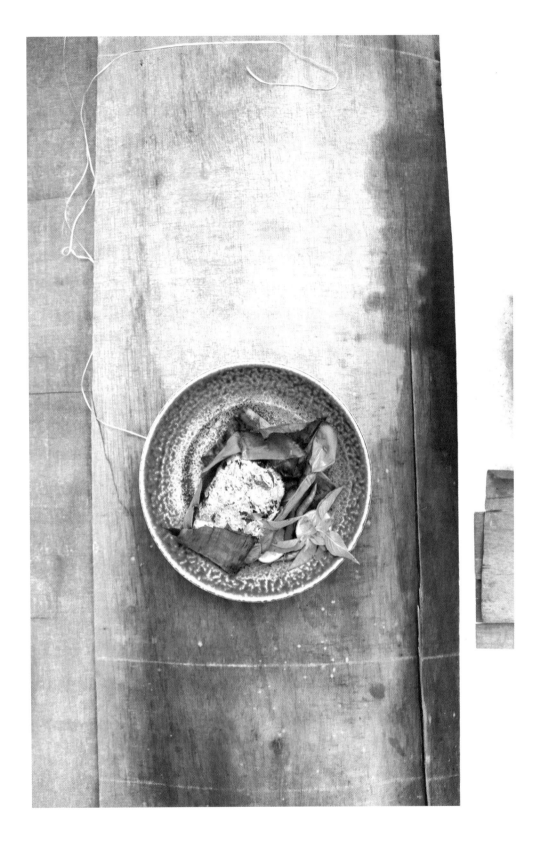

Any kind of crab will work in this. Restaurants in Balikpapan and Samarinda purchase the meat in flakes, and so I do here, too. Just make sure it is good quality. If you wish to cook your own crustaceans, I recommend using 3-4 large mudcrabs. If you can get female crabs, plump with roe, so much the better.

For a greater hit of umami, I sometimes add a rather untraditional ½ tsp of grilled *terasi* (fermented shrimp paste) into the already boldly seasoned crab.

Do not try to skip the steaming: the former is required for the cake to set, which will make it easier to turn over the grill. It is incontrovertible that these will taste better imbued with the insistent breath of burning coals or firewood. I admit, however, that it is a hot griddle pan that I most often consult.

PEPES KEPITING

MAKES 4

FOR THE SPICE PASTE
15g garlic cloves, peeled
50g shallots, peeled
2 bird's eye chillies
60g *cabe merah keriting*
  (page 520)
30g candlenuts
15g ginger, peeled and sliced
20g galangal, peeled and sliced
75g tomatoes, peeled, deseeded
  and chopped

FOR THE PARCELS
400g cooked crab meat
  (see above)
25g lemon basil leaves, shredded
½ tsp salt
½ tsp sugar
½ tsp ground black pepper
  (optional)
Four 20cm banana leaf squares,
  softened (page 520)

1 Prepare your steamer. Make the spice paste by pounding the ingredients with a pestle and mortar until fine. It does not have to be smooth; some texture is good.

2 Combine the spice paste with the crab meat, lemon basil, salt, sugar and pepper, if using, in a bowl. Taste and adjust seasoning. You want this to have some oomph.

3 Divide the filling among the softened banana leaves, which you then snugly wrap and fold into oblong parcels. Arrange these on a platter that will fit your steamer compartment. Steam for 12-15 minutes, until the parcels have firmed up slightly. Remove from the heat, cool slightly, then decant off any juice exuded by the parcels.

4 Heat a hot griddle pan over medium-high heat until smoking. Carefully arrange over the parcels, seal-side down, and leave them there for 4-5 minutes, turning over midway, until their wrappers are charred in places.

Traditionally, the rice, sweet potato and corn are cooked together, all at once, in the same pot. That the sweet potato may disintegrate and meld with the rice, and that the corn may be too wrinkly and soft, are of little concern. I do know, however, that for many a modern palate, they are. The two-part, boiling-and-steaming method enlisted in this recipe takes this into consideration.

NASI SUBUT

SERVES 4

400g jasmine rice, washed and
    soaked in water for 2 hours
150g purple sweet potato, peeled
    weight, cut into 1cm cubes
Shaved kernels from 1 sweetcorn cob,
    approx. 100g

1 Drain the rice. Fill a large saucepan with 2 litres water and bring to a boil over high heat. Meanwhile, fill a steamer with plenty of water and place it on a neighbouring burner, also over high heat. Line its perforated tray with a sheet of banana leaf.

2 Once the saucepan of water is boiling, add the rice, stir once, cover and simmer for 6-8 minutes, or until the grains are tender but with some bite. Drain in a large sieve or colander and quickly tip into the leaf-lined steamer tray. Scatter over the sweet potato and corn. Steam for 25 minutes, by which time everything should be perfectly cooked.

3 Leave to stand, beneath a lid, for 10 minutes, then stir gently to mix.

If you cannot get your fishmonger to debone – or rather de-cartilage – the stingray, it will be wise to get thick steaks, as opposed to thin flaps of wing. It is true that you will require a superb knife to flay and cut them, but do not worry unduly about torn bits of skin or flesh. All will be forgiven once they are skewered and cooked over coals, which have to be ferocious for these to char within the few seconds they have on the grill.

Different kinds of *sambal* are served with these, using ingredients such as *terasi* (fermented shrimp paste), *kecap manis* (sweet soy), tomato ketchup or chilli sauce. I like mine quite simple, hot with chillies, and heady with the warmth of blistered garlic, shallots and tomato.

SATE PARI

MAKES 12

FOR THE SATE
400g stingray, deboned weight, skinned and cut into 1½ cm cubes
2 tbsp lime juice
2 tbsp vegetable oil
12 bamboo skewers, soaked overnight

FOR THE SPICE PASTE
4 garlic cloves, peeled
30g shallots, peeled weight
15g turmeric, peeled
1 tsp salt
½ tsp sugar

FOR THE SAUCE
2 garlic cloves, peeled
6 shallots, peeled
1 medium tomato
4 red chillies, finely sliced
½ tsp salt
1 tsp sugar
1 tbsp lime juice

1 Marinate the stingray pieces in the lime juice for 5 minutes to eliminate the fishiness or *hanyir*.

2 Crush the ingredients for the spice paste with a pestle and mortar into a fine pulp, then tip onto the stingray, along with the vegetable oil. Give the pieces a stir. Cover and leave for at least 30 minutes.

3 In the meantime, get the coals going and make the sauce: heat the garlic, shallots and tomato in a dry frying pan over high heat, just until they begin to soften and char, then tip them into a mortar and pound with a pestle into a rough paste. Add the chillies, crush them in, and season with salt, sugar and lime juice.

4 Thread the yellow-tinted stingray pieces onto the soaked bamboo skewers, about 4 pieces per stick. Grill over hot coals briefly – they cook within minutes – brushing them with more oil lest they burn.

While mush is to be avoided, you want the rice bruised from the stirring, so that it clumps slightly. Not only do the flavours and aromas permeate the grains more effectively this way, they also seem to rest less gauchely on the spoon and mingle more readily in the mouth.

NASI BEKEPOR

SERVES 8

250g jasmine rice
400ml water
1 Indonesian bay leaf
30g salted mudfish
4 red bird's eye chillies
A handful of lemon basil leaves
Vegetable oil, for frying

1 Wash the rice several times or until the water runs clear. Drain well and put in a saucepan with the 400ml water and Indonesian bay. Bring to a boil over high heat, then lower the heat, cover and simmer for 15-20 minutes, or until the grains are tender and all the liquid has been absorbed. Leave the pan covered for 10-15 minutes so the grains can fluff up further in the steam.

2 Meanwhile, give the salted mudfish a light rinse. Dry well and fry in a small frying pan with some oil over medium heat until golden and fragrant. Remove from the fat and crush in a pestle and mortar into ragged splinters. Add the bird's eye chillies and lightly bruise them.

3 Tip these into the pan of cooked rice, along with the basil. Mix robustly with a wooden spoon.

As with the *gami cumi*, the best shallots to use for this are tiny, the size of small marbles.

SAMBAL RAJA

SERVES 8

200g small shallots, peeled
200g yardlong beans, cut into
   1cm sections
400g aubergines, cut into 2cm
   matchsticks
4 hardboiled eggs, peeled and cut
   into eighths
Vegetable oil, for frying

FOR THE SPICE PASTE

225g *cabe merah keriting*
   (page 520)
30g red bird's eye chillies
½ tsp fermented shrimp paste
   (page 522)
Pinch of salt

1 Pour 100ml vegetable oil into a wide saucepan over medium heat. Once hot, add the shallots and fry until they are tender but have not lost their form. Remove the lucent jewels with a slotted spoon, collecting them in a pile on one side of a large serving platter.

2 Afford the same treatment to both yardlong beans and aubergines, frying them separately, adding more oil if necessary. Arrange them neatly beside the fried shallots, along with the slices of hardboiled egg so that there is no more vacant space. Do not wash the pan, but give it a good wipe.

3 Crush the spice paste ingredients with a pestle and mortar into a fine pulp. Alternatively, grind them in a cosy blender until smooth, adding a little water if necessary.

4 Add 100ml more vegetable oil to the recently wiped saucepan. Place it over medium heat. Once hot, but not smoking, add the spice paste. Fry for a minute, then lower the heat and cook, stirring constantly, until it splits, deepens in redness and is very aromatic. Season with salt to taste, then daub over the fried vegetables and boiled egg. Serve with halves of lime.

Ideally, you should be cooking this over charcoal. The only reason for me giving a recipe involving an oven is that the result is so delicious – with a sauce like this it is hard to go wrong – that you will find the absence of smoke forgivable. Or so I hope.

AYAM CINCANE

SERVES 8

8 skinned chicken legs, each
   approx. 175g
100ml vegetable oil
4cm galangal, peeled and sliced
4cm ginger, peeled and sliced
3 lemongrass stalks, bruised
2 Indonesian bay leaves
30g coconut sugar, shaved
   (page 524)
2 tbsp tamarind water (page 524)
1½ tsp salt
600ml coconut cream

FOR THE SPICE PASTE
50g garlic cloves, peeled
125g shallots, peeled
175g *cabe merah keriting*
   (page 520)
1 tsp fermented shrimp paste,
   grilled (page 522)

1 Pierce the chicken legs all over, massage briefly with a little salt and set aside for 30 minutes. Crush the spice paste ingredients with a pestle and mortar into a fine pulp or grind them in a cosy blender until smooth, adding a little water if necessary.

2 Heat the vegetable oil in a wide saucepan over medium heat. Once hot, add the galangal, ginger and lemongrass. Fry until fragrant, then add the spice paste. Fry for a minute, then lower the heat and cook, stirring constantly, until it splits, deepens in redness and begins to smell more than the sum of its parts.

3 Stir in the chicken legs, then the Indonesian bay leaves, coconut sugar and tamarind water. Cover and leave to steam for 5 minutes, shaking the pan occasionally.

4 Stir in the 1½ tsp salt and coconut cream. Bring to a bubble, then cover and simmer gently for 20 minutes. Remove the lid and simmer for another 10 minutes until the chicken portions are tender and the sauce has thickened slightly. Remove from the heat and leave to sit for 1-2 hours, so the flavours can penetrate the meat and the sauce can thicken further.

5 Preheat the oven grill to its highest setting. Remove the chicken legs from the saucepan and arrange them on a large, lightly oiled, baking sheet. A shallow roasting tray with a removable wire rack is good, too. Once hot, paint the legs with some of the sauce and pop them onto the highest shelf. Grill for 5 minutes, until a light, slightly blotty, crust is formed.

6 Pull out the tray, give the chicken one more painting session and return them to the heat, leaving them there until a defined, deep brown, crust is produced. A touch of char is welcome. Serve with rice, cool slices of cucumber, calamansi limes and, if you wish, some of the leftover sauce.

BINGKA KENTANG

MAKES 12

325g waxy potatoes, boiled
    and peeled
600ml coconut cream
2 duck eggs
65g cake flour
75g caster sugar
¼ tsp salt
1 tsp pure vanilla extract
2 tbsp melted butter, for greasing

1 Boil the potatoes in a saucepan of water until cooked. Peel and crush them while they are still warm; the odd lump is charming. Set aside.

2 Give the saucepan a rinse and in it cook the coconut cream over medium heat, stirring occasionally, until it reduces by about a third. Continue cooking, stirring more regularly, until it reduces further and splits into fine, foamy curds and coconut oil. Remove 4 tbsp of the curds and set aside for later.

3 Whisk the duck eggs, cake flour, sugar, salt and vanilla extract in a bowl until smooth. Stir in the coconut curds and oil left in the saucepan, then the crushed potato. Set aside momentarily.

4 Preheat your oven to 220°C. Place a 12-hole muffin tray on a baking sheet and warm it up in the oven for 5 minutes. Once smoking, brush the muffin tray with the melted butter and divide the batter among its holes. Bake for 20 minutes, then retrieve the tray and dot the middle of each cake with 1 tsp of the reserved coconut curds. Return to the oven for another 5 minutes. Cool for about 10 minutes before removing from their tin. These are best eaten not hot but warm.

It is late afternoon in Kandangan. Hefni, Yudha and Arul have just melted into the shadows of a nearby musholla for afternoon prayers, leaving me to my own devices for half an hour or so. After this, it is back to Banjarbaru for dinner and much-needed rest.

Today I find myself saturnine, rather contrary, for reasons not entirely clear. The air feels laden with a tension that even regular supplies of cool, steady breezes seem incapable of ameliorating. Sylphs must be clogging up the atmosphere. And although the city keeps an amiable pulse, the sky, now an endless sprawl of sharkskin, peeling corridors of dormant businesses and barren sidewalks, are making my teeth itch. A storm seems to be upon us. Never have I so badly wanted the heavens to hemorrhage.

It seems natural for one's senses to be heightened amid such disconcertion. The meekest scent is a pong, tiniest sequin an inferno, faintest whisper a howl. The cement floors right outside the musholla, unsoothingly grooved to mimic seraya bark, speak to me. The same can be said of the richly hued *baju kurung*, hanging flowingly from poles beneath the windows of ochre-drenched shophouses, modelled by ghosts. Sparrows pose like courtesans in a row of vast lantern cages. The unmistakable wafts of aroma of fish smoking, undoubtedly for the city's famous *ketupat*, dance out the gates of a nearby shophouse. A crowd of *lahung*, *Durio dulcis*, shares a picnic mat with several *marawin*, the smaller-sized *Durio oxleyanus*. A cherubic vendor at the mouth of the market is taking out men-related frustrations on a thick beam of *lemang*, doling out fat segments of the sticky rice cake, piling on spoonfuls of some curry-like concoction congested with black-eyed beans. *Kacang putih* or *kacang laut*, as the pulse is known in these parts, features in several Banjarese dishes, their titles often carrying the term *masak tuha* – "cooked according to old traditions".

The halogen lamps of a kiosk in a parking lot opening out onto the city's arterial road have burst into life, illuminating a glass countertop cabinet that has just begun receiving nourishment. The owners, likely a husband and wife team, have begun carrying out God's work. I make a beeline and slide onto one of the rough wooden benches surrounding the counter and wait, together with a swelling clot of expectant eaters, for the couple to finish setting up. Some distance above us, angels are languidly flipping through their hymnals.

It takes me a while to get the attention of the male vendor. Of the five names boldly taped across the glass cabinet, I point to the topmost one. The gentleman nods, heaves an immense pail onto a stool and uncovers it. The bowl of a large ladle momentarily disappears into it and emerges brimming with batter. This creamy white paint is poured onto the middle of a flat, wide pan placed over middling flames.

Having formed a neat disc, the batter sets around the edges. Bubbles blossom across its surface. A weighty lampshade for a terracotta lid is carefully lowered over the pan, having spent several minutes warming up on an adjacent hob. I surmise that the heat retained by the lid will cook the surface of the *apam dangkak*.

The cooked pancake is lifted off the hot metal and dropped onto a lime melamine plate, not a freckle of brown to compete with the pores marring its pale countenance. A ladle of *air gula merah* (coconut sugar syrup) is sluiced over and the plate is pushed before me, just in time for my three companions to emerge from their prayer session. I eat hastily, in silent appreciation. Arul starts the car engine.

In the past, most *apam* vendors worked on counters not three feet from the ground, which led to customers tucking into the freshly made pancakes in the squatting position – *dangkak* in Banjarese means "squat". This is just one of the myriad *apam* of South Kalimantan. The town of Pengaron is known for *apam berahim*, eggy sponges quakingly drunk on syrup. Banjarmasin has *apam peranggi*, made with ground rice and coconut milk, traditionally leavened with fermented tapioca. These crack-topped, muffin-like delights tend to appear more during Ramadan. Amuntai has *apam sagu*, baked cakes made with sago flour, and *apam beras*, dewy-faced sponges raised with fermented rice. The *apam* of Barabai takes the form of sweet, spongy, finely pored, discs, sold in vast cloth-veiled baskets at umbrella-shaded kiosks dotting the city.

Elsewhere on the bench, patrons are tucking into *sulada gumbili*, steamed balls of loosely packed tapioca shreds; lozenges of *gagampam*, a steamed mustard-hued cake also made with tapioca; irregular wedges of *kole*, a firm, blancmange-like, pudding of rice flour and coconut milk; and *lupis*, glutinous rice cakes tinted with pandan juice and shaped into logs. Every plate on the counter is wet with the same coconut sugar syrup, like liquid billian. For the patrons who have decided on an array of *wadai* for teatime, it is this dark liquid that will unite them in the mouth.

WADAI

The term *wadai* is synonymous with *kue* in Java and Sumatra, and *kueh* or *kuih* in Malaysia and Singapore. It refers to snacks – pancakes, puddings, cakes, buns, whatnot – prepared from rice or root crops, though these days other starches and flours are permitted entry. Although South Kalimantan has developed a reputation for its *wadai*, many of them can be found in other parts of the country, at times in marginally different forms, but quite often with different names. The *wadai* at this little kiosk are no exception. In Java and Sumatra, *apam dangkak* will be recognised as *serabe*, *sulada* as *sawut*, *kole* as *gendar*, *lupis* as *lopes*. *Puteri salat*, a national favourite in

Indonesia, a thick layer of pandan-tinted custard steamed atop a futon of glutinous rice, is known in South Kalimantan as *wadai lakatan*; *lakatan* in Banjarese means "glutinous rice". The Javanese *nagasari pisang*, a delicacy of coconut milk and ground rice, studded with coins of banana, steamed in dainty parcels of banana leaf, has an analogue in *amparan tatak* here.

There are several *wadai* that one is more likely to encounter here than anywhere else in the Indonesia. *Pupudak* or *sunduk lawang* are boiled cakes of ground rice and sago flour, fragrant with coconut milk, contained in cylindrical purses of banana leaf. *Sari pengantin* takes those same ingredients and turns them into a steamed, two-tiered, pudding that has the tendency to be eye-wateringly hued. *Pengantin* might mean "wedding", but this particular item will be found gracing banquet tables on all kinds of festive occasions. The same can be said of *ipau*, which does not just challenge the notion of *wadai*, but takes it to a whole new level. It is best described as the birthchild of a lasagna and mille-crêpe, a stack of fine pancakes interspersed with layers of seasoned beef mince and vegetables, that is then cloaked in a thick coconut sauce and showered with crisp-fried shallots. It is quite the party animal.

On the other side of the personality grid is *petah*, a steamed, sugarless, sliceable pudding of ground rice, crunchily set with *air kapur* (limestone). On its own, it is a sombre affair, dense and bland, depending on its condiments to give it purpose. These assume the shape of *tahi lala*, coconut cream cooked to the point of separation, crisp-fried shallots and, at times, granulated sugar. A tray of *petah*, at its purest, is off-white and staid. Emerald ripples of *daun suji* extract frequently come to its cosmetic aid, as it does to those in the markets of Martapura, glorious malachite wheels sold in the company of boiled djenkol beans; *kacicak*, marble-sized cakes of ground glutinous rice; and *kicak gumbili*, gnocchi-like dumplings of tapioca.

Several *wadai* are regarded as endangered species, sold by a handful of vendors, hardly made at home. One is the otherworldly *gagaok*, for which a blend of ground glutinous and regular rice, lightened with grated coconut, is used to encase shavings of coconut sugar in banana leaf parcels. In the discomfort of a furious steamer, the sugar melts into a sticky fudge, and the snowy rubble turns into a succulent cocoon that only keeps its form until besieged by asbestos fingers.

Another is *pundut pisang sagu*, also completed in the steamer. Its title means "parcelled sago and banana", which says nothing of its exquisiteness, a pert, translucent ingot, amber with coconut sugar, with slices of banana sleeping within it. It receives a slick of coconut cream just before its parcel is sown shut, which then seizes and curdles in the damp heat, possibly due to the excitement derived from knowing how much pleasure it will give its consumer.

We arrive in Banjarbaru several minutes before nine, by which time most eateries have shut. The handful of those with lit entrances seem to be offering either barbecued seafood or *soto Banjar*. It is the latter that we decide on, and much as the collective ballast of *ketupat* (boiled rice cakes), *soun* (beanthread noodles), macaroni and potato lowers us further into torpor, the broth, made by slowly simmering chicken carcasses for hours, and warm with the sweet sighs of cardamom, clove, nutmeg and cinnamon, soothes our wary bones. The Banjarese seem mightily fond of featuring cinnamon in their savoury dishes.

Up till this point, the sky, despite being the richest aubergine, and emitting the odd rumble of thunder, has managed to maintain its passive-aggressiveness. It is only after we arrive at our accommodation that it finally shatters and weeps, turning everything beyond the hotel gate into a blur. If weather forecasts are to be believed, the whole of South Kalimantan will be sleeping very soundly tonight indeed.

SOUTHERN FEELS

Of the four provinces of Borneo Indonesia, South Kalimantan or Kalimantan Selatan is the most recognised for food, a patchwork of cuisines from the Javanese; Malays; Dayaks, namely the Bukit, Ma'anyan, Lawangan, Ngaju, Barangas and Bakumpai; and Banjar or Banjarese.

There are three categories of Banjarese: the Banjarese Pahuluan, "up-stream" folk, mostly farmers living along the Nagara river and in the Meratus Mountain range; Banjarese Batang Banyu, traders and craftsmen living in settlements along the Bario and Nagara river; and Banjarese Kuala, former farmers who now live in Martapura, formerly Kayu Tangi, the last capital of the now defunct Sultanate of Banjar, and Banjarmasin, the present-day capital of South Kalimantan.

There have been debates concerning the origins and evolution of the Banjarese. Some claim to have Dayak origins, though many researchers have come to the consensus that most are a product of Dayaks intermarrying with Sumatran Malays, who arrived from as early as the 4th century, and the Javanese, the earliest of whom founded the ancient Hindu kingdom of Negara Dipa. South Kalimantan is sometimes known as "the Land of Lambung Mangkurut", the second king of Negara Dipa. It was during his reign that Javanese-style courts began appearing in South Kalimantan, though it has been said that Javanese influences only seeped into the fabric of local life, from language to various art forms much later, after the Majapahit prince at the time married the daughter and sole heir to the throne of Negara Dipa.

Some researchers have said that many modern Banjarese have the blood of Arabs, who settled in the area during the early Islamic era, and the Chinese, who according to historical records from the Ming Dynasty era, were already making visits during the 14th century. By the 18th century, Chinese junks were arriving at the mouth of the Barito River. After being welcomed by the sultan, the merchants would do business with the locals in Kayu Tangi and Tatas (formerly Banjarmasin), using credit to purchase exotic goods, at times exchanging them for coarse and fine silks, tea, camphor, salt, copper utensils and porcelain. Their continuous arrival brought the region into a stopover circle for traders from neighbouring areas such as Java, Madura, Sulawesi, Lombok, Bali and Sumbawa, as well as Arabia and Gujarat further afield. In later years, there was a group of Chinese who settled in the Parit River area in Pelaihari, who ran tin mining companies. They were called Tionghoa Parit.

Of the exotic items that brought Chinese merchants to South Kalimantan, pepper was the most highly sought after, a spice so valuable that the British East India Company and Dutch *Vereenigde Oost Indische Compagnie* fought to monopolise it. It is rather interesting that pepper does not feature all that prominently in the dishes of the region today, besides being added to marinades for fish and meat, especially if they are to be deep-fried, and into soupy stews, to which they will impart huskiness, sharpness and warmth. Two such concoctions spring to mind: *gangan humbut*, a coconut-based braise made with the heart of the coconut palm, boosted with chicken or beef; and *gangan banyu banar*, a clear broth, prepared with river fish, sometimes *ketuyung* (mud creepers) and *haliling* (freshwater clams). The phrase *banyu banar* means "very water-like".

The lure of Banjarmasin, second to its food, is its floating market, Lok Baintan, which we visit the following day, at an hour I would rather not utter. There was some talk involving a breakfast of *laksa*, here pairing a fish-laden, sunlit sauce with nests of thick rice noodle. Unfortunately, this idea was abandoned on the realisation that there was not a single eatery open for business. Even the main market has only just started to rise. "Is it *that* early?", a bewildered Yudha muses, as our vehicle wends its way through the sprawl of dormant buildings. Above us, the sky, fresh from its outburst the previous night, is the most luxurious damson.

At the jetty, before getting hastened onto a *klothok*, we manage to snaffle *nasi itik gambut*, that unites boiled rice and wild duck curry in nifty parcels of banana leaf. The duck, lean and bony, is cut into small chunks and cooked in a sweet, mildly spiced, maroon sauce, a method the Banjarese would identify as *masak habang*, the Javanese *balado*. Those familiar with soft, fluffy rice whinge endlessly about the brittle, often broken, grains here. The concierge at our hotel, who hails from Cirebon in Java and who has been working here for two years, said he is still adapting to the rice from this corner of Kalimantan, grown in the wet fields in coastal areas.

The boat ride, which is to last a half-hour, turns out to be unexpectedly scenic, invigorating even. A generous dappling of sunshine, a fine veil of mist, and all life feels renewed. Our *klothok*, dipped in a blue as piercing as blades, glides past houses with buzzing kitchens, women doing laundry on riverbanks and a couple of teenagers briskly cycling back to their respective residences, probably hoping that the events of the night before will remain a secret between these houses, rickety planks, coconut palms and chocolaty water.

It is hard to tell when you have properly arrived at Lok Baintan. There is no entrance, no signage. The market happens when it is ready. You reach a point along the waterway where sampans slip into view, hovering close to the banks. Your eyes clap upon the rowers, mostly middle-aged women, in swirls of riotously patterned fabric, their heads shielded with *tanghoy* (farmer's hats), with ghastly quantities of fruit and vegetables for companions. Just as you think how serendipitous, how picturesque, all this is, you are quickly made a fool: this is no chance encounter. The ambulant grocers besiege from all directions, engulfing your *klothok*, and begin broadcasting the deals for the day until you relent.

Not every boat boasts vegetables and fruits. Some are selling cloth, some shirts and blouses, others snacks and beverages. Yudha makes several quick purchases from one of the numerous vendors surrounding our vessel and distributes these. Each of us receives a paper cup of hot brewed coffee, dregs and all, and a *wadai cincin*, "ring snack", its dark mahogany skin glossy with grease. While the appearance of its Javanese kin affords a copacetic explanation for its name, this one, from Kalimantan positively puzzles, having three, four, sometimes even five, holes, rather like a doughnut that decided to be a honeycomb in the fryer. Yudha and I nibble on the sweet, slightly crumbly, fritter on the carpeted roof of the *klothok* while our two friends haggle over golden rambutans, fondle velvet apples and santols, and apply their noses to combs of chubby bananas and armoured *tiwadak*.

Many a Southeast Asian is well versed with the glories of *Artocarpus integer*'s sun-lit arils, enjoyed as is or made into doughy fritters or pancakes (*limping*). A considerable number may be familiar with the joy that comes from eating its seeds, simply boiled or pounded into patties for fritters called *pastel*. *Mandai*, however, is made from *tiwadak kulit* that, despite meaning "skin", refers to the creamy white, pithy membrane just under its pustule-covered cloak and between its seeds. Before cooking, these fins would usually be stored in jars with brine, where they will soften as they sit, quite contently, for several weeks, until called upon. *Mandai* is the food of the Meratus Dayaks and Banjarese, found in eateries across South Kalimantan deep-fried or stir-fried, with onions and chilli.

Tiwadak is also cooked unripe, as are its close relatives tarap and jackfruit, with coconut milk and salted fish. This simple, mellow, creamy braise is known as bahampap. The skins of buah rambai also excel in this preparation. Unripe jackfruit is also the star in lontong orari, for which boiled rice cakes are snipped up and served with a thin coconut-based "curry" of langka muda. It truly is the breakfast of champions.

Besides being a conduit for coconut milk, coconut flesh (kelapa parut) has its own songs to sing. While its addition to cakes, wadai and desserts is well-traversed territory, its applications in the savoury realm are far less known and recognised. It makes the most sublime croquettes, paragadil, spiked with chillies and garlic and bound with beaten eggs. Dried shrimp can be added for umami, the scent of the nearby sea. A similar mixture is used to make tumpi, a kind of omelette, for want of a better term, and pajak, a savoury leaf-parcelled cake that comes to life over hot coals. They are both often eaten with cacapan which, at its simplest, is a fingerbowl-light infusion of snipped bird's eye chillies, garlic slivers and discs of jeruk purut, makrut lime.

The sweet, white snow may be dry-fried with warming spices and a paste of garlic, shallots, candlenuts and dried chillies, thereby producing serunding. It may also be pummelled with terasi (fermented shrimp paste), lightly grilled salted fish and shallots, and green mango and bird's eye chillies, to make cancalu, a speciality of the Meratus Dayak that is now quite hard to find.

There is a thoughtfulness behind the design of cancalu, the combination of a few ingredients that tastes far more than the sum of its parts, gutsy yet comforting. These qualities are exemplified with similar deftness by karik bilungka, a dish somewhere in between salad and soup, comprising grated cucumber, coconut milk and fried shallots. Enjoyed as part of a meal with rice, its calming quality will likely be complemented with sambal, perhaps sharpened with ramania (marian plums), binjai (Mangifera caesia) and mempelam (Mangifera indica L.), and several barbecued or fried aquatic creatures that Borneo's rivers so gladly supply. Some fine examples include giant prawns with electric blue claws (ulang), tilapia (nila), snakehead murrel (aruan), giant snakehead (toman), Mystus (baung) and climbing perch (papuyu). Milkfish (bandeng) from the estuaries, and squid and pomfret (bawal) from marine waters, are all welcome to join the party, but it is the freshwater catches that hog the spotlight.

At their freshest, these fish are best prepared with minimum fuss, either slipped into bubbling oil or grilled with bastings of kecap manis and tomato ketchup. In Tanjung, they may appear in gangan paliat, a braise the colour of a late afternoon sky, bright with galangal, lemongrass, turmeric and ginger and bracing with the acid of makrut limes.

These fish are celebrated with equal jubilance in their preserved states, too. A good example would be the aforementioned smoked *aruan* that is absolutely central to *ketupat Kandangan*. Salted fish, in particular *baung*, really shine in *batanak*, a coconutty braise with vegetables like squash and yardlong beans. Potpourri of dried *seluang* (*Rasbora*) and scaly mats of *sepat* (three-spotted gourami; *Trichopodus trichopterus*) are extraordinary deep-fried and flung around a wok with shallots and garlic. They make fantastic, if pungent, souvenirs.

Every group of Dayak in Borneo ferments fish with rice (*kasam*) in some way. Those in South Kalimantan are no exception. They clean and salt their fish of choice, turn them in a mixture of coconut sugar and crushed roasted rice, then immerse them in water for a week, by which time the fish should be sufficiently tangy.

These Dayak groups, as well as the Banjar Pahuluan, also have a dry fermentation preparation, involving a rub of salt and pounded roasted rice that clings to the fish, like a granular coating, after a week's souring. The Banjar Kuala and Batang Banyu would augment the salt and add a healthy dose of turmeric, for an appealing touch of gold. Fish preserved in this manner is called *samu*, which is excellent deep-fried, with slivered garlic and onions scattered into the gurgling oil just as the fish acquires a coppery, polenta-coarse, crust.

Many think that the mudfish for this is grilled, but the truth is that it is smoked. This smokiness seems to have a greater affinity for a thin, delicate gravy, not a rich one, and so I dial back on the coconut cream. Do as you feel fit.

I have not yet learned how to make *ketupat* the trad way. Like almost everyone else, I get them in ready-to-boil form, the rice packed into finely perforated plastic cases. All one has to do is follow the instructions. Despite lacking perfume from the nipa blades, they work fine here. And yes, they are hardly green: I am working on being a better man. If you prefer, use the *lontong* recipe on page 324.

KETUPAT KANDANGAN

SERVES 6

FOR THE SPICE PASTE
3 garlic cloves, peeled
8 shallots, peeled
15g ginger, peeled and sliced
10g galangal, peeled and sliced
5g sand ginger, peeled
1cm turmeric, peeled
1 tsp fermented shrimp paste, grilled (page 522)

FOR THE SAUCE
75ml vegetable oil
2cm cinnamon stick
3 cloves
2 Indonesian bay leaves
600ml water
650ml coconut milk (second extract; page 521)
1 tsp salt, plus more to taste
6 small pieces smoked mudfish, each approx. 75g
100ml coconut cream

TO SERVE
6 boiled *ketupat,* cut into 2cm cubes (see above)
6 hardboiled eggs, peeled and halved
1 portion fried shallots (page 524)
Sambal terasi (page 495)

1 Make the spice paste by pounding the ingredients together with a pestle and mortar, until a smooth balm is obtained. Alternatively, grind in a cosy blender, adding a little water if necessary.

2 Heat the oil in a large saucepan over medium heat. Add the spice paste, stir for several seconds, then reduce the heat and fry, stirring constantly, until it splits, deepens in colour slightly and becomes aromatic. Add the cinnamon stick, cloves and Indonesian bay leaves. Fry for several seconds, to release their aromas, then add the water, coconut milk and salt. Bring to a robust simmer, cover, lower the heat and simmer for 30 minutes.

3 Add smoked mudfish and simmer for another 15 minutes. Finally add the coconut cream and simmer for 2-3 minutes. The resultant gravy should be delicate and quite thin. Taste and adjust seasoning with salt.

4 Divide the *ketupat* among 6 shallow bowls. Divide the gravy among these, making sure each bowl gets some mudfish. Adorn with hardboiled eggs, crisp-fried shallots and *sambal terasi.*

We had this for breakfast one morning in Banjarmasin in the cosiest *warung*. We sat on floors lined with *rattan lumpit* and ate from low tables.

Although we did not get to see the all-important jackfruit stew, *sayur nangka*, being made, we got to witness how they cooked the *lontong*. Whereas in the past, nipa leaves would be used for the wrappers, these days banana leaves are preferred, likely because they are easier to wrangle. Once filled with rice and sealed with toothpicks, the conical parcels were neatly, tightly, layered in colossal pots, covered with water and boiled for a couple of hours over ferocious flames. The lids that went on, marginally smaller than the pots' mouths, and burdened by cast iron weights, helped restrict the movement of the parcels.

LONTONG ORARI

SERVES 8

FOR THE LONTONG
200g jasmine rice, washed and
    soaked in water overnight
Eight 25x30cm banana leaf
    rectangles, softened

FOR THE JACKFRUIT STEW
2 tsp coriander seeds
4 garlic cloves, peeled
8 shallots, peeled
10g ginger, peeled
6 candlenuts, lightly toasted
5g turmeric, peeled
½ tsp fermented shrimp paste,
    grilled (page 522)
500g unripe jackfruit, peeled
    weight
75ml vegetable oil
2cm galangal, bruised
2 lemongrass stalks, bruised
3 Indonesian bay leaves
750ml coconut milk
    (second extract; page 521)
500ml water or light chicken stock
1 tsp salt, plus more to taste

1 Drain the rice. Turn a softened banana leaf into a cone and secure with a toothpick so that it does not unfurl. Feed 4 tbsp of soaked rice into the cone and conceal it by rolling the excess leaf. You should get a compact, slightly flat, triangular parcel. Make all the *lontong* this way and place them in a cosy saucepan. You want them to fit snugly.

2 Pour water to barely cover the *lontong* and place the pan over high heat. Once boiling, cover, lower the heat and cook for 1½ hours. By this time, the grains would have swelled to fit the cones. Remove from the water and leave to cool.

3 Now for the *sayur nangka*. Roast the coriander seeds in a small frying pan over a lowish heat until fragrant and lightly coloured. Tip into a mortar and crush with the pestle into a fine powder. Decant this into a small bowl.

4 Use the mortar and pestle now to pound the garlic, shallots, ginger, candlenuts, turmeric and fermented shrimp paste with a pestle and mortar, until a smooth balm is

obtained. Alternatively, grind these ingredients in a cosy blender, adding a little water if necessary.

5 Cut the peeled jackfruit into chips, no thicker than 1cm. Place in a bowl and set aside.

6 Heat the oil in a large saucepan over medium heat. Once hot, add the spice paste, stir for several seconds, then reduce the heat and fry, stirring constantly, until it splits, deepens in colour and becomes aromatic.

7 Add the previously ground coriander and the galangal, lemongrass and Indonesian bay leaves. Fry for a minute, then add the coconut milk and water or stock. Once the liquid boils, stir in the jackfruit and salt. Cover and simmer for 20 minutes, or until the jackfruit is tender. Taste and adjust seasoning with salt.

8 Unwrap and divide the *lontong* among 8 shallow bowls and ladle over the hot jackfruit stew. Eat with *haruan masak habang* (page 328) and a healthy scattering of crisp-fried shallots (page 524).

Masak habang, meaning "red-cooked" in Banjarese, is a chilli-based preparation applied to fish, chicken, beef, even duck. It has two siblings, *masak hijau*, laced with green chillies, and *masak kuning*, bold with turmeric.

Despite being similar to the *balado* of Java in terms of overall flavour profile and appearance, what makes this dish unusual is the enlistment of cinnamon bark. Only a tiny section is used, but this is enough for its familiar, dulcet tones to be heard through the blanket of feisty flavours.

HARUAN MASAK HABANG

SERVES 8

FOR THE SPICE PASTE
6 garlic cloves, peeled
10 shallots, peeled
10g ginger, peeled
5g sand ginger, peeled
6 dried chillies, softened
  (page 520)
6 red chillies, sliced
6 red bird's eye chillies
10g fermented shrimp paste,
  grilled (page 522)

TO COOK
100ml vegetable oil
4 mudfish steaks, total weight
  approx. 500g
2 Indonesian bay leaves
2cm cinnamon stick
15g coconut sugar (page 524)
½ tsp salt
350ml water
3 tbsp tamarind water (page 524)
6 hardboiled eggs, peeled

1 Make the spice paste by pounding the necessary ingredients together with a pestle and mortar, until a smooth paste is obtained. Alternatively, grind in a cosy blender, adding a little water if necessary.

2 Heat the oil in a large saucepan over medium heat. Add the fish, and fry just to lightly brown. Remove to a plate. Add the spice paste, stir for several seconds, then reduce the heat and fry, stirring constantly, until it splits, deepens in colour and becomes aromatic.

3 Add the Indonesian bay leaves, cinnamon stick, coconut sugar, salt, water and tamarind water. Once the liquid boils, cover, reduce the heat and simmer for 20 minutes.

4 Return the fish to the pan and add the hardboiled eggs. Half-cover and simmer for another 10 minutes, or until the sauce is thick, veiled in a thin layer of oil. Taste and adjust seasoning with salt.

In Kalimantan, any accompanying sauce, especially one thin enough to accommodate dunking, qualifies as *cacapan*. It is *cocolan* in Java, and I suppose equivalent to *sawsawan* in the Philippines.

When you order *cacapan* in a *restoran*, especially one selling barbecued meat and fish, you will be presented with a shallow bowl bearing some thin, aromatic liquid, hot with chillies, sometimes garlic and shallots, tightened with one, or several, acidic, fragrant fruits. *Cacapan asam limau* is probably the most pared down example of this, containing the juice and wrung bodies of limes, namely calamansi and *limau purut* (makrut).

Cacapan asam jawa stars tamarind pulp, which turns it muddy and mahogany, a lip-puckering ointment into which fried fish and eggs – salted or hardboiled – may be slipped. Tamarind is also used in the *cacapan mangga* here, but in a far more restrained quantity, supplying just enough earthy tanginess to anchor the zippiness of the limes and green mango. *Pisang mentah* (green bananas), *belimbing waluh* (bilimbi) and *kundang* (marian plums) may be treated this way, too.

Common as it is for *cacapan* to contain a scant amount of sugar for balance, there are versions that use ripe fruits to counter the sour liquid. These include ripe mangoes and rambutans. A recipe for the latter rests on page 332.

There is one *cacapan* that happily lives in a world of its own, made with *terong bakar*, grilled-then-flayed aubergines. The limp corpses are cut up and left to wallow in a milky pond of coconut sauce, faintly pricked with lime.

CACAPAN MANGGA

SERVES 4-6

1 tbsp tamarind paste
200ml water
4 calamansi limes, halved
1 makrut lime, sliced
4 red bird's eye chillies, lightly crushed
1 small green mango, peeled and cut into
   rough slivers
½ tsp salt
2 tsp sugar
Black pepper

1 Dissolve the tamarind in the water, then strain into a bowl. Squeeze in the juice of the calamansi and makrut limes, then pop in their squashed bodies. Mix in the other ingredients. Taste and adjust seasoning.

This may sound peculiar, a cross between fruit cocktail and salsa, but it works a dream, especially paired with rice and fried salted *iwak seluang*. Eating rice with fruit, especially succulent, fleshy ones, like rambutan, durian, mango and banana, is quite common in Southeast Asia, especially in rural areas.

Some cooks forgo removing the rambutan flesh from their stones and simply halve the whole orbs. I once saw someone stir a dollop of *sambal terasi* into this before serving. Try it.

CACAPAN RAMBUTAN

SERVES 6

200g rambutan flesh lobes
6 bird's eye chillies, red or green
1 makrut lime, roughly sliced
6 calamansi limes, halved
200ml water
1 tbsp sugar
½ tsp salt

1 Combine the ingredients in a bowl and mix well, squeezing the juice from the limes into the liquid and dropping in their pressed bodies.

This is one of my favourite recipes in the book. It is best prepared with "teenage coconut", in other words, coconuts with firm, but still milky, flesh. If your drupe is on the dry side, enrich it with 3-4 tablespoons of coconut cream before adding everything else.

Strictly speaking, *tumpi* should be cooked in a pan lined with banana leaf over hot coals. This version dispenses with this, having been tailored for the kitchen stove, but always impresses, especially when served with *cacapan mangga*. The omelette takes to the liquid like a rusk to hot tea, the sweet, sharp, fruity flavours filling every pore.

HINTALU BATUMPI

MAKES 6

200g grated coconut
1 onion, peeled and finely chopped
2 garlic cloves, peeled
1 green chilli, sliced
1 red chilli, sliced
4 eggs, lightly beaten
30g dried *Acetes*
½ tsp salt
¼ tsp ground black pepper
¼ tsp caster sugar
Vegetable oil, for frying

1 Combine all the ingredients, except the oil, in a large bowl.

2 Heat a lightly oiled frying pan, about 12cm in diameter, over medium heat. Add 3-4 tbsp of the mixture. Once it has firmed up slightly and its underside is golden, flip it and allow the other side to brown. Make all the *tumpi* this way and eat with the *cacapan mangga* (page 329).

As with the *tumpi*, I recommend using coconut that is not too mature. Some milkiness is ideal. The salted fish most commonly used is known locally as *selongsongan*. *Telang* (mackerel) is good, too. I use salted *kurau*, threadfin bream, as that is most easily available to me.

CANCALU

SERVES 6

40g salted threadfin, cut into small
   pieces
8 shallots, peeled
5 red chillies
1½ tsp fermented shrimp paste
   (page 522)
150g grated coconut
125g green mango, peeled and
   roughly slivered
Pinch of sugar
Several pinches of salt
¼ tsp freshly ground black pepper

1 Thread the salted fish onto a bamboo or metal skewer and grill over medium flames on the stove until brittle and warmly fragrant. It should have lost all trace of putridity. Push it off the hot metal and into a mortar. Crush with a pestle into rough splinters.

2 Thread the shallots and chillies onto a pair of skewers and grill over medium flames until lightly scorched and tender. Add them to the mortar. Pierce the fermented shrimp paste onto a skewer, as if it were a marshmallow, and grill it over the flames until toasty and aromatic. Again, add it to the mortar. Now pound these into a rough paste – some texture is essential.

3 Add the grated coconut, slivered mango, sugar, salt and pepper. Thump everything in, just so the coconut and mango are lightly bruised. Now, taste. This should be sweet, sour, spicy and intensely savoury. Serve with hot rice.

What makes this laksa especially interesting is that the noodles are steamed in nests, like the *idiyappam* of South India, but thicker, like spaghetti. You will require a noodle press or *murukku* maker to make them. I admit that making the dough requires some elbow-grease and time, so I recommend taking an afternoon off to make this.

Some are keen on *kencur*, sand ginger, in this. I am not one of them, but if you wish it, bruise a knob, no longer than a finger nail, and drop it into the pot with the Indonesian bay leaves and flaked fish. Do not be tempted to add more, or to crush it into the *rempah*, unless you want the finished sauce to reek of a medicine hall.

LAKSA BANJAR

SERVES 8

FOR THE NOODLES
550g rice flour (page 523)
60g tapioca starch
Approx. 1½ litres water
Twelve 12cm banana leaf squares

FOR THE SPICE PASTE
10g garlic cloves, peeled
50g shallots, peeled
10g ginger, peeled
10g galangal, peeled
10g turmeric, peeled
2 bird's eye chillies
4 candlenuts
1 lemongrass stalk, tender
    portion only
¼ tsp fermented shrimp paste,
    grilled (page 522)

FOR THE SOUP
¼ tsp cumin seeds
1 tsp coriander seeds
5 tbsp vegetable oil
2 Indonesian bay leaves
1cm sand ginger, crushed
    (optional)
175g cooked mudfish, flaked
400ml water
600ml coconut milk
1 tsp salt, plus more to taste
Sugar

TO SERVE
Fried shallots (page 524)
Sambal terasi (page 495)

1 Begin with the noodles. Combine the rice flour and tapioca starch in a large bowl. With a fork, stir in 500ml water, until a lumpy, crumble-like, mixture is obtained. Cover and leave overnight or for at least 6-8 hours.

2 The following day, stir the remaining litre of water into the damp powder until a smooth, liquid batter is obtained. Pour half of this into a large, heavy, preferably non-stick saucepan and cook over medium-low heat, stirring with a wooden spoon or sturdy spatula until a stiff, smooth-surfaced paste is produced.

3 Pour in the remaining half of the batter, stirring it into its thickened counterpart. Continue cooking until you get a smooth-surfaced paste once again, gently coming away from the sides of the saucepan. Do not worry if the gathered batters fail to unite evenly and disregard any lumps or streaks of white. Take the pan off the heat and leave to cool slightly, until just warm. With water-moistened hands, give the dough a good massage, kneading until a soft, even-textured, Play-Doh-like, putty is obtained. Add a little water if you think it needs it. A kiss of dampness is alright.

4 Prepare your steamer. Arrange the banana leaf squares in 2 steamer compartments. Divide the noodle dough into 12 portions and feed each into a noodle press, fitted with a spaghetti-thick extrusion plate. Pipe the noodles out onto the leaves, forming white nests. Steam for 10 minutes, until shiny and tender, then remove the perforated pans to a work surface, leaving the water-filled vessel on the stove. (I do this as I like my noodles warm and so briefly re-stream them later.) Let the noodles cool, then cover them with tea towels. Alternatively, stack them up and cover the upper tray with the steamer lid. If you do not mind cold noodles, which is the situation in many eateries, remove them to a large oiled platter after stripping off their leaves, and cloak with tea towel. Now you may move onto the *laksa* sauce.

5 Make the spice paste by pounding the necessary ingredients together with a pestle and mortar, until a smooth paste is obtained. Alternatively, grind in a cosy blender, adding a little water if necessary.

6 Heat the cumin and coriander seeds in a large sauepan over medium heat, until aromatic and lightly coloured. Crush these with a pestle and mortar and set aside.

7 Pour the oil into the recently used saucepan over medium heat. Add the spice paste, stir for several seconds, then reduce the heat and fry, stirring constantly, until it splits, deepens in colour and becomes deeply aromatic.

8 Add the crushed cumin and coriander seeds, Indonesian bay, sand ginger, if using, and mudfish flakes. Fry for 4-5 minutes, so the flavours mingle and marry, and the fish flakes crisp up and colour slightly. Pour in the water, coconut milk and salt. Raise the heat, bring it to a boil, then reduce the heat and simmer for 40 minutes. Taste and adjust seasoning with salt and sugar.

9 Divide the noodle nests among 8 bowls, keeping the extra 4 nests for those who want seconds. Over each nest, ladle over the hot, lightly golden, gravy and sprinkle with crisp-fried shallots and a dollop or two of *sambal terasi*.

Some cooks add carrot to their soup, but I omit it. I do, however, enjoy swirling in a little evaporated milk, which not all cooks agree on – it so happens that some of the best *soto Banjar* I had contained it.

With regards to carbohydrate, the *ketupat* and *soun* (beanthread noodles) are non-negotiable. The addition of *ampal gumili*, tapioca fritters, elevates it, converting a humble meal into a proper feast. Feel free to add potato or macaroni if you wish, both cooked separately to prevent clouding and thickening the broth.

SOTO BANJAR

SERVES 8

FOR THE STOCK
1½kg free-range chicken
2 tsp salt
2¼ litres water
4 spring onions
1 tsp black peppercorns
5cm galangal, sliced
4cm cinnamon stick
4 cloves
4 Java cardamom pods
2 Indonesian bay leaves
2 star anise

FOR THE SPICE PASTE
1 tsp fennel seeds
2 whole nutmeg, lightly crushed
½ tsp white peppercorns
2 candlenuts
6 garlic cloves, peeled
100g shallots, peeled
15g ginger, peeled and sliced
100ml vegetable oil

FOR THE GARLIC PASTE
3 tbsp vegetable oil
10 garlic cloves, peeled and
    thinly slivered

TO FINISH THE SOUP
3 tbsp evaporated milk
Salt

TO SERVE
6 boiled *ketupat*, cut into
    large cubes (page 323)
75g beanthread noodles, boiled
    and drained
6 hardboiled eggs
6 tbsp Chinese celery, chopped
6 tbsp fried shallots (page 524)
Ampal gumili (page 344)
Sambal terasi (page 495)
Calamansi limes

1 Put the ingredients for the stock in a large saucepan. Bring to a boil over high heat, then cover, turn the heat to its lowest and simmer for 1–1¼ hours, by which time the chicken should be tender, on the cusp of fragmenting.

2 Meanwhile, make the two pastes. Begin with the spice one. Lightly toast the fennel seeds, nutmeg, white peppercorns and candlenuts in a dry saucepan over medium heat until aromatic. Remove from the heat, cool slightly, then pound with the garlic, shallots and ginger with a pestle and mortar into a smooth paste. Alternatively, grind everything in a cosy blender, adding a little water if necessary.

3 Heat the 100ml oil in a medium-sized frying pan over medium heat. Scrape in the spice paste, stir for several seconds, then reduce the heat and fry, stirring constantly, until it splits, deepens in colour slightly and becomes very aromatic. Transfer to a bowl, give both mortar and frying pan a solid wipe.

4 Now for the garlic paste. Heat the 3 tbsp vegetable oil in the cleaned frying pan over medium heat. Once hot, fry the garlic until light gold and crisp, then tip into the cleaned mortar. Pound into an oily balm. As with the spice paste, tip out into a small bowl and set aside.

5 When the stock is ready, remove the bird to a platter, then strain the stock into a fresh pot. Discard the contents in the sieve. Bring the stock to a rolling boil over medium-high heat, then stir in the spice paste and fried garlic paste. Cover and simmer gently for 30 minutes. Meanwhile, divide the cooked *ketupat* and beanthread noodles among 8 shallow serving bowls. Flay and finely shred the meat of the cooled bird and add a small handful to each serving.

6 Taste the soup. Adjust seasoning, adding salt and a little pepper if it needs some pep or pouring in boiling water if it has reduced too much. Add the evaporated milk, if you want it, at this juncture.

7 Pour several ladles of the hot broth over the contents of the serving bowls. Serve with the hardboiled eggs, Chinese celery, fried shallots, *ampal gumili*, *sambal terasi* and calamansi limes, contained in individual bowls and saucers.

Known in Indonesian as *perkedel singkong*, these make a wonderful starter with *sambal terasi* (page 495) or even chilli sauce squirted from a bottle. In Banjarmasin, *ampal* may be made from grated coconut and minced fish or shrimp.

AMPAL GUMBILI

MAKES 13-15

225g tapioca, peeled weight
1 small red onion, peeled
  and finely sliced
1 garlic clove, peeled and minced
1 tbsp Chinese celery, finely chopped
2 green bird's eye chillies, finely sliced
¾ tsp salt
Vegetable oil, for frying

1 Finely grate the tapioca into a medium-sized bowl. Gently mix in the red onion, garlic, Chinese celery, green bird's eye chillies and salt.

2 Heat 2cm worth of oil in a medium-sized frying pan over medium-low heat. Once hot, dollop in 6 x 1 tablespoons of the tapioca mixture. Fry until lightly crisp and golden, around 2 minutes per side, basting them in the hot oil. Transfer to a dish generously lined with kitchen paper. Make them all this way. These are best eaten fresh, but keep reasonably well. I often make them in large batches and freeze them for up to 2 weeks. I remove them from icy cold 2 hours before eating and warm them for 15-20 minutes in an oven preheated to 180°C.

Samu is made in a manner similar to the *wadi* on page 408, except the rice is pounded into a slightly coarser flour and often enhanced with turmeric powder. This recipe uses *samu* made with *papuyu*, climbing perch.

This way of cooking may also be applied to unfermented (in other words, fresh) small fish, whatever their provenance, cleaned and rubbed with salt and turmeric.

IWAK SAMU BASANGA

SERVES 6

125ml vegetable oil
300g *iwak papuyu samu* (see above)
6 garlic cloves, peeled and finely sliced
4 shallots, peeled and finely sliced
4 red bird's eye chillies, sliced

1 Heat the oil in a large, deep frying pan or wok over a medium heat. Once hot, introduce the *samu* and baste it with the hot oil. Once it develops a crust, sprinkle over the garlic, shallots and chilli, and continue cooking for 6-8 minutes, turning over midway. By this time, the garlic and shallots should have turned golden and slightly crisp, the chilli slices crinkly. Drain on kitchen towel and serve with halves of calamansi.

Karuh, in Banjarese, is "murky". A fitting title for a braise the tone of a moonlit river, owing to the addition of coconut milk and sap from a sliced banana heart.

GANGAN KARUH

SERVES 8

FOR THE SPICE PASTE
3 garlic cloves, peeled
5 shallots, peeled
3 candlenuts
1 tsp fermented shrimp paste,
    grilled (page 522)

FOR THE SOUP
1 litre coconut milk
1cm turmeric, crushed
2 Indonesian bay leaves
2 lemongrass stalks, bruised
1 mudfish steak, approx. 200g
1 tsp salt, plus more to taste
1 banana heart, approx. 400g
6 bilimbi, halved
400g taro yam, peeled weight,
    cut into 1cm slices
4 *saba* bananas, peeled and cut
    into 2cm chunks
100g water convolvulus, cut into
    4cm pieces
100g *daun supan-supan*
    (water mimosa)

1 Make the spice paste by pounding the ingredients together with a pestle and mortar, until a smooth paste is obtained. Alternatively, grind in a cosy blender, adding a little water if necessary.

2 Bring the coconut milk to a gentle simmer in a large saucepan over medium heat. Add the turmeric, Indonesian bay leaves, lemongrass, fish and salt. Cover, lower the heat and simmer for 10 minutes.

3 Meanwhile, remove the outer bracts of the banana heart, stopping once you arrive at a creamy, pale yellow core. Slice this into 1cm coins and soak immediately in a bowl of acidulated water to prevent discolouration. Set aside.

4 Add the spice paste to the saucepan, half-cover and simmer robustly for 5 minutes. Drain the banana heart and add it to the soup. Simmer for 3-4 minutes.

5 Add the bilimbi, taro and *saba* and simmer for another 5, until they are just tender. Finally, add the water convolvulus and water mimosa. Simmer for 4-5 minutes, just until they wilt slightly and deepen in greenness. Taste and adjust seasoning with salt.

This soup gets its name from its alleged provenance, Paliat, in Tabalong. The village lies about twenty kilometres from Tanjung, where I first had it, on an especially sweltering, still-aired afternoon. It has also been decided by some that *paliat* is really a portmanteau, "*pa*" from *kepala*, meaning fish heads, perhaps used in the most traditional versions, and "*liat*" being a corruption of *lekat*, meaning sticky or thick, referring to the coconut milk. This ingredient, along with turmeric, is the most prominent voice in this sunlit choral piece. Mellow, nuanced, and only the slightest bit betrayed by the squirt of makrut lime that readies it for obscene helpings of rice.

This version uses giant river shrimp, *udang galah*. It is also popularly made with freshwater fish, *patin* (iridescent shark) and *baung* (*Mystus*) being top favourites.

GANGAN PALIAT UDANG GALAH

SERVES 6

FOR THE SPICE PASTE
2 lemongrass stalks, tender portion only
2 red bird's eye chillies
3 shallots, peeled
2 candlenuts
2cm galangal, peeled
2cm ginger, peeled
1cm turmeric, peeled

TO FINISH
4 tbsp vegetable oil
600ml coconut milk
½ tsp salt
1 tsp coconut sugar (page 524)
6 giant river shrimp, claws removed
2 red chillies, slit
1 tbsp makrut lime juice or tamarind water (page 524)

1 Make the spice paste by pounding the necessary ingredients together with a pestle and mortar, until a smooth paste is obtained. Alternatively, grind in a cosy blender, adding a little water if necessary.

2 Heat the oil in a large saucepan over medium heat. Add the spice paste, stir for several seconds, then reduce the heat and fry, stirring constantly, until it splits from the oil, deepens in colour and becomes aromatic.

3 Add the coconut milk, salt and coconut sugar. Bring to a simmer, lower the heat, cover and simmer for 5 minutes. Add the shrimp and red chillies. Cook for just 4-5 minutes, then finish it with the lime juice. Turn off the heat. Taste and adjust seasoning. Serve with rice, and a dish of blanched vegetables, in particular yardlong beans, aubergine and winged beans, and more wedges of makrut limes for those who want it higher-pitched.

Basanga is Banjarese for "fry". These days, many use its Indonesian equivalent, *goreng*. In this recipe, the *mandai* is deep-fried, then stir-fried in a spicy red paste of chillies and garlic.

Making *mandai* is not challenging at all. Put the *tiwadak* pith in a bowl and massage it with salt – ½ tsp for every 250g of pith – and leave it overnight beneath a lid. This seems to soften it slightly and relieves it of bitter juice (though there is never very much.) The following day, give it a light squeeze, put it in a jar, cover it with brine, approx. 30g salt to a litre of water. Cover the jar and leave it to ferment in a cool, dark place for 5-7 days.

Fresh pith may be used by those who find themselves at odds with the scent and taste of fermented fruit. It will be crisper, but also chewier. That is its nature.

MANDAI BASANGA

SERVES 6

450g fermented *tiwadak* pith
   (*mandai*, see above)
8 garlic cloves
6 bird's eye chillies
6 shallots, thinly sliced
2 red chillies, thinly sliced
½ tsp salt
1 tsp sugar
Vegetable oil, for frying

1 Wash the *mandai* in 3 changes of water to remove surfeit salt, then squeeze well and contain it in a bowl. Crush the garlic and bird's eye chillies into a rough paste and set aside.

2 Heat 3cm worth of oil in a wide saucepan over medium heat. Once hot, stir in the *mandai*. Cook until lightly crisp and golden, then transfer to a dish generously lined with kitchen paper.

3 Decant all but 2 tbsp of the oil in the pan. Place it over medium heat once more and add the garlic-chilli paste. Fry until fragrant and a slightly richer red. Stir in the shallots, red chillies, salt and sugar. Once the shallots have vaguely softened, stir in the fried *mandai* to heat through.

A dish that is described as "*masak tuha*" is cooked according to old traditions, by cooks from a different era. A decent number of these seem to contain *kacang putih*, black-eyed beans, and *kelapa sangrai*, toasted coconut.

Fried pieces of mudfish are used here, but this is also good made with beef or chicken. Some cooks desire a rich gravy. Others make it less so, with just enough sauce to cloak and cuddle the starring protein. This recipe produces the latter.

HARUAN MASAK TUHA

SERVES 6-8

FOR THE BEANS
150g black-eyed beans, soaked
   in water overnight

FOR THE SPICE POWDER
2 tsp coriander seeds
1 tsp fennel seeds
¼ tsp turmeric powder

FOR THE SPICE PASTE
20g garlic cloves, peeled
75g shallots, peeled
15g blue ginger, peeled and
   sliced
10g turmeric, peeled and
   sliced
12 dried red chillies, softened in
   boiling water
30g red chillies, sliced

2 lemongrass stalks, tender
   portion only
1 tsp fermented shrimp paste,
   grilled (page 522)

TO COOK
150ml vegetable oil
1kg mudfish, cut into large
   chunks
2cm cinnamon stick
2 Indonesian bay leaves
1 tbsp tamarind water (page 524)
175g grated coconut, made into
   kerisik (page 521)
30g coconut sugar, shaved
   (page 524)
250ml coconut milk
750ml water
1 tsp salt, plus more to taste
6 hardboiled duck eggs, peeled

1 Drain the beans and place in a medium saucepan. Cover generously with water. Bring to a boil over medium heat, cover, lower the heat and simmer until tender, 30-45 minutes. Drain and set aside.

2 While waiting for the beans to cook, make the spice powder and paste. Roast the coriander and fennel seeds in a small frying pan over medium-low heat. Once fragrant and lightly coloured, crush with a pestle and mortar into a fine powder. Tip into a small bowl, mix in the turmeric powder and set aside.

3 Make the spice paste by pounding the ingredients together with a pestle and mortar, until a smooth balm is obtained. Alternatively, grind in a cosy blender, adding a little water if necessary.

4 Heat 100ml of the oil in a large saucepan or wok over medium heat. Rub the mudfish pieces with a little salt and brown them in batches in the hot fat. Remove to a platter.

5 Add the remaining oil, let it heat up, then scrape in the spice paste. Stir for several seconds, then reduce the heat and fry, stirring constantly, until it splits, turns a deep red and is aromatic.

6 Add the cinnamon stick, Indonesian bay leaves and crushed dried spices. Cook for a minute, then add the tamarind water, *kerisik*, coconut sugar, coconut milk, water and salt. Bring to a robust boil, then cover, lower the heat and simmer for 45 minutes.

7 Stir in the cooked beans, cover and simmer for 10 minutes. Uncover, slip in the fried fish and boiled duck eggs. Simmer, without a lid, for a final 10 minutes. By this time, the sauce should be dark red and slightly thick, veiled by a film of vermillion oil. Taste and adjust seasoning.

This reminds me a little of the *nasi lemak* I grew up eating, except here most of the magic happens within steamer-borne banana leaf pouches – everything is chucked in and tied up. The rice absorbs the coconut milk, forming a cake, on top of which the coconut cream silkily, unctuously, sets.

It makes for a wonderful breakfast or teatime treat, especially when partnered with a good *sambal*. For something more substantial, serve it with *haruan masak habang* (page 328) and salted duck eggs.

PUNDUT NASI

MAKES 10

200g jasmine rice, washed and
  soaked in water overnight
200ml coconut milk
1 Indonesian bay leaf
200ml coconut cream
½ tsp salt
Ten 20x24cm banana leaf rectangles,
  softened (page 520)
Ten 3x22cm banana leaf strips, softened

1 Drain the rice and place in a bowl.

2 Warm the coconut milk in a medium saucepan with the Indonesian bay leaf over medium heat. Remove it from the heat just as it begins to simmer. Stir in the coconut cream and salt. Set aside.

3 Prepare the steamer. Take a banana leaf rectangle. Fold it in half lengthwise. Pinch it in the middle where both sides meet, from the top, with one hand, creating an opening on either side. With the other hand, close one opening by pushing the leaf on that side over to meet the pinched area. Into the remaining opening, spoon 2½ tbsp jasmine rice and 5 tbsp of the coconut liquid. Push the leaf at the other side over to meet the pinched area, thereby producing a neat and slim purse. Wrap with a strip of banana leaf and secure with toothpicks. Make all the parcels this way and arrange in a cosy tray.

4 Lower this tray into the steamer and leave it there for 1¼ hours. Remove and cool completely before defrocking.

Use the tenderest, milkiest, coconut flesh possible for this increasingly rare treat. It makes a world of difference.

GAGAOK

MAKES 10

FOR THE PASTRY
85g rice flour (page 523)
85g glutinous rice flour
2 pandan leaves, snipped into
    large sections
1½ tbsp water
150g grated coconut
¼ tsp salt
Ten 20x24cm banana leaf
    rectangles, softened (page 520)

FOR THE FILLING
75g coconut sugar, shaved
    (page 524)

FOR THE TOPPING
75g grated coconut
1 tsp sugar
Pinch of salt

1 Combine the two kinds of rice flour and pandan leaves in a large frying pan. Push them around over medium-low heat, until they smell warm and feel slippery and light. They should not have acquired any colour. Push through a fine sieve into a bowl and discard the leaves.

2 Sprinkle in the water and mix until a crumble-like rubble is obtained. Push through a sieve once again. The resultant powder should be fine and light. Flick in the grated coconut and salt. Set aside.

3 Prepare your steamer. Place the ingredients for the filling and topping in 2 small separate bowls. Mix the topping ingredients well.

4 Onto the middle of a softened rectangle of banana leaf, add 2 tbsp of the rice flour mixture, lightly spreading to create a 3x5cm rectangle. Sprinkle 2 tsp of the coconut sugar filling onto the middle of this white space. Cover with 2 tbsp of the coconut topping. Bring up the sides of the banana leaf and secure the parcel with toothpicks. Make all the parcels this way and arrange them in the perforated steamer compartment. Steam for 15 minutes over medium heat. Cool slightly before eating.

Sagu basah, wet sago, is usually summoned for this. I use regular sago flour and soak it in water overnight. The result, though not identical, is a more-than-decent approximation.

I have observed that unsoftened, nearly-mature, banana leaves work best. Not only do they form the requisite parcel with greater ease, the security provided by their malleability and rigidness benefits the batter, which is frightfully runny. If you, like me, have to contend with brittle leaves, then softening them is the only way to go. The path ahead will be messy, there is no point in lying. I am also afraid the result will likely look less smart. I can assure you, however, that it will still be delicious.

PUNDUT PISANG SAGU

MAKES 10

FOR THE BATTER
120g sago flour
80ml water
100g coconut sugar, shaved
   (page 524)
100ml water
4 *pisang rajah*, cut into ½cm coins
Ten 20x24cm banana leaf
   rectangles, softened (page 520)

Ten 3x22cm banana leaf strips,
   softened
Vegetable oil, for brushing

FOR THE COCONUT SAUCE
100ml coconut cream
Pinch of salt

1 Combine the sago flour and water in a bowl. The resultant mixture will seem somewhere between solid and liquid. Cover and leave overnight, or for at least 8-10 hours, until all the water has been absorbed by the flour.

2 Warm the coconut sugar and water in a smallish saucepan. Once the sugar has dissolved, strain into a jug and allow it to cool. Do not wash the saucepan.

3 Break the soaked sago flour into a rubble and whisk it into the cooled syrup in the jug. Add water to arrive at the 500ml mark. Pour out 90g of this mixture and cook in the saucepan until thick. Remove from the heat and whisk in the remaining batter, until smooth. The odd translucent globule will not matter.

4 Warm the coconut cream in a small saucepan, stirring so it thickens slightly but removing it before it has the chance to split. Stir in the pinch of salt.

5 Prepare your steamer. Lightly oil the banana leaf rectangles. Fold one in half lengthwise. Pinch it in the middle where both sides meet, from the top, with one hand, creating an opening at either end. With the other hand, close one opening by pushing the leaf on that side over to meet the pinched area. Into the remaining opening, add 3 tbsp of the batter, 3 slices of *pisang rajah* and 1 tbsp of the cooked coconut cream. Close this opening as with the first, forming a neat purse. Wrap with a strip of banana leaf and secure with toothpicks. Make all the parcels this way and arrange in a cosy tray. Steam for 25 minutes over medium-low heat. Cool slightly before eating.

What first drew me to this was its name. When I discovered what it was, a steamed coconut sugar custard, spiced with fennel and cinnamon, I had a hunch that we would have a thing going. And I was right. I have been prudent with the spicing; some people prefer a weightier fragrance.

KARARABAN

SERVES 8

FOR THE SPICE POWDER
1 tsp fennel seeds
1 tsp ground cinnamon

FOR THE CUSTARD
60g plain flour
25g rice flour (page 523)
200ml water
350ml coconut cream
¼ tsp salt
100g coconut sugar, shaved
  (page 524)
50g caster sugar
2 eggs, plus 2 yolks

1 Begin with the spice powder. Lightly toast the fennel seeds in a small, oil-free, frying pan over medium-low heat. Once fragrant and light brown, crush into a fine powder with a pestle and mortar. Stir in the ground cinnamon and press through a small, fine sieve into a bowl. Discard the detritus in the sieve but do not wash it yet.

2 Lightly oil a 12x22cm loaf tin and line its floor and sides with baking paper, which will enable you to remove the cooked article cleanly and efficiently. While it will certainly be damp, it will not melt into, or meld with, the pudding it is protecting.

3 Combine the plain and rice flours, 150ml water, 300ml coconut cream and salt in a bowl. Whisk until smooth.

4 Dissolve the coconut and caster sugars in the remaining 50ml water in a medium saucepan over medium heat. Once the sugars have dissolved, strain the syrup through the sieve into the bowl of batter. Whisk, then return to the saucepan. Cook over medium heat, stirring gently, just so it thickens to the consistency of runny yoghurt. Take off the heat and cool slightly while you prepare your steamer.

5 Once the steamer is hot, whisk the eggs, yolks and ¾ tsp of the crushed spices into the remaining 50ml coconut cream, then stir this into the batter in the saucepan. Pour this batter into the prepared tin. Press over the remaining crushed spices through the previously used sieve, as one would cocoa over tiramisu. Carefully lower the tin into the steamer and cook, over medium heat, for 30-40 minutes, or until firm to the touch.

6 Remove from the steamer and cool completely before freeing it from its tin – upend, disrobe and invert – and slicing into wedges.

These delectable little green bean cakes are more commonly known by their Javanese title, *gandasturi*.

KAKUMBU KACANG HIJAU

MAKES 16-18

FOR THE CAKES
200g green mung beans
1 litre water
75g caster sugar
¼ tsp salt
75ml coconut cream
Canola oil, for deep-frying

FOR THE BATTER
160g rice flour
 (*tepung beras*, page 523)
15g plain flour
Pinch of salt
1 egg
Approx. 200ml water

1 Wash the green mung beans. Place in a medium saucepan with the 1 litre of water. Bring to a boil over medium heat, cover, reduce the heat and simmer for 20-30 minutes, or until tender, but not mushy. There should be hardly any water left in the pan. (If there is, drain the cooked beans.)

2 Add the sugar and salt to the cooked beans and crush everything together with a wooden spoon into a soft, grainy balm. Stir in the coconut cream and return the saucepan to a medium-low heat. Cook gently, stirring and crushing, until a cohesive, firm dough is obtained. Let this dough cool slightly, then with lightly dampened hands pinch off golfball-sized lumps and shape these into fat patties. You should get 16-18.

3 Make the batter. Combine the dry ingredients in a medium-sized bowl. Whisk in the egg, then just enough water to produce a paint thick enough to coat the back of a spoon.

4 Heat 4cm canola oil in a deep, wide frying pan over medium heat. Once hot, dip several patties in the batter, allow excess to drip off, and slip them into the hot fat. Fry until light gold and crisp, about 2-3 minutes, shaking the pan occasionally. Drain them on kitchen towel before eating (as fresh as possible). Make them all this way.

While the cool, green Calacatta tiles of rice cake taste of little, it is their dalliance with granulated sugar, oleaginous cooked coconut milk (*tahi lala*) and fried shallots that makes for a fascinating gustatory experience.

PETAH

SERVES 8-10

FOR THE PETAH
125g rice flour, plus 1 tsp
   (page 523)
40g tapioca starch
1 tsp sugar
¼ tsp salt
500ml water
6 tbsp limestone water (page 524)
2 tbsp pandan extract (page 522)

TO SERVE
400ml coconut cream
¼ tsp salt
Fried shallots (page 524)
Granulated sugar

1 Place the 125g rice flour in a medium-sized bowl. Add the tapioca starch, sugar, salt, 450ml water and limestone water and whisk until smooth.

2 Pour 225g of the batter into a medium saucepan. Into this, stir the remaining 50ml water. Place the saucepan over medium-low heat and cook, whisking, until the mixture bubbles and seizes into a thick paste. Remove from the heat and stream in the remaining batter, whisking gently, until smooth. Do not fret at the presence of lumps. Just let it relax for 5 minutes and give it another whisk. Set aside.

3 In a small bowl, combine the remaining 1 tsp rice flour with the 2 tbsp pandan extract. Whisk until smooth, then mix in 3 tbsp of the batter produced in Step 2. At this point, you should have 2 batters: one white, housed in a saucepan, and another pistachio green, contained in a small bowl.

4 Prepare your steamer, lightly oil a round 15x5cm cake tin. When the steamer is ready, lower in the cake tin. Pour in the white batter, cover and steam over high heat for 3 minutes. Uncover and gently, steadily, stream in the green batter, moving in a circular fashion. Go in with a chopstick, swirling to produce a soft marble effect. Return the lid and steam for 20 minutes over medium heat, then turn the heat to medium-low and cook for another 40 minutes. Remove the tin from the steamer and allow to cool completely. This should take about 4-5 hours, but I prefer to leave it overnight.

5 Shortly before eating, cook the coconut cream in a saucepan over medium heat, stirring, just until it splits. Season it with the salt, then tip into a serving bowl. Contain the crisp-fried shallots in another, the granulated sugar in yet another.

6 Cut the *petah* into tiles and arrange these on a plate. Serve with the bowls of condiments.

This *wadai* is wildly popular at Ramadan bazaars and all manners of festive occasions. Though known beyond Kalimantan as *talam Banjar*, a term which, broadly speaking, could point to any Banjarese delicacy set in trays, locals call it *puteri salat*. There are several versions, majority involving a band of glutinous rice and two of flavoured custard, like pandan, coconut sugar, even chocolate. I have used the former two. Some versions comprise two layers of flavoured custard and one of wobbly, white coconut pudding.

Some like their *puteri salat* so firm that it could second as a doorstop. Some like it so tender that it quiver, sulks and frets as a knife is being lowered into them. This recipe makes something sliceable, neat and tidy, but with more than a soupçon of tenderness.

PUTERI SALAT

SERVES 10-12

FOR THE RICE LAYER
250g glutinous rice, washed thrice and soaked in water overnight
150ml water
60g grated coconut
50ml coconut cream
1 tbsp sugar
½ tsp salt
Softened banana leaf, for lining

FOR THE BROWN LAYER
2 tbsp caster sugar
75ml water, plus 1 tbsp
60g coconut sugar, shaved (page 524)
20g plain flour
1 tsp wheat starch
Pinch of salt
2 eggs plus 2 yolks
275ml coconut cream

FOR THE GREEN LAYER
100g caster sugar
Pinch of salt
20g plain flour
2 tsp wheat starch
3 eggs
4 tbsp pandan extract (page 522)
250ml coconut cream

1 Prepare your steamer and line its compartment with a generous sheet of muslin. Drain the glutinous rice and spread over the lined compartment. Steam for 30 minutes.

2 Give it a gentle stir with a chopstick, then sprinkle over 100ml of the water. Steam for another 25 minutes, until tender. Place the rice in a bowl and mix in the remaining 50ml water, grated coconut, coconut cream, sugar and salt while still hot.

3 Line the base and sides of a 20x5cm square tin with softened banana leaf or greaseproof paper. Scoop the cooked and seasoned glutinous rice into the tin and press it down evenly over the base. Set aside.

4 Make the brown layer. Make a caramel with the caster sugar and the 1 tbsp water in a small saucepan over medium heat. Once seething and dark amber, add the shaved coconut sugar and the remaining 75ml water. Stir, just until the coconut sugar has mostly dissolved, then remove it from the heat.

5 In a medium-sized heatproof bowl, whisk together the plain flour, wheat starch, salt, eggs and yolks. Then stir in the coconut cream, followed by the coconut sugar syrup. Strain this smooth butterscotch-coloured liquid through a fine sieve into a measuring jug. You should get approximately 500ml. If not, add water to make up the difference. Return this liquid to the heatproof bowl and cook in a double boiler (made by suspending the bowl on the mouth of a saucepan with barely trembling water) until it reaches the consistency of pouring custard, stirring constantly with a whisk or spatula. Scrape out into a fresh bowl and give the heatproof bowl a thorough wash.

6 Now, make the green layer. In the washed heatproof bowl, mix the plain flour, wheat starch, sugar and salt. Lightly whisk in the eggs, then the pandan extract and coconut cream. Strain the Kermit-coloured liquid through a fine sieve into a measuring jug. As with its brown-toned counterpart, you should get approximately 500ml. If not, add water to make up the difference. Once again, return this liquid to the heatproof bowl and cook in a double boiler until it reaches the consistency of pouring custard, stirring constantly with a whisk or spatula. Scrape out into a bowl.

7 Return to your steamer, filling it with more water and putting it over medium heat. Once the water in it is boiling, lower the tin of pressed rice into its compartment. Steam for 15 minutes.

8 Remove the lid, gently smooth the swollen grains with a spatula, then gently pour over the brown coconut sugar custard. Cover, turn the heat down to its lowest setting and steam for 7-10 minutes, or until the custard is springy to the touch.

9 Lightly run the tines of a fork across the surface of the brown layer, then gently pour (or ladle) over the pandan-green custard. (If you are wondering, the raking action creates minor ridges that help the two bands of custard adhere to one another.) Cover and steam for another 7-10 minutes over the softest possible heat, or until springy to the touch. The surface of the custard should be smooth. Undulations are usually due to overcooking or the heat being too intense.

10 Gingerly remove the tin from the steamer and turn off the heat under it. Leave the *wadai* to cool completely before lifting it out of its metal casing (using the leaf or greaseproof paper) and turning it into slices with a sharp, lightly oiled, blade.

The star gooseberry leaves add an intriguing, spicy greenness, to the fermented grains, reminiscent of fresh cut grass.

TAPE KETAN

SERVES 10-12

350g glutinous rice
25g star gooseberry leaves
350ml water
2 tbsp crushed *ragi* (yeast)
Softened banana leaf

1 Wash the glutinous rice three times or until the water runs clear. Drain well and place in a medium-sized bowl.

2 Blend the star gooseberry leaves with the water into an emerald liquid. Tip into a measuring jug. You should get about 400ml liquid, though this is not utterly crucial.

3 Reserve 125ml of this healthfully hued liquid and keep in a cool place (or fridge). Tip the rest into the bowl of drained rice. There should be just enough liquid to barely cover the grains. If not, simply add more water. Set aside for 4 hours.

4 Prepare the steamer and line its perforated tray with muslin. Drain the rice in a fine sieve and spread the grains, along with any fine bits of fibre, over the muslin-lined tray. Steam for 30 minutes.

5 Remove the tray from the steamer momentarily. Give the rice a gentle stir, preferably with a pair of chopsticks or a spatula, and pour in the reserved 125ml green liquid, which the grains should readily imbibe. Steam for another 10-15 minutes, or until the grains are just tender. Remove the grains to a large, shallow bowl. Fling over a teatowel and leave to cool completely.

6 Sprinkle over the crushed yeast and mix in gently but thoroughly. With hands lightly moistened with water, shape the rice into golfball-sized orbs. You should get 18-22.

7 Arrange them snugly in a suitably sized Tupperware, its base and sides lined with softened banana leaf. Conceal with yet another layer of banana leaf, cover with a lid, and leave in a cool, dark place for 3-4 days, by which time the balls would have softened slightly and be sitting in a shallow pool of boozy liquid. I live in humid conditions and so keep my *tape* in the fridge from this point on. If you live in cooler, drier climes, you may be able to continue keeping it outside.

Baayak in Banjarese means "strained", from *ayak* "sieve", describing how the pasta is made, by extruding dough through a large perforated ladle or colander. This is rich, and may even stretch to feed 10 as a light snack.

BUBUR BAAYAK

SERVES 6-8

FOR THE DOUGH
220g rice flour
  (*tepung beras*, page 523)
40g plain flour
4 tbsp limestone water
  (page 524)
Approx. 6 tbsp water

FOR THE SAUCE
200g coconut sugar, shaved
  (page 524)
50g caster sugar
500ml water
¼ tsp salt
1 pandan blade, knotted

TO SERVE
Approx. 250ml coconut cream

1 Begin with the dough. Combine the rice and plain flours in a medium-sized bowl, then mix in the slaked lime water, followed by the regular water, until you get a smooth, white lump. It should be damp and soft, almost on the brink of pastedom, so add a little more water if necessary. Cover and leave for 30 minutes.

2 Combine the shaved coconut and regular sugar, water, salt and pandan blade in a medium-sized saucepan. Place over medium heat and bring to a boil, stirring until the sugars have dissolved. Strain this syrup through a fine sieve into a bowl, to remove any impurities in the coconut sugar, then tip it back into the saucepan.

3 Return the saucepan to medium heat, so that the syrup steadily bubbles. Lightly oil the concave side of the colander and fit it over the mouth of the saucepan. Scrape the dough into the colander and force it with a sturdy spatula or wooden spoon through the perforations, sending droplets cascading into the simmering syrup beneath. There is a decent amount of dough to finish, so I recommend stopping every now and then, giving the pan a little shake to redistribute the pasta and preventing them from clumping.

4 Once all the dough has been used, give the contents of the pan a gentle stir, then lower the heat and continue simmering for 5-7 minutes, or until the squiggles of rice pasta are cooked through. The sauce, at this stage, will still be runny. Turn off the heat, remove the pandan blade and cover. Leave the *bubur* to compose itself for 10 minutes. When you return to it, the pasta would have plumped up, and what was once a syrup should now resemble a thick butterscotch sauce. Divide among 6-8 bowls and serve with a jug of coconut cream.

These squishy, syrup-sodden sponges are a Ramadan bazaar stalwart.

Gently warming the flour with pandan leaves is not a traditional step, but I think it makes these cakes especially light and delectable, something their bath of clove-pricked syrup accentuates. Speaking of this, you may elect to tint the syrup with a little yellow from a bottle, something to which many locals are predisposed.

BINGKA BARANDAM

SERVES 6

FOR THE BATTER
2 tbsp plain flour
½ pandan leaf
2 duck eggs
Pinch of salt

FOR THE SYRUP
125g sugar
500ml water
1 pandan leaf, knotted
3 cloves
A few drops of yellow food
   colouring, optional

1 Place the flour and pandan leaf in a small frying pan. Over medium heat, push the flour around until it is light and slippery. It should not have coloured. Sift into a bowl and discard the pandan leaf.

2 Beat the eggs and salt in a freestanding electric mixer until thick, pale and voluminous, about 3 times its original volume. Sprinkle in the flour and give it a terse whisk.

3 Lightly lubricate the indentations of an *apam* pan, then place this over medium heat. Once the pan is hot, spoon in the airy *bingka* batter, filling each indentation to its brim. When their sides have set, their bottoms lightly browned, cover and continue cooking for a minute or so, just until their surfaces are dry. With a pair of spoons, remove them to a large shallow bowl. Make them all this way; you should get 10-12. Allow them to cool completely.

4 Make the syrup by combining the ingredients in a saucepan and simmering for 5 minutes, stirring to dissolve the sugar. Take off the heat, leave to cool slightly, then pour over the *bingka*. Leave the sponges to their fate for 30 minutes. They should be moist and a little squishy. They should also have collapsed slightly.

Resist the temptation of compacting the mounds of shredded tapioca, for fear that they will fragment. This will only make them dense. Have faith!

SULADA GUMBILI

SERVES 6

FOR THE CAKES
750g tapioca, peeled weight
Softened banana leaf, for the
    cooling

FOR THE SAUCE
125g coconut sugar, shaved
    (page 524)
2 tbsp water
300ml coconut cream
250g jackfruit flesh, cut into slivers
Pinch of salt

1 Prepare your steamer. Grate the tapioca on the coarse side of the grater; you want the shreds to be approx. $\frac{1}{2}$cm thick. Using your fingers, pick up a handful of the grated tapioca and place on the perforated tray in a voluminous stack. It should be beautifully disheveled, but confident. You do not want it fragmenting as you convey it to the steamer. Do the same for the remaining tapioca. You should get 12-14 such stacks.

2 Steam over medium-low heat for just 6-7 minutes. The heat should have warmed them through, turning them tender but not at the expense of any crispness. An inserted skewer should slip in a treat and feel warm when withdrawn. Whatever translucency they acquire should be ghostly at best. Let them stand for 5 minutes, then convey to a sheet of heat-softened banana leaf, where they are to cool further.

3 Now make the sauce. Place the coconut sugar and water in a small saucepan. Cook over low heat for 5 minutes, stirring until the sugar dissolves. Then add the coconut cream and simmer for another 5-7 minutes, until slightly viscous. Add the jackfruit slivers, simmer for 5 minutes, just until the fruit softens and deepens in yellow. Stir in the pinch of salt. Allow to cool (and thicken slightly) before serving with the *salatat gumili*.

Traditionally, this is made on the stove, in an *apam* pan with indentations, beneath a heated clay *tutup* (lid) shaped like a lampshade. This manner of cooking achieves crusty bottoms and cracked, burnished tops, rugged as water-neglected land. I have modified the recipe to suit our modern needs, using a muffin tray and a hot oven.

Fermented tapioca, *tape gumili*, is required for this. I get mine from a Malay vendor at my nearest market. It can be easily made at home, though. Whatever the quantity of tapioca you desire, peel and cut them into 4cm sections, then halve these vertically. Steam until tender, then cool completely. Roll them in several crushed wine tablets, sold at Asian grocers or Chinese medicine shops, and pack them into a suitably sized container. Some line (and seal) this container with softened banana leaves for a greater fragrance. Cover and stow in a cool, dark place for 5-7 days, juddering occasionally. The tapioca has adequately fermented when it is the texture of wet cotton. Any tough fibres are to be removed before they are mixed into batters.

APAM PERANGGI

MAKES 12

150g rice flour
   (*tepung beras*, page 523)
175ml water
300ml coconut cream
100g fermented tapioca (see above)
200g sugar
¼ tsp salt
80g plain flour
1 tsp easy-blend instant yeast
Vegetable oil, for greasing

1 Combine the rice flour and 125ml of the water in a medium bowl and mix until you get something resembling damp crumble topping. Cover and leave overnight or for at least 8 hours.

2 The next day, warm the coconut cream and remaining 50ml water in a saucepan over medium heat. Remove from the heat and set aside.

3 Crush the fermented tapioca, sugar and salt in a bowl into a smooth paste. Any missed fibres in the tapioca should be removed now. Stir in the plain flour. Break up the wet rice dough and mix it in until a thick paint is obtained. Stir in the instant yeast. Cover with clingfilm and set aside for 2 hours or until frothy.

4 Preheat the oven to 230°C. Lightly grease a muffin tray with vegetable oil. Put it on a baking tray and place this on the second highest shelf in the oven, about 15cm from the grill. Allow it to heat up for 5 minutes.

5 Give the batter a stir. Open the oven door, withdraw the tray and divide the batter among the greased cups, until almost full. Push the tray back into the oven and bake for 15 minutes or so, until risen, crack-topped and brown in parts.

These steamed, fine-pored sponges may also be made with white sugar.

APAM BARABAI

MAKES 10

100g rice flour
   (*tepung beras*, page 523)
75ml water, plus 2 tbsp
75g coconut sugar, shaved
   (page 524)
3 tbsp coconut cream
Pinch of salt
50g fermented tapioca (page 379)
¼ tsp easy-blend instant yeast
Softened banana leaf, for lining

1 Combine the rice flour and 75ml water in a medium bowl and mix until you get something resembling damp crumble topping. Cover and leave overnight or for at least 8 hours.

2 The next day, dissolve the coconut sugar into the 2 tbsp water and coconut cream in a saucepan over low heat. Stir in the salt and allow to cool completely.

3 Whisk the cooled syrup into the wet rice dough. Crush the fermented tapioca in a small bowl and mix it in, together with the instant yeast. Leave for 2 hours or until frothy.

4 Prepare your steamer. Line the bases of ten shallow 8cm moulds with circles of lightly greased banana leaf. Arrange these in the perforated steamer compartment, then divide the batter among them. Steam for 10 minutes, by which time they should be slightly puffy and dewy-faced. Eat warm.

You will find shaping these fried biscuits to be surprisingly easy work. The only tricky task is knowing when to retrieve them from the hot fat – the coconut sugar in the batter means they brown quite fast.

These crisp and softly crumbly, little darlings, are best eaten warm.

CINCIN

MAKES 8

100g rice flour
  (*tepung beras*, page 523)
125ml water
60g coconut sugar, shaved
  (page 524)
1 pandan leaf, snipped
Eight 12cm banana leaf squares,
  softened (page 520)
Canola oil, for deep-frying

1 Combine the rice flour and 50ml of the water in a small bowl. Mix with a fork, until a damp rubble is obtained. Cover and leave overnight, or for at least 8 hours, for the flour to fully absorb the liquid.

2 The next day, bring the coconut sugar, remaining 75ml water and pandan leaf to a simmer in a small saucepan over medium heat, stirring to dissolve the sugar. Strain this hot syrup into the rice rubble, stir to mix, then tip the resultant batter into the pan. Cook until a damp, but shapeable, paste is obtained. Leave to cool for 5-10 minutes.

3 Drop a bulging tablespoon of batter on a banana leaf square and gently press it into a disc. With a chopstick, or your favourite finger, create 4 or 5 little holes. Shape all the *cincin* this way.

4 Heat 4cm of canola oil in a large saucepan over medium heat. Once hot, slip in as many leaf rafts as the pan can accommodate with overcrowding. Fry for a minute, until their sides are set and deep gold, continually basting them with hot oil. It is in their nature to puff up slightly. Using tongs, tug the leaf rafts out from beneath the set fritters. Flip the fritters and fry for another minute. Careful not to over-fry them; you do not want cinder *cincin*. Drain on kitchen towel.

Nagasari pisang and *amparan tatak* both involve setting bananas in coconut pudding. There are two main differences. *Nagasari* is usually contained within nifty parcels of banana leaf and its pudding is uniformly cool, glassy. *Amparan tatak* is most commonly set in large trays and assumes two tiers, the robust, firm, bottom, and a tremulous, tender, top.

Pisang raja is the best banana for the job. Its flavour, backed with lilting notes of vanilla, honey and jasmine, intensifies in the heat. The cooked fruit also possesses a moreish, yielding, waxiness here that works very well with the pudding. It is essential that you use ripe fruit, as their flavour and sweetness are central to the success of this *wadai*. Close to half a kilo is called for. It sounds ludicrous, and as you begin cramming them into the tin, doubt will start trickling in. But do not worry, as this amount is vital in getting not just the prettiest, but most delectable, mosaic.

AMPARAN TATAK

SERVES 10-12

FOR THE BOTTOM LAYER
750ml coconut milk
   (second extract; page 521)
170g rice flour (page 523)
20g tapioca starch
250g sugar
½ tsp salt
400g *pisang raja*, peeled weight
Softened banana leaf, for lining

FOR THE TOP LAYER
350ml coconut cream
30g rice flour
30g cornflour
2 tsp sugar
¼ tsp salt

1 Line the base and sides of a 20x4cm square tin with softened sheets of banana leaf. Prepare your steamer.

2 Make the bottom layer. Combine the coconut milk, rice flour and tapioca starch, sugar and salt in a medium saucepan. Cook over medium heat, whisking constantly, until thick as pastry cream. Scrape this onto the base of the prepared tin. Leave for a couple of minutes to firm up slightly, then arrange over the whole torpedoes of banana, pressing them in gently. As well tiled as you want this to be, it is crucial that each banana is given several millimeters of private space, lest the top and bottom layers fail to adhere to one another.

3 Now for the top layer. Give the saucepan a rinse and into it pour 250ml of the coconut cream. Place over a very low heat to warm up.

4 In a small bowl, whisk the rice flour and cornflour, sugar and salt into the remaining 100ml coconut cream. Once the coconut cream is just warm, whisk in the flour slurry and remove from the heat just as the mixture begins to thicken. You want it pourable and smooth. Spread this over the bananas and give the pan a light shake. Steam for 15-18 minutes, until the top is firm. Cool completely before slicing it in its pan.

The name, I suspect, is a corruption of *klaapertart*, the baked custard of young coconut from Manado, Sulawesi.

This is best eaten lukewarm, dished out in messy spoonfuls. The more civilised way of serving it is to let it cool down completely and slice out wedges while its body is tin-bound.

KALAKATAR

SERVES 6-8

30g plain flour
15g rice flour (page 523)
75g caster sugar, plus 1 tbsp
250ml coconut water
1 pandan leaf, knotted
75ml coconut cream, plus 1 tbsp
2 medium eggs, lightly beaten
¼ tsp salt
300g young coconut flesh, in curls
2 tsp cornflour

1 Preheat the oven to 200°C.

2 Place the two flours, 75g caster sugar and coconut water in a medium saucepan. Whisk until smooth, then drop in the pandan leaf. Cook over medium-low heat until a bubbling sauce, thick as gravy, is obtained. Take off the heat, discard the pandan leaf and whisk in the 75ml coconut cream, eggs and salt.

3 Combine the young coconut curls and cornflour in a bowl and massage together. Leave for 5 minutes, then stir into the coconut custard.

4 Pour this mixture into a shallow 20cm round cake tin. Bake on the second highest shelf until set, about 30-35 minutes.

5 Remove the tin from the oven, turn on the grill to its highest setting. Sprinkle the *kalakatar* the extra 1 tbsp coconut cream and 1 tbsp sugar. Return it to the oven, only removing it once beautifully scorched.

The billowy citrus blouse on the cook puts her in stark contrast against what is essentially a sweltering, ashen-walled, shoebox. In this hallowed space, she is the light, barely glistening with perspiration despite being the one having to make lunch, while I, a happy observer, look fresh out of a sauna.

I head into the backyard for a brief reprieve, only to find the air bereft of movement, the sun's glare stern and unrelenting. I find relief in patches of river peeking out from behind the wild foliage enveloping the property. Whatever water my eyes catch, I drink, even if it would most likely be as warm as a bath. The sight and sound of it, trembling, flowing, are enough to calm and soothe. "Negative ions," as one of my aunts would point out, with painful satisfaction.

The truth is that the weather in and around Palangka has been merciless for several days now. It is likely the reason for people being so mightily irate, from motorists to market vendors. Yesterday evening, Yudha asked a gentleman outside the bank for directions to a restaurant and was told, basically, to buzz off. Apparently our hotel has been experiencing difficulties getting someone to remedy an increasingly furious flicker in their illuminated signage because of the crazy heat, although this is likely just an excuse. I reckon the 'L' will be completely silent by tonight.

Palangkaraya is the capital of Central Kalimantan. Bordered by the Java Sea in the south as well as East, South and North Kalimantan, this province, the third largest in Indonesia, is relatively new. Once part of South Kalimantan and ruled by the Muslim Sultanate of Banjar, it was carved out in 1957, in response to the demand for autonomy by the Dayaks, of whom the most prominent are the Ngaju, Ot Danum and Ma'anyan.

While it seems the majority of the Dayaks lead isolated existences even in present times, inhabiting the inaccessible, often impenetrable, interiors of Kalimantan Tengah, an area rich with rainforests, mangroves and swamps, a good number have chosen to live closer to the southern coast, finding work in cities like Palangkaraya and Pangkalan Bun, coexisting with other ethnic groups such as the Javanese, Banjarese, Malay, Madurese, Toraja and Chinese. Siwoh is one such person, and I feel terribly privileged watching her work.

Back inside the kitchen, a contingent of aubergines has been arranged on the barbecue. We watch and wait for the skins of the svelte creatures, all a princely shade of purple, to go black, and for their flesh to go buttery. Some hiss in anger, dripping clear beads of blood through little wounds. Others rest stoically, letting the bars brand them until they finally collapse. Not one for passive aggressiveness, I would much rather they explode their hot love all over.

A large *cobek* is lifted from the wet concrete floor onto a counter and duly wiped with a kitchen rag. Basalt has never looked thirstier and the cook seems all too eager to supply. Flung over its gentle curvature is a dozen cloves of garlic and a fistful of bird's eye chillies, tropical fairy lights, in shades of red, orange and mustard. A liberal sprinkling of salt goes over, followed by a nugget of *terasi* whose aroma bloomed and swelled like a twisted, black-hearted, flower as it roasted earlier. The pestle, or *ulekan*, like a door handle pilfered from an ancient temple, is brought out and the fruits and bulbs are pressed against the rough surface until their bodies are broken. They are then rubbed into a reddish pulp, pullulated with tiny, fiery bones.

Elsewhere in the windowless space, the roasted aubergines are flayed and freed from their charred, blistered skin. A hillock of *daun singkong*, young tapioca leaves, is being scrunched and crushed. Milk is being wrung from grated coconut meat. Poles of *singkah uhut*, the shoots of a species of rattan, are being stripped of their casings, their creamy white marrows cut into sections, not unlike how one would tackle leeks for a stew. There are many other edible species of rattan or *rotan*, such as *singkah marau*, *irit* and *nang'e*. I grew up associating the plant with garden furniture and corporal punishment and only learned about the culinary delights held in its shoots when I was researching food in Mindanao a few years back. This is my first time seeing them being cooked. While these can be simply sautéed with garlic, perhaps with a handful of dried anchovies, today their fate lies in a *juhu*, currently occupying an immense enamel pot sitting magisterially on the stove. A vessel of bubbling vermillion, fragrant and full of promise.

JUHU

Juhu is very much Central Kalimantan's equivalent to the *gangan* of East and South Kalimantan. At its heart, it is a soupy, lightly soured, vegetable braise. It is quite the movable feast, as one would expect from a Dayak dish, born in the wild with the intention of promoting survival, not so much pleasure. The combination of aromatics for its foundation runs the gamut from risibly basic to delightfully complex. It may use just turmeric and *daun salam* (Indonesian bay) or further enlist the powers of garlic, ginger, galangal, bird's eye chillies, candlenuts, black pepper and lemongrass. Sourness, a defining quality of many soups in the region, can be supplied by many kinds of fruit, from young pineapple to *terong asem*, tamarind to bilimbi. Even *tempoyak*, fermented durian, may be dolloped in for velvety funk and tang. Those who want the acidity counteracted with a little creaminess can opt for a swirl of coconut milk. As with many similar braises in Southeast Asia, *juhu* relies on animal for umami, such as freshwater fish, beef and pork ribs and, sometimes, chicken bones. The Ma'anyan are quite famous for a *juhu* made with *bangamat*, or greater flying fox, that insists on *pikauk* leaves as its sharpening agent.

Besides rattan, many other kinds of vegetable can be used. Bamboo shoots, cucumbers, bottle gourds and squash. Young papayas and durians. Unripe bananas and their crisp, succulent stems. Taro yams and their tops known as *kujang*. The leaves and bitter fruits of *jawau*, *Nauclea orientalis*. *Kamenyo* and *leping* leaves. Water convolvulus, bittergourd tendrils and mustardy *segau*, forest spinach, or what the Sarawakians call *ensabi*. *Singkah enyuh*, coconut palm shoots; *singkah hambie*, sago palm shoots; and *singkah udus*, shoots of the *sawit* palm that the Ngaju make for special occasions like traditional Karahingan Thanksgiving and wedding ceremonies.

Just as the rattan pieces are slipped into the enamel pot, a palm-sized climbing perch, fried to a golden crisp, is unceremoniously chucked onto the *cobek* and crushed – fins, bones and all. The smoky flesh of the aubergine is scraped in and the lot is massaged into a rough paste. A Ngaju speciality, this is known as *kandas*. As with *juhu*, it can be made with all manners of things, the most common being *potok* (torch ginger), *sarai* (lemongrass) and a combination of *rimbang* (*terong asem*) and *suna* (native, chive-fine, spring onions).

Kandas is reminiscent of a coarse relish, rough-edged, uncompromising, tender-hearted and seldom vicious with spicy heat. Chilli fiends will likely find greater pleasure in *dadah belasan*, a heady red paste of garlic, shallots, bird's eye chillies, candlenuts, lemongrass and roasted *terasi*. What makes this dish especially intriguing is how it is completed: after getting crushed in a *cobek* it is concealed with a tray of hot coals. The coals grill the surface of the *sambal*, as if it were a crème brulee, making it tantalisingly fragrant. *Dadah belasan* can be eaten with any vegetable, but the Dayaks have a weakness for ivy gourds or *pepasan*.

Siwoh nudges us towards the dining table and we comply. Paper cups are watered. Chipped ceramic plates and stainless steel cutlery are distributed. An enormous bowl bearing a mound of rice arrives at the table, plumes of steam wafting from it, alongside packets of *krupuk kelaikai*, fiddlehead fern crackers, a welcome change from the fish and tapioca crackers that have graced all our meals in the region thus far. The rice is distributed among our number just in time for the incoming *juhu* and *kandas*, the latter heaped onto a devastatingly small saucer. "More is coming", she says through Yudha, before turning and heading towards the kitchen. "Eat first."

The *juhu* is pure joy. The huskiness of the turmeric, acid from tamarind, sweetness of the *baung* (*Mystus*) plucked from the rivers this morning, and pleasing bitterness of the rattan shoots. We continue to drench the fluffy white grains with the steaming liquid, sullying the lot with daubs of the spiced aubergine, while the oppressive heat and bluebottles fade into insignificance.

Siwoh soon drifts out of the kitchen with a pair of plates, one bearing deep-fried fish steaks, the other a swamp. The fish, also *baung*, was brined for a day or so, dried and fermented for a week in pounded roasted rice. The procedure here is almost identical to that for *samu* in South Kalimantan. Indeed, *samu* is what the Ma'anyan call it. It is more commonly addressed in these parts by its Ngaju name, *wadi*. It can also be prepared with pork or wild boar.

The swamp turns out to be made of tapioca leaves, crushed and cooked with pieces of pork belly, shallots, garlic, lemongrass and a glass of coconut milk until most of the liquid evaporated. It is called *tepen* and has a more extravagant sister in *kalumpe*, which the Ngaju call *karuang*. The preparation is almost identical, except for the addition of pea aubergines and crushed roasted peanuts.

The rice we are eating is grown further inland, together with corn, sweet potatoes, tapioca and peanuts. It is in the deep, lush interiors of the province that the culture and traditions of the Dayaks are quietly kept alive. A good example is the preparation of *kenta*, an integral part of the Ngaju rice harvest festivities. Freshly harvested young glutinous rice is first roasted over burning wood until toasty and golden. The grains are then pounded in a large billian mortar and shook in a winnowing basket to expel the husk. The hammered *ketan* left in it is combined with grated coconut meat, coconut water, hot water and a little sugar and mixed well. *Kenta* tastes best after being allowed to sit for a couple of hours, during which the flavours mingle and make merry. I think of it as a cross between rice pudding and muesli: ambrosial, slightly sticky and with a wonderful bite. Eccentric as it sounds, some elderly folk derive great pleasure eating it with fried *wadi*. It is one of the few sweet treats the Dayaks of Kalimantan Tengah make, the other being *tumpi*, or what is known in most parts of Borneo as *pinjaram* or *panyam*.

In terms of tediousness, *kenta* is rivalled by two other foods, *baram*, a potent rice wine, and *kopu*, a tapioca product I first learned of from an online documentary by the Asli Food Project. The making of *kopu* predates the arrival of rice, around the late 3rd century BCE, from the Yangtze Valley in China, recognised as the origin of domesticated rice. In those ancient times, *kopu* served as a staple for the Dayaks, together with sweet potatoes, yams, sago and, of course, tapioca in its regular state. The fondness for these forms of carbohydrate is still alive and visible in dishes like *soto manggala*, a soup from Pangkalan Bun prepared with chicken talons and tapioca chunks, as well as the multitude of *kue* found across the island. The primary reason for rice rising to prominence is that it is more lucrative, being straightforward to grow, taking four months to mature (tapioca takes up to ten).

Kopu demands time and patience. Tapioca is first peeled, cut up and soaked in a basin of water for several days until completely soft. The water must be changed daily. The softened tapioca is drained and shredded, fibres extricated and expelled. It is then immersed in water once again and left until the shreds have settled at the bottom of the basin. The tapioca is drained, wrung in muslin to remove excess moisture, spread out on a basket and left to dry under the sun, producing a white, crumble-like, substance.

To cook, one has to soak the desired amount in water for a third time, but for only a couple of minutes. The rehydrated *kopu* is then cooked in a dry wok with grated coconut over diffident flames and stirred constantly to prevent clumping and colouring – it should remain as white as possible. Once fluffy and tender to the touch, the *kopu* is seasoned with salt and sugar as one wishes. It is now ready for consumption.

Juhu can be made with many things. This one uses *iwak patin* (iridescent shark) and young rattan shoots. It is crucial to remember that sourness is a common feature in *juhu*, and while this is commonly supplied with *terong asem*, I have used tamarind and a couple of underripe tomatoes.

JUHU SINGKAH UMBUT ROTAN

SERVES 6-8

FOR THE SPICE PASTE
15g garlic cloves, peeled
50g red onion, peeled and
   chopped
10g ginger, peeled
10g turmeric, peeled
1 lemongrass stalk, tender
   portion only
3 candlenuts
½ tsp fermented shrimp paste,
   grilled (page 522)

FOR THE SOUP
1 litre water or light fish stock
1 tbsp vegetable oil
2 Indonesian bay leaves
2 underripe tomatoes,
   quartered
1 tsp salt, plus more to taste
½ tsp freshly ground black
   pepper
Pinch of sugar
450g young rattan shoots, peeled
   weight
6 tbsp tamarind water (page 524)
600g iridescent shark, cut into
   2cm steaks

1 Make the spice paste by pounding the ingredients in a pestle and mortar until fine and smooth. Alternatively, grind in a cosy blender, adding a little water if necessary. Set aside.

2 Bring the water to a boil over high heat. Add the spice paste, oil, Indonesian bay leaves and underripe tomatoes. Boil for 2 minutes, then lower the heat, cover and simmer for 30 minutes.

3 Meanwhile, tend to the rattan shoots. Cut them into 3cm sections and blanch in a medium-sized saucepan of water for 5 minutes. Drain and repeat the process two more times. This is to drive out any bitterness and itchiness the consumer may experience. By this point, the shoots should be barely on the cusp of tenderness.

4 Uncover and crush the tomatoes into the soup. Add the salt, black pepper, sugar and blanched rattan shoots. Cover and simmer for 15 minutes, or until the shoots are properly tender.

5 Add the tamarind and fish steaks. Simmer, without a lid, for 5-7 minutes, or until the fish is cooked. Allow to cool for a couple of minutes before tasting and adjusting seasoning.

For this *juhu*, sourness is supplied by underripe pineapple, which appears to be all too easily obtained. If you feel it requires further sharpening, then feel free to add tamarind water or a good squirt of lime.

JUHU NANAS BABI

SERVES 6-8

FOR THE SPICE PASTE
15g garlic cloves, peeled
50g red onion, peeled and chopped
10g galangal, peeled
10g turmeric, peeled
1 lemongrass stalk, tender portion only
2 candlenuts
½ tsp fermented shrimp paste, grilled (page 522)

FOR THE SOUP
250g pork ribs
350g pork shoulder, cut into 5cm chunks
1½ litres water
1 tsp salt, plus more to taste
½ tsp freshly ground black pepper
400g underripe pineapple flesh, peeled weight, cut into large chunks

1 Make the spice paste by pounding the ingredients in a pestle and mortar until fine and smooth. Alternatively, grind in a cosy blender, adding a little water if necessary. Set aside.

2 Fill a large saucepan with water, then add the pork ribs and shoulder. Bring to a boil over high heat, continue robustly simmering for 5 minutes, then drain and wash thoroughly. Give the saucepan a quick rinse and return the meat and bones to it.

3 Pour over the 1½ litres water. Bring to a boil over medium heat, then add the spice paste, salt and black pepper. Boil for another 2 minutes, lower the heat, cover and simmer for 1½ hours or until the shoulder meat is tender.

4 Add the pineapple chunks. Cover and simmer for 10 minutes, or until the fruit is tender. Taste and adjust seasoning.

This recipe is based on one I had in Palangkaraya, using *rimbang bulu*, basically *terong asem* (*Solanum ferox L.*), and *suna*, the local spring onions with especially slender leaves. There are versions solely made with *kalorang* (pea aubergines), *potok* (torch ginger), *sarai* (lemongrass) or *terong bakar* (grilled aubergine).

Unable to obtain *suna*, I use chives instead. Regular spring onions, however fine, do not seem adequately sturdy. The *terong asem*, however, is non-negotiable, and must be cooked first, either by boiling or grilling, preferably over charcoal. Some cooks peel it, others do not. I wrap it in foil and roast it in a hot oven, keeping its skin on after.

What helps the various components cohere in *kandas* is fish, mostly from fresh waters, either grilled or fried. Dayaks use whatever they have at their disposal, from whole *papuyu* (climbing perch) or *nila* (tilapia) to steaks of *baung* (*Mystus*). I tend to use small walking catfish, cut into sections and utterly fried, so that even its bones can be crushed in.

KANDAS RIMBANG BULU

SERVES 6

1 small *terong asem*, approx. 150g
4 garlic cloves, peeled
8 shallots, peeled and sliced
½ tsp salt
6 red bird's eye chillies
75g deep-fried fish (see above)
Small bunch of chives, cut into 1½cm
    sections (see above)

1 Preheat the oven to 220°C. Make criss-cross incisions all over the surface of the *terong asem*, then wrap it in foil and put it in the oven on the centre shelf. Roast until very tender, which can take up to 40 minutes. Unwrap, put on a plate and leave to cool slightly.

2 Pound the garlic and shallots with the salt into a fine paste. Add the bird's eye chillies and crush them in. Add the fried fish and pound until it has broken into a floss of sorts, bones and all.

3 Cut the cooled *terong asem* into small pieces and add, together with the chives, to the mortar. Lightly pound them in, just to release their juice and aroma. Taste and adjust seasoning with salt.

Traditionally, *daun rawen rungkai* or *sungkai* (*Albertisia papuana Becc.*) is added to this, the leaves behaving as a flavour enhancer. In its absence, monosodium glutamate (MSG) is often called upon. I have nothing against this substance but tend to use a good fish stock instead.

KALUMPE

SERVES 6

4 garlic cloves, peeled
6 shallots, peeled
2cm cinnamon stick
4cm galangal, sliced and bruised
1 lemongrass stalk, bruised
500ml dried anchovy stock (page 520)
150g young tapioca leaves
125g pea aubergines
6 red bird's eye chillies, bruised
¼ tsp salt
200ml coconut milk
50ml coconut cream

TO SERVE
75g fried peanuts (page 522)
50g fried anchovies (page 520)

1 Pound the garlic and shallots into a fine paste with a pestle and mortar. Alternatively, grind in a cosy blender, adding a little water if necessary.

2 Combine the garlic-shallot paste, cinnamon, galangal, lemongrass and stock in a medium saucepan. Bring to a boil over high heat, then cover, reduce the heat and simmer for 15 minutes. Stir occasionally.

3 Meanwhile, lightly pound the young tapioca leaves, just to bruise and break them. Add the pounded leaves, pea aubergines, red bird's eye chillies, salt and coconut milk. Cover and simmer for 10 minutes.

4 Add the coconut cream and simmer uncovered for another 2 minutes. Dish up and sprinkle with the fried peanuts and anchovies. Taste and adjust seasoning.

Apui, in some Dayak languages in Kalimantan Tengah, means "fire". While it seems clear that *papui* means "grilled", I have not yet found anyone who knows what *mapui* is. It could be the same word in a different dialect, for *terong mapui* is a dish of grilled aubergines stirred or lightly crushed into a spicy sauce, and eaten with grilled fish and rice.

Numerous versions of this dish exist. One involves grilling the aubergines whole, peeling, shredding and adding them to the sauce. Another similar recipe involves frying, not grilling, slices of aubergine. This version involves grilling the halved fruit and then simmering them in the sauce.

TERONG MAPUI

SERVES 8

4 medium aubergines, each
   approx. 125g
100ml vegetable oil
1 tbsp coconut sugar, shaved
   (page 524)
1 tbsp tamarind water (page 524)
150ml water
½ tsp salt

FOR THE SPICE PASTE
15g garlic cloves, peeled
20g shallots, peeled
100g *cabe merah keriting*
   (page 520)
5 bird's eye chillies
2 lemongrass stalks, tender
   portion only
2 candlenuts
1 tsp fermented shrimp paste,
   grilled (page 522)

1 Halve the aubergines lengthwise and cook them over hot coals until scorched and tender. Alternatively, grill them on a fiercely heated griddle pan, or on the highest shelf of an oven preheated to 220°C for 20-25 minutes, turning them over midway. Transfer the cooked fruit to a plate.

2 Pound the ingredients for the spice paste with a pestle and mortar. You may alternatively use a cosy blender, adding a little water if necessary.

3 Heat the oil in a large deep frying pan or wok over medium-high heat, then add the spice paste. Fry for a minute, stirring constantly, then lower the heat and fry until fragrant, aromatic and deep red. This may take up to 7-10 minutes.

4 Add the coconut sugar, tamarind water, water and salt. Once the sugar dissolves into the bubbling liquid, push in the grilled aubergines. Cover, lower the heat and simmer very gently for 7-10 minutes. The aubergines should be quite soft by now and drunk with flavour. Uncover and simmer for another 5, or until most of the liquid has either been absorbed or evaporated.

This unusual preparation that involves grilling *sambal* is prominent among the Dayaks who live in the areas flanking the Kahayan River. I have not yet encountered an individual who knows the meaning of its name, though to my mind it seems to suggest addictiveness: *dadah*, in Malay and Indonesian, means "drugs" (though the acronym *narkoba*, for *narkotik dan obat-obatan*, is more commonly used in Indonesia), while *belasan*, in those languages, means "dozen", "dozens" or "multiple times."

I use the Indonesian *cobek* here, as most do. The wide mouth of the mortar means you can grill the *sambal* directly in it. In its absence, pound the ingredients in a regular pestle and mortar, then spread it over a heatproof dish and push this beneath a scorching grill.

DADAH BELASAN

SERVES 6

175g *cabe merah keriting* (page 520)
25g red bird's eye chillies
100g shallots, peeled weight
25g garlic cloves, peeled
6 candlenuts, approx. 15g
10g fermented shrimp paste (page 522)
¼ tsp salt
¼ tsp sugar
1 tbsp vegetable oil

1 Preheat the oven grill to its highest setting.

2 Place a wide frying pan over medium heat. Once smoking, add the two kinds of chilli, shallots, garlic and candlenuts. Lower the heat, and leave them for 2-4 minutes, until the vegetables are slightly soft and have acquired some colour, even charring in parts. The candlenuts should feel toasty and lightly scorched. Tip these into a *cobek*.

3 In the same pan, dry-fry the fermented shrimp paste over medium-low heat, pressing it against the hot metal, until it no longer smells fetid, and is dry and crumbly. Add this to the contents of the *cobek*. Add the salt, sugar and oil. Pound until a fine paste is obtained. Taste and adjust seasoning.

4 Spread this paste thinly over the *cobek* and create grooves on its surface with a spoon. Pop the *cobek* onto a sturdy tray and push beneath the hot grill. Leave it there until scorched and charred in parts. The aroma released during this process is quite remarkable. Serve with vegetables, such as cucumbers, yardlong beans, winged beans and cabbage. And, of course, rice.

In kampungs deep within the forests of Kalimantan Tengah, unhusked glutinous grains are used, the resultant powder the colour of coffee. Here, regular glutinous rice is called upon.

Unlike *samu*, which is often fried as is, in their granular jackets of ground rice, *wadi* has to be washed and dried before being cooked. The most common way to do this is to deep-fry or grill them.

WADI

MAKES APPROX. 1KG

1kg *iwak baung* (*Mystus*)
150g sea salt flakes
200g glutinous rice

1 Cut the fish into 2cm steaks. Wash thoroughly, pat dry with kitchen towel, then massage with half the sea salt. Arrange on a tray and leave in a cool place overnight.

2 The following day, discard the water the fish would have exuded. Lightly pat the fish dry with kitchen towel. Set aside momentarily.

3 Toast the glutinous rice in a pan over medium heat until golden. Allow to cool slightly, then tip into a pestle and mortar and pound into a fine powder. Allow this powder to cool completely, then rub with the remaining sea salt over the fish.

4 Pack the coated fish into a sterilised 2 litre Kilner jar. Cover and keep in a cool, dark place for 5-7 days to ferment. Beyond this period, I transfer the jar to the refrigerator due to the humid conditions in which I live.

5 To cook, simply wash them, pat dry and fry in hot oil, until lightly crisp. Eat with hot rice. Wonderful as this is with *sambal belacan* (page 495) or *kandas* (page 401), I recommend a bowl of *cacapan mangga* (page 329) as an accompaniment.

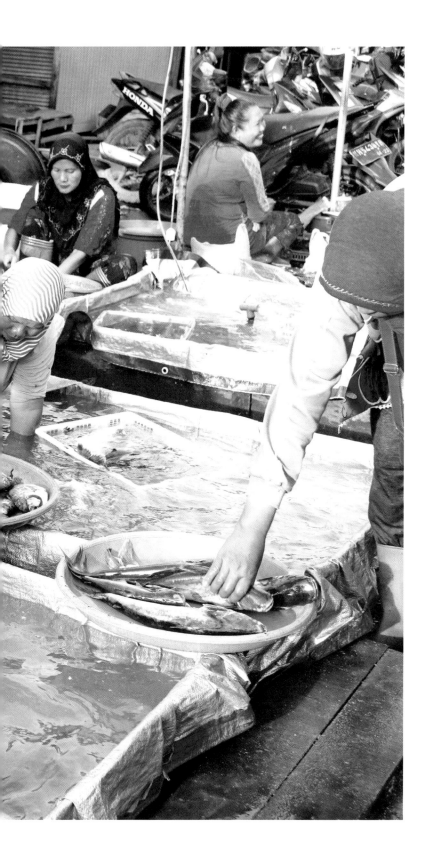

The *tiwadak* or *cempedak* (*Artocarpus integer*) should be ripe, but not mushy, or the fritter will go soggy quite fast. Here, the arils are fried with their seeds in, as is done in Kalimantan, so serve them with a little bowl into which guests may pop them.

GUGUDUH TIWADAK

SERVES 6-8

750g *cempedak* arils

FOR THE BATTER
50g plain flour
50g cornflour
100g rice flour
   (*tepung beras*, page 523)
15g glutinous rice flour
1 tsp sugar
¼ tsp salt
¼ tsp baking soda
Approx. 200ml cold water

1 Make the batter by combining the dry ingredients in a bowl and adding just enough cold water to achieve the consistency of thick paint.

2 Heat about 4cm of canola oil in a medium saucepan or wok over medium heat. Once hot, turn 2-3 *cempedak* arils in the batter and slip them into the hot fat. Fry for 3-4 minutes, pushing them about with a frying slice until golden and crisp. Fry all the *cempedak* this way. Drain on kitchen towel and cool for several minutes before eating.

Never did I expect World Cup Fever to grip Kalimantan, much less Singkawang, a small city in its western province. Pubs and *kedai kopi* have been chock-a-block, the mostly male clientele transfixed by the gospel flashing from ceiling-mounted televisions. At our hotel, it seemed as though all its patrons had congregated in the café on the ground floor, spilling out onto the adjacent driveway. We decided to partake in the merriment. It seemed the polite thing to do. As payment, I spent the first few hours of morning floating through whorls of colour.

It took two cups of *kopi pancong* to restore my senses, although one could argue that I really just had one – *pancong* means "half-full". Serving coffee in this fashion supposedly started in Pontianak several decades ago because locals could not afford a full cup. It has already wended its way to Jakarta. The black, biting brew was part of a breakfast of *pisang goreng*, fried bananas, cut up and speared with toothpicks. Though more than decent, they could not hold a candle to the ones I had in Pontianak several nights back. The *pisang kepok* were sliced into blades and fanned out before receiving their robes of batter and bath in bubbling fat. Besides packing a rapturous crunch, they were yielding, creamy even, the usual caterwaul of grease muted to a whisper. We ate them alongside breadfruit (*sukun*) and orbs of grated taro studded with peanuts (*ou ie*), both of which had been fried with similarly staggering skill.

The Teochew gentleman responsible for the heavenly goods divulged that he had been doing it since he was ten; the business was started by his great grandfather at least seventy years ago. Introducing himself as Aditya – it is common for Indonesian Chinese to have names that sound most non-Chinese – he magnanimously furnished us with a saucer of *srikaya*, often described as coconut curd or jam, prepared with duck eggs so that it was shot through with gold and dense like pastry cream. He said it married well with the *sukun*. Indeed, the combination was heavenly. I am hoping to have more tonight, on our return to the province's capital. But for now, I shall channel all my attention to lunch.

The eatery, set on the ground level of a shop house exudes old world charm, a quilt of heron grey tiled floors, cream marble tabletops, weatherworn wooden stools and vintage, dragon-embellished clay pots filled with devil's ivy and desert roses. It is a place that would benefit from being viewed through sepia-tinted glasses, though the teal polyester tents, designed to shelter al fresco patrons, kill the vibe somewhat.

We are directed to a table a considerable distance from the kitchen, farther than I would ordinarily prefer. It is quite possible the owners caught sight of my notebook and camera and decided to distance me from their source of income. Their sullen demeanors and brusque manners of speech made it plain that no form of inveigling would be condoned.

It takes no longer than five minutes for the *choipan* to arrive, wreathed in steam, their fresh, dewy faces anointed with filings of fried garlic and some of its oil. Also known as *cai kue*, "vegetable cakes", these dumplings have skins made from a pastry of rice and sago flours, filled with a variety of things, namely taro yam, skinned mung beans, jicama and garlic chives, flavoured with dried shrimp. Non-halal establishments may sneak lard into their little celestial bodies.

We ordered a large platter bearing all four kinds today. Restraint is something unknown to us. Common as it is to find *choipan* shaped into half-moons, today they present themselves as dainty money pouches with rumpled tops, in the vein of *xiao long bao*, but with a ghost of translucency. As with all dumplings, time is no friend of theirs and Yudha urges us to eat them while still warm, which we do, quite happily, as the *adzan* from a nearby mosque sends his song into the sultry afternoon air.

Choipan is a delicacy linked to the Teochews and the Hakkas, the two most prominent Chinese dialect groups in Kalimantan Barat. The Teochews came from the northeastern coastal area of Guangdong, around Shantou, settled in urban areas and tended to focus on trade. The Hakkas, on the other hand, hailed from the interiors of Guangdong and to a lesser extent Fujian, and lived in rural parts of the province where they grew rice, among other crops, and worked in mines.

THE WET CRACKER

It has been documented that China had contact with West Borneo from as early as the 3rd century, and engaged in some form of trade with it since the 7th century, during the Tang Dynasty. The Chinese sought incense, medicinal herbs, sea cucumber, rattan and bird's nest. In exchange for these precious items, the Dayaks received silks and other fabrics, porcelain and pottery. However, it was only in the late 18th century that the region received its greatest swath of Chinese immigrants, under the encouragement of the sultans who required labourers for their gold mines. Most of these miners were Hakka, and many eventually established mining companies known as *kongsi*. A number of these Hakka would later move deeper inland, engage in trade with the Dayaks, even marrying into their families.

Besides *choipan*, the Teochews are represented by *bubur ikan*, which is not a gruel per se but a clear broth, tinted chartreuse with preserved mustard greens, into which boiled rice, slices of poached fish, either napoleon, shark or barracuda, and nuggets of their soy-cooked liver, are added. The Hakka have *yong theu fu*, tofu and vegetables, such as aubergines, chillies and bittergourd, stuffed with seasoned ground pork or fish, and blanched in a broth delicately flavoured with chicken bones and dried anchovies. These may be served dry or in said broth, and eaten with two sauces, one of chilli, and a chocolate-coloured number made with hoisin and oyster sauces.

Most Hakka food, such as chicken in rice wine, pork belly stewed with red rice wine lees or steamed with preserved mustard greens, is mostly found in homes. The Hakka classic, *lei cha*, "thunder tea", a dish of rice served in a herbal, chlorophyll-dense brew, is not commonly eaten in these parts.

The Chinese food with the most presence in the commercial sphere is supplied by Hokkiens. A trot down Jalan Gajah Mada in Pontianak, home to a small though strong Hokkien community, will reveal the glories of *hekeng*, succulent cakes of minced prawn and pork, enrobed in beancurd skins and deep-fried, and *ko kue*, cubes of rice flour pastry, fried on a metal cast-iron plate with garlic chives, soy and egg. On the streets near the city's central market, hawkers fling *kwetiu*, flat, wide rice noodles, into charcoal-fuelled woks with beef strips, egg and beansprouts. These ribbons, infused with smoke, umami and caramel, are always served in elegant pouches of *daun simpur* (*Dillenia*).

We arrive back in Pontianak late in the afternoon. There is no time to waste, as we have a date with one of the city's most esteemed *kerupuk basah* makers. The epitome of graciousness and hospitality, Mak Nett welcomes us into her home in Bangka Belitung Laut, leading us into her living room via her kitchen, its immaculateness and tranquility sabotaged by a solitary steamer puttering away on the stove. We make ourselves at home on her upholstered settees, as per her instruction. A tray of glasses, rocky with ice and orange with Fanta, appear on the table, as well as a platter of *kerupuk basah*, snipped into coins, accompanied by a bowl of a sauce comprising roasted peanuts and chilli, sugar and salt.

Despite translating into "wet cracker", *kerupuk basah* is really a fish cake. It comes from Putussibau, a town along the River Kapuas in the eastern part of the province. Nett, who has been running her cottage industry for five years, says that the fish has to be freshwater, ideally *toman* (giant snakehead), *gabus* (murrel snakehead) or *patin* (iridescent shark). Those catering to palates accustomed to marine fish may make it with *ikan tenggiri* (Spanish mackerel), but for the majority, notes of weed-licked rock and riverbed are utterly desirable, and unlike the fishcakes made by the Thais and Chinese, these are incredibly chewy, similar to the *keropok lekor* of Terengganu and *pempek* from Sumatra. I would not be surprised to find them part of the same story.

Making *kerupuk basah* is straightforward but time consuming business. Once rid of skin and bone, the fish meat is blended with garlic, salt, pepper and tapioca starch before being shaped into a collection of slender, foot-long sausages. I am told that the more traditional sago flour tends to produce a greyish article, while tapioca starch helps to preserve the pinky whiteness of the fish. Chicken bouillon powder can be worked into the paste as one wishes, as can little jewels of *patin* belly fat. The *kerupuk* are then boiled in batches until they float to the surface, like glossy, swollen bratwursts. Once cool, they can be stashed in the freezer and steamed whenever the urge arises.

SWIMMING UPSTREAM

While we nibble and drink, the focus of the conversation loosens and we find ourselves discussing local favourites. Mention is made of the *pengkang* from Peniti, which I managed to try on the way up to Singkawang several days back. These are triangular banana leaf parcels, bearing cargoes of glutinous rice, moistened with coconut milk and punctuated with dried shrimp, that are clamped between bamboo rods and turned over smouldering coconut husks. They are heavenly piping hot, dismantled with boorish fingers and dabbed with an oily, brick red *sambal* made with *kepah*, a kind of river clam.

 We broach the *bubur pedas* of Sambas Regency, within spitting distance of the Sarawakian border. It is, as its name suggests, a gruel, one made with roasted rice and coconut, a *bumbu* of chilli, galangal, shallots, lemongrass, black pepper and candlenuts, and up to twelve kinds of vegetables and leaves, including Vietnamese mint and the oregano-like *buas buas*, *Premna foetida*. The broth is sometimes flavoured with chicken, more often *tetelan*, beef trimmings. Besides being spicy, as is its wont, it is also earthy and herbal. Nett proceeds to mention another porridge, *bubur lemak*, comfortingly prepared with whole chickens and coconut milk and eaten with *sambal*, preserved mustard greens and sliced bird's eye chillies. "It's from Kapuas Hulu, like me," she says, eyes twinkling. *Hulu* means "upriver".

 The food found in the river-hugging settlements in Kapuas Hulu regency is mostly of the Orang Melayu or Malays. The only real difference between the Malay dishes from Kapuas Hulu and those elsewhere in the province, and most of Borneo, are the ingredients. The names of the dishes, their essence and soul, their silhouette, are pretty much the same.

 For the residents of Kapuas Hulu, the forests, rivers and mangroves have much to give. There is an abundance of unusual fruit. *Buah mawang* (*Mangifera pajang Kosterm.*) and its sharper, more odorous, smaller-sized sister, *kemantan*, are two varieties of mango that frequently find their way into *sambals*. *Buah manga kasturi*, *Mangifera kasturi*, also known as the Kalimantan mango, is one that has become rare. It is known for being pure nectar when ripe, as is the case for *buah honey gitak*, a fruit from the *Willughbeia* family that apparently tastes like a soursop-mangosteen milkshake. These two fruits are only ever eaten as they are, unadulterated, and the same applies to *buah keledang, Artocarpus lanceifolius Roxb*, which looks like a *tarap* lit up from within by fluorescent vermillion arils.

There is also the *Gnetum gnemon* or melinjo tree to consider, whose leaves and fruit shine in the Javanese *sayur lodeh*. It was during the late 18th century that the Javanese migrated to Kalimantan in droves, in the company of the Madurese, Bugis and Minangkabau. In Kalimantan today, these peoples and many of their foods, from the Javanese *buntil* (here called *botok*) and aforementioned *lodeh* to Minangkabauan *rendang*, seem to be simply called Malay, with little distinction. In a way, the same can be said of dishes that originated with the Arabs, such as *nasi kebuli, nasi mandhi*, even *biriyani*. The Arabs were at one point dubbed "honorary Malays" and even considered native.

Slipping down from the tree canopies to the forest floors, fallen trees and damp patches of earth are opulent with *kulat*, mushrooms, such as *tuan* and *tambir*, usually fried with garlic and chilli, as well as *pakis*, fern fiddleheads, often dropped into braises of garlic, turmeric and coconut milk, sometimes imbued with shards of smoked *lais*. Like the *jelawat* and *arwana* from the rivers in the area, *Kryptopterus lais* is not easy on the wallet: a single kilogram can easily amount to 200,000 – 300,000 rupiahs.

Another dish uniting the fruits from the forest and rivers is *asam pedas*, "sour, spicy", braise associated with the Malays in Indonesia and Malaysia. Though most commonly made with fish, meat, in particular beef, may be used for festive occasions. While the *asam pedas* found in cities would regularly contain aubergines and ladyfingers as part of the vegetable contingent, rural versions delight in bamboo shoots, fern fiddleheads, rattan shoots, *tupus telor* and *umbut ransa*. Whatever is available is used.

The differences do not stop there. While some choose to perfume their *asam pedas* with torch ginger, others may plump for Vietnamese mint. While some slip in add leathery pieces of *asam kandis* (*Garcinia xanthochymas*) or shiny currant-like fruits of *lambai-lambai* (the name cutely means "come, come"; *Cayratia trifolia*) for quintessential sourness, the ideal sharpening agent for the upstream folk tends to be *terong asem* (*terung Dayak, Solanum ferox L.*). Based on Mak Nett's description, this upstream *asam pedas*, is simpler on the palate, with fewer layers of flavour, and strikingly similar to the *juhu* of the Dayaks in Central Kalimantan.

Of the Dayaks in Kalimantan Barat, the Iban, Ot Danum, Kanayatn and Kendawangan are some of the more prominent ones, leading isolated existences deep within the province's interiors. Much of their culture and traditions remain a mystery to most, more so here than in the other provinces of Kalimantan – or so it appears to me. Not even younger generations of Dayaks, whose families have been living in or closer to the cities, seem to know much, having already assimilated into the fabric of modern society and living. Back in the day, the Dayak women who married Hakka men had to assimilate into Hakka culture. The same is true for those who married Malay men. The little I know about Dayak fare has come from a gentleman of Kanayatn descent who ran a small restaurant in Pontianak. It was, at the time of writing, likely the only Dayak eatery in the entire city.

As with most of its ilk, Dayak cooking in Kalimantan Barat is uncomplicated. Fish and tortoises from the rivers and game from the forests, such as snake, dog, wild birds and boar are usually cooked directly over flames or first contained in bamboo culms. They are flavoured simply, with scrunched up bunches of local spring onion, crushed fingers of various gingers, turmeric root and leaves and salt. Vegetables are cooked similarly, usually seasoned with just a little salt. These viands would be consumed with a *sambal*, perhaps some *jukut*, and rice, their chief carbohydrate, although in ancient times tapioca and job's tears, known locally as *jali* or *jelai*, assumed this role.

Jukut is, in essence, the *pakasam* of the West Kalimantan Dayaks, prepared with fish or wild boar. The best fish to use, according to Mak Nett, are freshwater species, such as wallago (*tapah*), iridescent shark (*patin*) and *Chitala* (*belida*). After being cleaned and cut up, they are massaged with salt, cooked rice and a lick of honey, then packed into an airtight jar and kept in a dark place for up to a week. Although *jukut* is grand fried with shallots, garlic, ginger and turmeric, Mak Nett expresses an especial fondness for having it deep-fried and spritzed with calamansi juice. Yudha heartily concurs.

HAMMERED SQUID

Several hours later, beneath a moonless sky, Yudha and I find ourselves in a narrow, dark alley, lit by the fluorescent tubes of a hawker's kiosk and a blaring flat-screen television. Apparently, France is playing against Argentina as we speak.

Of the seven cosy plastic tables cluttering the space, we pick the one closest to the counter. Yudha pops over to the kiosk vendor and mutters something while I make myself comfortable in a Monobloc. As Yudha joins me the table, the gentleman, struggling to contain his annoyance at us interrupting, proceeds to harvest two dried squids from the collection hanging across his glass cabinet like deathly buntings. Securing them in a wire barbecue frame, he warms their bodies over a clay brazier on the raw cement floor, rocky with red-hot charcoal.

The frame is turned several times over a stretch of five minutes, until the desiccated cephalopods whiten and begin to smell of hot sandy beaches. The man then takes them back to his counter and pummels them furiously with a wooden mallet, shattering their bodies into shards, tender as beaten wool. He piles these onto a plate and brings them to our table, together with a teeny bowl bearing an elixir of fish sauce, soy, vinegar, sugar and crushed dried shrimps. A plate of baby cucumber and *emping melinjau*, melinjo crackers, arrives shortly afterwards.

This, as I understand it, is the Chinese way of enjoying *sotong pangkong*, "hammered squid". The Malays prefer to eat it with a spicy, sweet peanut sauce, particularly during Ramadan. We tear at the shards, dipping them in the sharp, saline ointment before munching, while other patrons stare at the television, possessed, in the night air thick with clove and tobacco. One of their number has clearly got a little too carried away with their *gudang garam*.

Before delivering me back to the hotel, Yudha decides to pick up some durians for his family. "It's that time of the year", he chimes, as we step out of the car. Two of the most popular varieties include yellow-fleshed *landak* and *ngabang*, both of which are grown in orchards in Capkala district. The one Yudha goes for, the ivory-fleshed *kuching tuding*, comes from Batang Tarang.

Aided with a cleaver, the vendor splits open a fruit for Yudha's assessment, revealing a solitary seed resting all too comfortably in its chamber. Plump and content, oblivious to its fate, it becomes clear why this variety has been named "sleeping cat". At the urging of Yudha and the vendor, I extricate the creature and slowly apply it to my lips.

A common snack in Singkawang, especially welcome on a scorching day.

Petis udang, or *hei ko* in Hokkien, is a paste, treacly in colour, stickiness and palate-coating richness, produced by the reduction of the slurry of leftovers from shrimp processing, sweetened with molasses. It is easily found in Asian food grocers.

RUJAK MENTIMUN

SERVES 8

8 small cucumbers, approx.
   15cm in length
4 tbsp dried shrimp, rinsed,
   dried and pounded to floss (page 521)

FOR THE SAUCE
4 tbsp vegetable oil
50g raw peanuts, skinned
6 red bird's eye chillies, finely sliced
3 tbsp tamarind water (page 524)
30g coconut sugar, shaved (page 524)
5 tsp *petis udang* (page 523)
Salt, to taste

1 Heat the vegetable oil in a medium frying pan over medium heat. Once hot, add the peanuts. Stir, lower the heat slightly, and continue frying until the peanuts are light gold and cooked through. Retrieve them from the pan and drain on kitchen towel. Allow to cool slightly before pounding to a rubble with a pestle and mortar. Tip out onto a plate and set aside.

2 Add the chillies to the mortar, pound into a paste, then add the tamarind water, coconut sugar and *petis*, working them in until the sugar has dissolved. Stir in the crushed fried peanuts and set aside for 5 minutes for the flavours to mingle. Taste and adjust seasoning with salt. This may be kept in the fridge overnight.

3 Peel the cucumbers and halve them. Arrange them on a plate and smear with the sauce. Sprinkle with the pounded dried shrimp and eat.

I use iridescent shark, which is *de rigueur* in Kapuas Hulu. In Singkawang and Pontianak, cities close to the sea, *kerupuk basah* is made with Spanish mackerel. You may use any firm white fish. These typically have beams of fish belly fat running through them, which I omit as I cannot get them. This makes quite a large number for a single household, but take heart in the knowledge that these freeze a dream. Besides eating them snipped into sections with *kuah kacang*, I have to say they are wonderful thinly sliced and deep-fried.

KERUPUK BASAH

MAKES 16

FOR THE KERUPUK
600g tapioca starch, plus more
    for dusting
475ml water
400g iridescent shark flesh,
    skinned and boned weight
1 garlic clove, peeled and minced
1 tsp salt
½ tsp ground white pepper

FOR THE PEANUT SAUCE
2 garlic cloves
50g shallots, peeled
4 *cabe merah keriting*, sliced
    (page 520)
4 red bird's eye chillies
4 tbsp vegetable oil
350ml water
50g coconut sugar, shaved
    (page 524)
4 tbsp tamarind water (page 524)
150g peanuts, skinned, roasted
    and crushed (page 522)
½ tsp salt, plus more to season

1 Combine the tapioca starch and the 475ml water in a bowl, then mix into a thick, phase-defying substance. Cover and leave overnight in a cool place, or for 8-10 hours, by which time the starch should have absorbed all the water.

2 Grind the iridescent shark into a creamy balm in a food processor, adding 1-2 tbsp cold water if necessary. Scrape into a large mixing bowl. Break the hydrated tapioca starch into a fine rubble, then add it with the garlic, salt and pepper to the blended fish. Massage, adding water if necessary, until a smooth, damp but shapeable dough is obtained. If little lumps of tapioca remain, allow the mixture to rest for 10 minutes, then massage again. Cover with clingfilm and refrigerate for 30 minutes.

3 Fill a large and wide saucepan with at least 10cm of water and bring to a boil. Sprinkle a large, wide tray with a little tapioca starch. With a pair of water-moistened hands, divide the paste into 16 balls, roll these into 20cm sausages, and arrange on the starch-dusted tray, juddering around until they are well-coated. Cook the *kerupuk* in boiling water in batches for 12-15 minutes, until they float and swell to 1½ times their original size and wobble in between the tongs. Allow to cool.

4 For the sauce, crush the garlic, shallots and two chillies into a paste, then fry in the oil in a medium saucepan over medium heat until fragrant. Once red, and about to split, add the water and coconut sugar. Lower the heat, cover and simmer for 5 minutes, then add the tamarind water, peanuts and salt. Simmer for another 5 minutes, until thick. Turn off the heat and cool completely before tasting and tweaking with salt. Serve with the fish cakes, first snipped into sections.

In an ideal world, these would be cooked over live coals, for 8-10 minutes, receiving light anointments of vegetable oil to discourage burning. As my world is hardly ideal, I have consulted a griddle pan.

PENGKANG

MAKES 8

250g glutinous rice, washed thrice
    and soaked in water overnight
75ml water
100ml coconut milk
½ tsp salt
2 tbsp dried shrimp, softened (page 521)
Eight 22cm banana leaf squares,
    softened (page 520)
Vegetable oil, for brushing

1 Prepare the steamer. Drain the glutinous rice and spread the grains over its perforated tray, first lined with muslin. Gather excess cloth over the rice, pop the tray onto the steamer and cook for 30 minutes. Uncover, sprinkle in the water, give a brief stir, then cover and steam again, this time for 25 minutes, until the rice is just tender.

2 Convey the cooked glutinous rice to a bowl. With a pair of chopsticks, or a rice scoop, gently work in the coconut milk and salt. Once well mixed, mix in the dried shrimp. Divide this into 8 portions on a large tray and cast over a tea towel to keep them warm.

3 Take a banana leaf and roll into a cone. Feed it with a portion of seasoned rice, gently packing it in. Fold or roll over excess leaf, then seal with a toothpick. Wrap all the *pengkang* as this way, quickly: it is best to do this while the rice is warm and cooperative. Brush them with a teeny bit of vegetable oil.

4 Heat the griddle pan over high heat, until smoking. Grill the parcels in batches, occasionally pressing them onto the hot metal, for about 5 minutes a side, until the leaves are aromatic and blackened in parts. Cool slightly before eating with the *sambal kepah* on the following page.

In the absence of *kepah*, simply use their weight in *kerang* (blood cockle) flesh.

SAMBAL KEPAH

MAKES APPROX. 200G

FOR THE SPICE PASTE
2 garlic cloves, peeled
30g shallots, peeled
75g *cabe merah keriting*, chopped
 (page 520)
4 dried red chillies, softened
 (page 520)

TO FINISH
100ml vegetable oil
½ tsp salt, plus more to taste
1 tsp coconut sugar (page 524)
2 tbsp tamarind water (page 524)
150g raw *kepah* flesh, drained

1 Make the spice paste by pounding the necessary ingredients together with a pestle and mortar, until a smooth balm is obtained. Alternatively, grind in a cosy blender, adding a little water if necessary.

2 Heat the oil in a medium saucepan over medium heat. Once hot, stir in the spice paste. Cook for several seconds, then reduce the heat and fry, stirring always, until it splits and is dark red. Add the salt, coconut sugar and tamarind water. Raise the heat, add the raw *kepah* flesh and cook for 3-4 minutes until most of the liquid they would have exuded has evaporated. Taste and adjust seasoning with salt.

For this *sambal*, the aromatics and spices are crushed and left raw, the anchovies quickly blanched. The best anchovy for the job is *teri Pontianak*, *teri Medan* or *teri nasi*, *nasi* meaning "rice", an indicator of its tininess.

A tiny curl of makrut lime zest, worked into the paste, is a good idea.

SAMBAL TERI MENTAH

SERVES 6

FOR THE SPICE PASTE
1 garlic clove, peeled
4 *cabe merah keriting*, chopped
 (page 520)
2 red bird's eye chillies

TO FINISH
125g dried anchovies
2 shallots, peeled and sliced
¼ tsp salt
1 tsp sugar
2 tbsp lime juice

1 Make the spice paste by pounding the necessary ingredients together with a pestle and mortar. You want a fairly rough paste. Scrape out into a medium-sized bowl.

2 Give the dried anchovies a light rinse then drain. Bring a small saucepan of water to a boil over high heat, then drop in the anchovies, stir, count to thirty, then drain and rinse under a cold tap. Tip into the spice paste in the bowl and mix in the remaining ingredients. Taste and adjust seasoning with salt, sugar and lime juice.

In place of *midin*, fiddleheads of the vegetable fern may be used. Instead of dried shrimp, you may use fresh ones, peeled and deveined, and added to the pot together with the coconut milk and salt.

MIDIN MASAK LEMAK

SERVES 4-6

FOR THE SPICE PASTE
2 garlic cloves, peeled
3 shallots, peeled
1cm turmeric, peeled
4 red bird's eye chillies

TO COOK
250g young bracken fern
3 tbsp vegetable oil
2 tsp dried shrimp, softened and
    pounded (page 521)
200ml coconut milk
½ tsp salt

1 Make the spice paste by pounding the necessary ingredients together with a pestle and mortar, until a smooth paste is obtained. Alternatively, grind in a cosy blender, adding a little water if necessary. Set aside.

2 Trim the tough bases off the young bracken fern and snip them into 5cm sections.

3 Heat the oil in a medium saucepan over medium heat. Once hot, add the spice paste, fry for a minute. Reduce the heat and fry, stirring always, until it splits and deepens in colour. Add the pounded dried shrimp and fry until it loses its raw scent.

4 Add the coconut milk and salt. Once the mixture simmers, raise the heat slightly and add the young bracken fern. Cook just until they wilt slightly, going tender crisp, and the sauce has reduced to a light, flavoursome syrup.

Pedas translates into "spicy". Here, this heat is not supplied by chilli, but black pepper, a spice that is extremely popular among the folks of Sambas. Apparently, this rice porridge is called *pedas* for another reason: the word, in the Sambas dialect, means "of a great quantity", referring to the greens that give it body and soul.

BUBUR PEDAS SAMBAS

SERVES 10

FOR THE STOCK
500g beef shin, cut into 2cm
    cubes
2 litres water
1½ tsp salt

FOR THE SPICE POWDER
2 tbsp coriander seeds
2 tsp cumin seeds
2 tsp black peppercorns

FOR THE SPICE PASTE
10g garlic cloves, peeled
25g shallots, peeled
15g ginger, peeled
15g galangal, peeled
20g candlenuts
2 tsp fermented shrimp paste,
    grilled (page 522)

TO COOK
150g jasmine rice
100ml vegetable oil
2 lemongrass stalks, bruised
2 Indonesian bay leaves
150g grated coconut, made into
    kerisik (page 521)
Kernels from 1 sweetcorn cob,
    approx. 100g
1 medium carrot, peeled and
    finely chopped
100g young sweet potato leaves
200g young bracken fern, prepared
    as on page 433

TO SERVE
A bunch of Vietnamese mint
    leaves, shredded
Raw beansprouts
Fried anchovies (page 520)
Fried peanuts (page 522)
Calamansi limes

1 Place the beef shin and 2 litres water in a large saucepan. Bring to a boil over high heat. Add the salt, then cover, lower the heat and simmer for 2 hours, until the meat is very tender.

2 Meanwhile, there are several things to do. First, make the spice powder by toasting the whole spices in a dry frying pan over medium-low heat until fragrant, then pounding into a powder with a pestle and mortar.

3 Next, make the spice paste by pounding the necessary ingredients together with a pestle and mortar, until a smooth paste is obtained. Alternatively, grind in a cosy blender, adding a little water if necessary. Set aside.

4 Lastly, toast the jasmine rice in large frying pan over medium heat, stirring constantly, until golden. Tip into a pestle and mortar, leave to cool slightly, then roughly crush. You want each grain broken into 2-3 shards. You do not want a fine powder. Set aside.

5 Remove the beef from the pot. Cool slightly and roughly chop. Strain the stock into a large measuring jug and add enough water to reach the 2 litre mark. Give the saucepan a rinse and a solid wipe. In it, heat the oil over medium-high heat.

6 Add the spice paste. Fry for a minute, then lower the heat and continue cooking, stirring constantly, until it splits, deepens in colour and becomes fragrant. Raise the heat again. Drop in the lemongrass and Indonesian bay leaves. Stir in the beef stock, crushed rice, crushed spices and *kerisik*. Bring to a robust simmer, then cover, lower the heat and simmer for 1 hour, until a creamy gruel is obtained.

7 Add the chopped beef, corn kernels, carrot, sweet potato leaves and bracken fern. Simmer for another 20 minutes. Taste and adjust seasoning with salt, then divide among 10-12 serving bowls. Consummate each serving with Vietnamese mint leaves, beansprouts, fried anchovies and peanuts and calamansi limes. A little saucer of *sambal terasi* (page 495) will not go astray.

For something gentler on the palate, replace the crisp small shrimp with their weight in medium shrimp, peeled and deveined, stirring them in along with the *tempoyak*.

UDANG SAMBAL TEMPOYAK

SERVES 6-8

FOR THE SPICE PASTE
10g garlic cloves, peeled
30g shallots, peeled
6 dried red chillies, softened
    (page 520)
50g *cabe merah keriting*, sliced
    (page 520)
6 red bird's eye chillies

TO COOK
125ml vegetable oil
250g small shrimp
4 red bird's eye chilli, thinly sliced
1 tbsp coconut sugar (page 524)
100ml water
3 tbsp fermented durian
    (*tempoyak*; page 75)
Salt and sugar

1 Pound the ingredients for the spice paste with a pestle and mortar. Alternatively, use a cosy blender, adding a little water if necessary.

2 Heat the oil in a large deep frying pan or wok over medium-high heat. Once hot, add the shrimp and fry for 3-4 minutes, until crisp and deep orange. Add the sliced bird's eye chillies. Once these release their aromas, remove them to a plate with a slotted spoon.

3 Add a little more oil if the pan seems thirsty. Then, add the spice paste. Fry for a minute, stirring constantly, then lower the heat and fry until fragrant, aromatic and deep red. This may take up to 7-10 minutes.

4 Add the coconut sugar and water. Once the sugar dissolves into the bubbling liquid, add the *tempoyak*. Cover, lower the heat and simmer gently for 5 minutes. Taste and adjust seasoning with salt and sugar. It should be slightly sweet and tangy and intensely savoury.

5 Serve in a bowl and pile the crisp-fried shrimp and chilli over.

Although *belulang* means bones in Indonesian, in Sambas it usually points to ribs. This dish requires some time and effort but is totally worth it. Instead of the fine rice noodles (*meehoon* or *bihun*) recommended, this is also commonly enjoyed with *nasi kassum*, rice perfumed with Vietnamese mint and crisp-fried shallots.

ASAM PEDAS BELULANG

SERVES 8-10

FOR THE BEEF
1kg beef shortribs
2 litres water
1 tsp salt

FOR THE SPICE POWDER
1 tsp cumin seeds
2 tbsp coriander seeds
1 tbsp fennel seeds
½ tsp ground cinnamon
½ tsp freshly grated nutmeg

FOR THE SPICE PASTE
20g garlic cloves, peeled
60g shallots, peeled
6 dried chillies, softened
50g *cabe merah keriting*, sliced
   (page 520)
15g red bird's eye chillies

TO COOK
150ml vegetable oil
150g grated coconut, made into
   kerisik (page 521)
1 tsp salt
2 tsp coconut sugar (page 524)
1 tsp sugar
2 tbsp tamarind water (page 524)
A small bunch Vietnamese mint
   leaves, shredded
1 turmeric leaf, roughly shredded

TO SERVE
Fried shallots (page 524)

1 Combine the beef shortribs, water and salt in a large saucepan. Bring to a boil over high heat, then cover, lower the heat and simmer for 1 hour. Skim off any scum that has drifted to the surface.

2 Meanwhile, make the spice powder by dry-frying the whole spices in a frying pan over medium heat until fragrant, then pounding with a pestle and mortar and mixing in the cinnamon and nutmeg.

3 Make the spice paste by pounding the necessary ingredients together with a pestle and mortar, until a smooth paste is obtained. Alternatively, grind in a cosy blender, adding a little water if necessary.

4 When the ribs have had their hour's simmering, remove them to a plate. Strain the stock into a large measuring jug. You should get 1½ litres. Otherwise, top up with water.

5 Give the saucepan in which the ribs were cooked a good wipe and add the 150ml vegetable oil. Let it heat up over medium heat, then add the spice paste. Fry for a minute, then lower the heat and continue cooking, stirring constantly, until it splits, deepens in colour and becomes fragrant.

6 Add the spice powder, boiled ribs, 1½ litres beef stock, *kerisik* and salt. Bring to a boil, then lower the heat, cover and simmer gently for 1¼-1½ hours, until the meat is tender.

7 Stir in the coconut sugar, sugar, tamarind water and salt. Finally stir in the Vietnamese mint and turmeric leaf. Once they wilt, the dish is done. Serve sprinkled with crisp-fried shallots. Eat with boiled fine rice noodles. Slices of hardboiled egg are a fine idea, too.

The pastry, which uses both rice flour and tapioca starch, has to be cooked before being divided and shaped. There is no denying that some patience and elbow grease are required, as the resultant dough is on the rebarbative side. I have found, however, that a large non-stick saucepan and a heatproof spatula help tremendously.

I sometimes replace the jicama with 400g taro yam, peeled weight, first boiled until tender and cut into little cubes. I omit the carrot for this version.

CHOIPAN

MAKES 22-24

FOR THE PASTRY
120g rice flour (page 523)
80g tapioca starch
¼ tsp salt
Approx. 375ml water

FOR THE FILLING
3 tbsp vegetable oil
2 garlic cloves, peeled and
    chopped
4 tbsp dried shrimp, softened
    and pounded (page 521)
100g carrot, peeled and finely
    chopped
400g jicama, peeled and finely
    slivered
¼ tsp salt
½ tsp light soy
2 tbsp water

TO SERVE
Fried garlic (page 522)

1 Place the rice flour and tapioca starch, salt and water in a large non-stick saucepan. Whisk until smooth. Place the pan over medium heat, whisking until it begins to thicken. Exchange the whisk for a heatproof spatula. Lower the heat and cook, stirring, until an off-white, springy, dough is produced. There should be no trace of chalky whiteness. Tip into a bowl, first sprinkled with tapioca starch, and cover with a tea towel. Leave to cool.

2 Now make the filling. Heat the oil in a large frying pan over medium heat. Add the garlic and fry until fragrant, stirring, then add the pounded dried shrimp. Lower the heat and fry until the shrimp smell toasty and warm, about 2-3 minutes. Add the carrot and jicama. Fry for 1 minute, then add the remaining ingredients and cook until the vegetables are tender. Taste and adjust seasoning. Leave to cool.

3 Give the pastry a good knead on a work surface lightly dusted with tapioca starch. Divide it into walnut-sized balls, you should get 22-24. Roll them into thin 8cm discs, with the help of a small rolling pin. Place 1 tbsp of the filling on their middles. Dampen the edges of these pastry rounds with a little water, then fold them into half-moons, expelling as much air as possible.

4 Prepare your steamer. Lightly brush the perforated tray with vegetable oil and arrange the pastries over, with 1-2cm of separation. Steam for 10-12 minutes, until dewy-faced and a little translucent. Convey to a serving platter. Brush the *choipan* with a little vegetable oil and sprinkle with crisp-fried garlic.

The number of noni leaves you require depends on the number of fish chunks you get. I tend to get around 10-12 parcels with this amount.

Any turmeric-golden coconut-based sauce can be used. I use the gravy for the *laksa Banjar* (page 339) but without the flaked fish.

BOTOK MENGKUDU

MAKES 12

FOR THE SPICE PASTE
300g grated coconut
1 tsp coriander seeds
½ tsp cumin seeds
25g Vietnamese mint
2 turmeric leaves, shredded
4 tbsp tamarind water (page 524)
2 tsp coconut sugar (page 524)
½ tsp salt

TO COOK
400g *ikan baung* (*Mystus*), skinned and boned weight, cut into 4cm pieces
½ tsp salt
20 medium noni leaves
Approx. 350ml *laksa Banjar* gravy (see above)

1 Begin by making the spice paste. In an oil-free pan over medium-low heat, fry the grated coconut until faintly crisp and uniformly brown, stirring constantly. This may take 15 minutes or so. Sprinkle in the coriander and cumin seeds and continue stirring, for just a minute or so, until they release their warm aromas.

2 Tip the toasted coconut and dry spices into a mortar. Pound with a pestle into a fine rubble. If your mortar is not large enough, you will need to do this in batches.

3 Add the Vietnamese mint and turmeric leaves to the mortar and pound them in, producing a deep green paste. Work in the tamarind water, coconut sugar and salt. Taste. It should be quite fiercely flavoured: herbal, smoky, astringent. Add a little more salt if you feel it needs it.

4 Place the fish chunks in a bowl and lightly sprinkle with the ½ tsp salt. Give them a light massage and set aside for just 5 minutes. Arrange a piece of fish on a noni leaf and smear on 1 tbsp of the coconut-herb paste. Wrap the seasoned fish in the leaf, as you would a gift. Then place this parcel on another leaf, sealed side down, and wrap again. Wrap all the fish pieces this way and arrange on the floor of a 22x5cm round cake tin.

5 Prepare your steamer. Once hot, lower in the tin and steam for 5 minutes. Pour over the gravy and steam for 5 more minutes, so the fish is cooked, the leaf casings are greenish black and the gravy is hot.

This delightful recipe was given to me by Chef Yudha Indra Pramanto. Any white-fleshed fish can be enlisted. I have plumped for milkfish. If you cannot get hold of small ones, a large darling, hewn into steaks, will work a dream.

TANAK LADE SAMBAS

SERVES 8

FOR THE SPICE PASTE
15g garlic cloves, peeled
25g shallots, peeled
10g ginger, peeled
10g galangal, peeled
1cm turmeric, peeled
1½ tbsp black peppercorns

TO COOK
100ml vegetable oil
2 small milkfish, each approx.
  350g, cleaned
4 tbsp water
Salt

FOR THE COCONUT SAMBAL
1 garlic clove, peeled
4 shallots, peeled
6 red bird's eye chillies
¼ tsp salt
1 tsp fermented shrimp
  paste, grilled (page 522)
2 tsp calamansi lime juice
175g grated coconut

1 Make the spice paste by pounding the necessary ingredients together with a pestle and mortar, until a smooth paste is obtained. Alternatively, grind in a cosy blender, adding a little water if necessary.

2 Heat the oil in a large, deep, frying pan over medium-high heat. Pat the cleaned fish dry and rub each one with a good pinch or two of salt. Fry the fish in the hot fat, turning over midway, for 1-2 minutes per side. You want the fish light gold. It does not matter if it is fully cooked. Remove to a plate.

3 Add a little more oil to the pan if it looks a tad dry. Once hot, add the spice paste. Fry for a minute, then lower the heat and continue cooking, stirring constantly, until it splits, deepens in colour and becomes fragrant. Return the fish to the pan. Give the pan a shake, add the water, cover and let the fish steam for 5 minutes. Remove the lid, gently turn the fish over, and continue cooking until the pan is dry and the crushed spices are clinging to the fish.

4 Transfer the fish to a serving dish and then quickly make the coconut *sambal*. Pound the garlic, shallots, chillies, salt, grilled fermented shrimp paste and calamansi lime juice into a fine balm with a pestle and mortar. Lightly crush in the grated coconut, so that it releases some of its sweet milk. Taste. It should have a nice kick to it. Serve with the fish and rice.

Some versions of *srikaya* (sometimes spelled *sarikaya*) are thin enough to be squirted and squiggled through a bottle, others so thick they need a spoon to be retrieved, like this. Many recipes contain vanilla, but I prefer pandan. I want the barest hum, which explains the brief appearance of a blade towards the end of its cooking time.

SELAI SRIKAYA

MAKES APPROX. 350G

6 duck egg yolks
125g caster sugar
Pinch of salt
200ml coconut cream
5cm pandan blade

1 Combine the duck egg yolks, sugar, salt and coconut cream in a heatproof (preferably ceramic) bowl fitted onto the mouth of an accommodating saucepan (thereby creating a double boiler). Whisk gently, just to combine.

2 Cook the pale yellow mixture over medium heat, whisking until it becomes warm. Then lower the heat and exchange the whisk for a wooden spoon. Continue cooking for about 30 minutes, stirring constantly, until a yellow substance, the thickness of pastry cream, is obtained. The thicker the mixture gets, the less frequent your stirring may be. Give the pandan leaf a good crush in your hand and drop it in. Continue cooking the *srikaya* for 5 more minutes, then remove the bowl from the pan.

3 Extract the pandan leaf and discard it. Allow the *srikaya* to cool completely before storing in a sterilised 250ml jam jar. Once open, it will keep in the fridge for up to 2 weeks.

The taro commonly used by cooks in Pontianak is called *keladi hitam*, a variety which seems to fry crisply, but dryly, therefore requiring some of it to be half-boiled and mashed into the mixture. With the regular Thai taro that we commonly get, this step can be, thankfully, skipped. Speaking of handling yams, I highly recommend wearing a glove for combining and shaping. I have had many an itch.

OU IE

MAKES 16-18

50g skinned peanuts
450g taro, peeled weight
1 tbsp cornflour flour
1 tbsp sugar
½ tsp salt
Canola oil, for deep-frying

1 Preheat the oven to 180°C. Once hot, sprinkle the peanuts in a roasting tin and toast them until golden, about 10-12 minutes. Remove from the heat, allow to cool completely, then crudely shatter them with one end of a rolling pin. Set aside.

2 Coarsely grate the taro into a large bowl. Add the cornflour, sugar and salt. Then, with a gloved hand, lightly massage until it clumps. Gently mix in the roasted peanuts. This mixture should be cohesive, like a tightly dressed slaw.

3 Heat 4cm of canola oil in a deep frying pan over medium heat. Lightly shape the grated taro into orbs, roughly the size of golfballs, and arrange on a platter. You should get 16-18. When the fat is hot but not smoking, fry the balls in batches, stirring constantly but lazily, for 5 minutes, until crisp and deep gold.

This is a lot easier than it sounds. Trust me.

PISANG GORENG PONTIANAK

MAKES 12

12 ripe *saba* bananas, each
    approx. 60g
Canola oil, for deep-frying

FOR THE COATING BATTER
100g plain flour
50g rice flour
    (*tepung beras*, page 523)
Half an egg, approx. 30g
1 tbsp sugar
¼ tsp salt
⅛ tsp baking powder
Appox. 225ml water

FOR THE CRISPY BATTER
100g tapioca starch
50g rice flour
    (*tepung beras*, page 523)
1 tbsp sugar
¼ tsp salt
Remaining half of egg
⅛ tsp baking soda
Approx. 250ml water

1 Make the 2 batters in 2 separate large bowls, adding the dry ingredients first, then whisking in the wet ingredients until well-combined and slightly airy. The coating batter should be thick as double cream, so that it will coat the fruit adequately. The crispy batter will be worryingly liquid, but fear not.

2 Peel the bananas. Make several incisions down each one, about 5mm apart, and then gently press them so they fan out. Arrange them on a work surface, poised for battering.

3 Fill a medium wok with canola oil and place over medium heat. Once hot, turn 4 fanned-out bananas in the thick batter and slip them into the fat. Give them a little stir. Once the batter sets and is on its way to acquiring some colour, which should happen in a matter of seconds, give the crispy batter a stir and lash over 1-2 ladlefuls over the bananas. They will sizzle upon impact, and the surface of the oil will be veiled in bubbles, which will dissipate to reveal a lacy network of batter wisps.

4 With a pair of tongs, divide this network into 4 territories and turn the fried bananas in them, so that each one gets cocooned. Once a joyous gold, remove the fritters to a tray lined with several sheets of kitchen towel. Fry all the bananas this way, making sure to remove any burnt bits of batter before each batch.

This is a more complex version of *es bongko*, a wonderful afternoon cooler of pandan pudding set with mung bean starch (*kue bongko*), crushed ice and coconut milk sweetened with coconut sugar and scented with pandan.

I have noticed that some *kue bongko* eat less glassily, offering a wobblier, creamier finish. I suspect these are not solely made with said mung bean starch, also known as *tepung hoen kwe*, but with rice flour too. Should you fancy something similar, make a double portion of the pandan pudding for the *lompat tikam* recipe in my previous book, *Bekwoh*, letting it set in a 17cm square tin. As stated in the glossary, some intensify the green of their pandan extract by adding several blades of *daun suji*. I do not, but if you feel like it, be my guest.

Besides the *kue bongko* and ice, there are five other components to this recipe. It involves black glutinous rice and red adzuki beans, that you will have to cook into sweet, thick, beaded balms. It includes *che hun tiau*, wiry strips of tapioca noodle, often known as tapioca *cendol*, that you only need to boil. These are admittedly challenging to find outside West Kalimantan and may be replaced with sago pearls instead. It also requires grass jelly, which you can purchase ready-made from Asian grocers with relative ease. And, finally, to bind all these disparate elements, there is coconut milk, that you need to scantily salt. And although most cooks settle for tinned paint, it has to be said that fresh milk is the best way to go here.

CHE HUN TIAU

SERVES 10-12

FOR THE RED BEANS
150g dried adzuki beans
1 litre water
1 pandan blade
75g caster sugar
Pinch of salt

FOR THE BLACK GLUTINOUS RICE
100g black glutinous rice
700ml water
1 pandan blade
75g caster sugar
Pinch of salt

FOR THE KUE BONGKO
100g mung been starch
  (*tepung hoen kwe*)
60g caster sugar
¼ tsp salt
450ml water
250ml coconut milk
4 tbsp pandan extract
  (page 522)

TO SERVE
200g tapioca cendol
  (*che hun tiau*)
100g grass jelly
1 litre coconut milk
Salt
Crushed ice

1 Begin with the red beans. Place them in a medium-sized saucepan with the 1 litre water. Bring to a boil over high heat. Continue to boil for 5 minutes, then cover, turn the heat down to its lowest setting and simmer gently for 1-1½ hours or until tender. The beans should be sitting in a shallow puddle of liquid. Add the pandan leaf, sugar and salt. Simmer for another 10 minutes, without the cover, stirring to crush some of the beans into the liquid, thickening it slightly. Turn off the heat, half-cover and leave to cool.

2 Now for the black glutinous rice. Wash the rice until the water runs clear – though it will always be purplish – then place in another medium-sized saucepan with the water. Bring to a boil, cover, lower the heat and simmer gently for about 1 hour or so, or until the grains are tender. Stir in the pandan leaf, sugar and salt. Simmer for 10 more minutes, uncovered, so it thickens slightly. Turn off the heat, half-cover and let the rice cool completely in its pot.

3 While the rice and beans cool, tend to the other components. Start with the *kue bongko* or pandan pudding. Combine the mung bean starch, sugar and salt in a medium-sized saucepan. Whisk to combine, then stir in the water and coconut milk. Place the saucepan over medium-low heat and cook, stirring, until the liquid has thickened, arriving at a flowing but viscous, custard-like, consistency. This should take no more than 5-7 minutes. Whisk in the pandan extract, simmer for just 10-15 seconds, then remove from the heat and scrape into a 17cm square cake tin. Leave to set (in a room cool enough, this takes no more than an hour) and slice into tiles.

4 Move onto the tapioca *cendol* by cooking it according to the packet's instructions, which usually involves boiling them in a large saucepan of water until mostly translucent, then straining and cooling under a cold tap. Their middles will still be white. Cut the grass jelly into 1cm cubes. Lightly salt the coconut milk and keep it nice and cold. Crush the ice into smaller chunks and return these to the freezer.

5 It seems ridiculous to instruct how to serve this, as much depends on the size of the serving bowls and appetites. Roughly speaking, I use a bowl suited to serving medium portions of noodle soup. In this, place 2 tbsp of the black glutinous rice, red beans, tapioca *cendol* and cubed grass jelly. Drown the lot in the cold coconut milk and spoon over some crushed ice. Finally, top with a tile of the *kue bongko*. You should be able to fill 10 such bowls handsomely. Even 12.

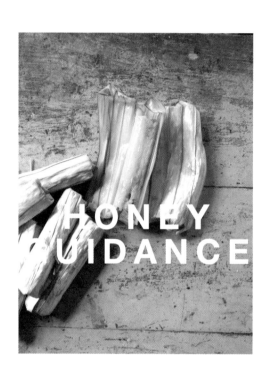

It is positively baking here in Tutong. In the longhouse where I have spent the last hour chatting with a group of Dusun gentlemen, lunch has all but just arrived. My hosts Syafien and Samhan talk me through the dishes, deftly crafted from an array of wild pickings. A salad (*punyud*) of wild bananas (*pisang tajak*), red chillies, calamansi juice and fermented shrimp paste (*belacan*). *Sayur bedudun*, a forager's braise that today presents itself as a buttery tangle of *Gnetum gnemon* leaves (*sayur bagu*), *taum* shoots and various wild mushrooms (*kulat*). An immaculate stir-fry marrying bitter rattan shoots (*umbut rotan*) and sweet, herbaceous *Helminthostachys zeylanica*. The shape of the latter's blades has resulted in some cute monikers, like *sipat manuk*, "chicken feet", and *lapak itik* "duck webs". "Those are easy to spot in the wild," Syafien says. "Their leaves are always pointing up." Indeed, the literal translation of its Malay name, *tunjuk langit*, is "pointing skywards".

The only meat dish at the table is one of braised chicken, *ayam masak rebus kunyit*. Its sauce, vicious with turmeric and politely sharp with desiccated chips of *asam aur-aur* (*kandis*; *Garcinia forbesii*), is to serve as paint for our mounds of boiled red rice. I am told that it is exceptional dribbled over triangular *lapat*, glutinous rice cakes dulcet with coconut milk, once freed from their cocoons of *palas* palm blades.

In Brunei, *masak rebus kunyit* is a treatment most commonly linked to the Kedayan, who also apply it to beef. It seems to be the most well-known Kedayan dish among the Bruneians, if not the only. The Dusun and Kedayan are two of the most predominant ethnic groups in Brunei, the others being Belait, Bisaya, Malay, Murut and Tutong. Intercultural interactions, as well as intermarriages, migrations and the phenomenon of ethnic fluidity, have made the subject of culinary identity challenging terrain. This, I have learned after four years of research, applies to much of Borneo. Today these communities share countless dishes, the overlaps in their cuisines so drastic as to mock the faintest suggestion of uniqueness. Everybody seems aware of the similarities. More than accept it, they seem to celebrate it, and no better illustration of this exists than the country's unofficial national dish, *ambuyat*, a thick, translucent glue derived from *ambulong*, the starch of rumbia palm pith, which I have seen sold in Sabah as *sagu basah*.

The traditional extraction of *ambulong* is a painstaking process. After being heaved out of its tree, rumbia pith is finely grated onto a mat fashioned from *mengkuang* leaves. Water is allowed to dash over and the moistened filings are subjected to feverish stamping beneath multiple pairs of naked feet, releasing a milky liquid that is then directed into a basin known as a *tampin*. The liquid is left to sit overnight and by the following morning the starch would have settled, setting firmly beneath a column of surfeit water that may be elegantly removed through the simple act of decanting. At this point, the *ambulong* is ready to be crumbled and used, but Syafien tells me the process is repeated to remove impurities.

To make *ambuyat*, the *ambulong* is first placed in a bowl known as a *kalumpang*. The next step is the *menumpah*, wherein scalding water is poured over and beaten in, turning the starch gloopy and translucent. Vendors of *ambulong* in markets always sell related products, including blistered wafers called *kuripit* and a chalky potpourri, like fine crumble topping, called *kubal*, that elderly Dusun folk used to take with them on long treks.

"See that?" Syafien asks, leaning over the balcony, pointing to a semi-constructed wooden shed across the weed-greened water, connected to the rest of the Alai Gayoh house by a chunky bridge of plank and rope. "We hope to demonstrate the *ambulong* extraction process there one day," he continues, tossing bits of bread into the river to satisfy a group of ravenous mudfish.

TALLOW OF TREES

Many ethnic groups in Borneo believe the mudfish or snakehead murrel to possess medicinal properties. The Bruneian Dusun are no exception, turning them into clear soups for post-partum women, believing that they will restore their health and heal their wounds. In the kitchen, this fish, known by the Dusun as *dolog*, joins the ranks of freshwater eel (*ambutan*), walking catfish (*lambutan*) and climbing perch (*puyuh*), as well as the marine false trevally (*angkutak*), as some of the tastiest fish around which to build a meal.

A favourite way of handling *dolog* is *tupung*, which involves a rub of chilli and turmeric, plush robes of banana leaf and a sojourn over wood fire. They may also be hit with salt, impaled by bamboo skewers, leafily wrapped and placed not over flames but in close proximity, against the side of the hearth (*puan*) so they are almost perpendicular to the counter. This process, called *padar*, does not just cook the fish: it helps to preserve them. "They are done when juices stop trickling down," Syafien informs me. Other traditional ways of preserving fish include salting and drying them; fermenting them in a jar (*birid*) with salt and cooked rice covered with *tarap* leaves to produce *jaruk*; and gently smoking them for a week or so on a tray (*pa'an*) suspended above the stove (*tungku*). The latter process is called *salau*, its product *mpayang*.

The latter two techniques may be applied to excess meat from a kill, especially if it involves mousedeer (*palanok*), Javan rusa (*tambang*) or the Dusun favourite, wild boar (*gromoh*), which is gradually being substituted with reared pork. Prepared with chunks of belly meat, skin and fat intact, both fermented and smoked articles are addressed as *antongol*. Trimmings of skin, especially those with inordinate amounts of fat, are transformed into scratchings (*kigis*). The Dusun have recently started treating chicken skin this way. When pickings are lean and the larder is emaciated, a leaf pouch of crushed rice (*nubur lopot*), a handful of *kigis* and a daub of *sambal* make for a sound meal.

As with many of their Bornean kin, the Bruneian Dusun have taken the ethos of "waste not, want not" into the realm of the vegetable. Several greens are made into *jeruk*, with pounded roasted rice. *Lasia spinosa* (*sayur bungar*) with its glossy, webbed leaves and thorny, succulent stalks, is particularly delicious treated this way. The Kedayan call such ferments *budu*, making them with the white pith of ripe *tibadak* (*cempedak*), razor clams (*ambal*), beansprouts and tiny river mussels (*kupang*).

The Dusun have also developed some interesting techniques to preserve fruit. They derive *kurom*, an aromatic powder from *sibut*, combining it with salt. The fruit is known in the Bandar area as *sabal*. "It is an acquired taste," Syafien admits. The Dusun produce *liking*, sun-dried *tibadak*, these days commonly made with tongues of sliced banana. They also make *luah*, durian granules, for want of a better term, the colour of dark chocolate, by cooking ripe durian flesh in an oil-free wok over the shiest of flames for a protracted period of time – usually an entire night – with constant stirring. "There is a reason why the youth will not do it", Syafien says, his tone sympathetic as he pries open a Tupperware for me to sample. While its taste remains faithful to its source, framed with notes of leather, smoke and butterscotch, its notorious aroma has been whittled down to a pleasant purr. It is its chewiness, however, that leaves the strongest impression, and I was surprised to learn that they adore it on *tumpi*, thick griddled discs of *ambulong* and grated coconut that are gelatinous when fresh and rubbery when cold.

The ingenuity and resourcefulness – not to mention patience – reflected in the making of *luah* is also visible in the extraction of *kiton*, known more commonly throughout north Borneo as *engkabang*. More condiment than preserve, *kiton*, evocatively described as "tree butter", comes from *buah kawang*, the illipe nut cluttering the canopies of *Shorea macrophylla* that flourish along river banks and on alluvial plains. Once harvested and cleaned, the nuts are thoroughly dried, first under a baking sun, then in a hot pan, before being pounded into a damp powder. This is conveyed to a basket-like device known as a *kandulan* that when wrung encourages out an oil with chemical characteristics similar to cocoa butter and a scent reminiscent of lightly warmed cashews. This elixir is then streamed into sections of hollow bamboo tube, where it hardens into a kind of pale daffodil tallow. Stowed away in a cool place, these tubes can last for years.

Using them is not as fiddly as one would think: the central marrow must be first pushed out from beneath, like a glue stick, and then rubbed against the surface of choice, be it a hot pan for cooking or a mound of freshly cooked rice for aromatic enrichment. There is supposedly another variety of *engkabang*, derived from a shorter tree with smaller fruit, with a greenish tint and a fuller, more zaftig, flavour. This, sadly, almost never makes it to the marketplace.

Besides serving as protection, the cardboard-stiff petals surrounding the illipe nut afford it the silhouette of a shuttlecock, enabling it to dance on the breeze and drift on the water. The unprocessed nuts, simply boiled, are said to be toothsome nibbled alongside bowls of *sambal* or fermented durian (*tempoyak*). It is not just humans who are in on this delectable secret: the majestic *empurau* has a reputation for being quite the *kawang* connoisseur – it is supposedly these nuts that impart a velvety oiliness to the fish's flesh. This prized trait, combined with its increasing elusiveness, has sent *Tor tambroides* prices through the roof.

"Take a rest. Coffee will be on its way soon", Samha instructs before heading into the kitchen to check on things. I give the notebook a rest and move closer to the water, drinking the jungle in all its verdant splendour, with some restless honeyguides and emerald doves for company, feeling atrociously spoiled.

IT CAME FROM THE WATER

The past week in Brunei has been exceptionally fruitful. I got to share boat space with a fisherman down in the nipa-rich mangroves of Temburong where he hoisted up pots of large, blue-clawed shrimp (*udang galah*). While most enjoy these majestic creatures boiled, peeled and jolted with lime juice, a group of special individuals have decided that an afterlife as burger patties would suit them best. A bevy of Kedayan ladies, also in Temburong, gave me a tutorial on the local *wajid*, made not with glutinous rice but *padi jawa*, a kind of millet, and not with coconut sugar but regular white sugar caramelised in coconut milk. Auroral visits to the *tamu* dotting the country revealed to me a world of fresh discoveries. *Kelimpanas* that is burnt to fend off bad spirits. Wiry roots called *pelibas kuning* that are believed to cure food poisoning. Waxen, pink-flushed blades of *mambangan* leaf that have remarkable chemistry with shallots, chillies and pounded dried shrimp. Leathery and bone-hard mangrove apples, whose sourness and palate-aggravating astringency make them the ideal candidates for an unusual *sambal*.

Known more commonly in Malaysia as *buah pedada*, mangrove apples are a rare find these days. But when I chanced upon a fruited tree in Kampong Ayer a few days earlier, I knew that Lady Luck was shining down on me. Whether it is their star-cut sepals or Pinocchio-inspired antennae, there is something otherworldly, mischievous, about this fruit. Pamela Isley would have approved of its design. As they bounced on their stalks in the breeze, I found their colour, an olive shade of green, to be the perfect foil against the orange-pink shrimp wafers (*keropok*) set out to sun nearby, their baskets arranged along a series of wooden planks not two metres above dashing water.

Kampong Ayer was historically the *de facto* capital of Brunei. Scholar and explorer Antonio Pigafetta, who joined the Magellan-led expedition to the Spice Islands, famously described it as being "entirely built in salt water", containing "twenty-five thousand hearths" with the houses "all constructed of wood and built up from the ground on tall pillars." Allegedly thought of then as a Venice of the East, it was only in 1906 that its main inhabitants, the Bruneian Malays, moved in earnest onto land. The Chinese merchants who existed among them, in a much smaller number, followed suit.

Much of what we know of Brunei prior to the arrival of the Spanish in the early 16th century is by and large the fruit of detective work. The consensus is that Brunei was most likely the "Bo-ni" or "Po-ni" mentioned in Chinese historical records, described as being "equidistant from Champa and Mindoro"; "humid and undulating; comprising a group of fourteen geo-administrative lands"; "a place where people buried their dead in surrounding hills". It is also agreed upon that it was active in trade. The *Universal Geography of the Taiping Era* mentions sending a first emissary from Bo-ni in 977, with gifts to the emperor of camphor, tortoiseshell, sandalwood and elephant tusks carried by a Sino-Muslim ship. The Chinese also stated that it was being Islamised around the 15th century, due to increased contact with Muslim Arab traders sailing in from Quanzhou, a city on the southeastern coast of China that was once one of the most important ports along one of the historic Maritime Silk Roads.

It was Brunei's geographical location that led it to prosper. In its Golden Age, it lay at the intersection of four maritime routes, used by both pirates (Javanese, Malays, Cham, Acehnese, etc.) and merchants. It is said that two to four junks sailed between Brunei and Malacca exchanging camphor, gold, rice, sago, wax and pearls, among other things, in exchange for Indian cotton fabrics and glass beads. Notwithstanding the prohibitions at the time, Brunei continued to be frequented by ships from Southern China during the Ming Dynasty, as mentioned in several route charts from the 15th and 16th centuries reprinted in the *Shun Feng Xiang Sun*. Pigafetta spoke of the luxury he and his companions encountered in Brunei, then under the reign of Sultan Abdul Kahar, the humblest of which included a warm welcome of live music, flying peacock feathers and a *prahu* decorated with gold leaf and great gifts of betel, food and cloth.

Brunei also traded with Siam, Patani, Champa and the Burmese coasts. It was a stop on the Northern route from Malacca to both Manila and the Moluccas and was included on the route charts of Arab navigators. Interactions with the Muslim world via these traders may have influenced the design of brassware, such as voluptuous *kuron* for cooking rice and *lanjang* for making braises and soups, once popular among affluent Dusuns. These traders were also once responsible for the occasional availability of spices in the area, in particular clove and nutmeg, and they may have inspired the manners in which they are applied to foods today, especially sweetmeats. These include *biraksa*, a steamed, halva-like pudding, laced with cumin, coriander, cinnamon and fennel; *koya*, sun-baked tablets of sweetened ground rice, cumin, coriander and fennel; and the medicinal and medicative *madu kesirat*, a sweetmeat of ground rice, coconut sugar and pounded roasted coconut, febrile with fennel, cumin, coriander, cardamom, clove, pepper, lemongrass and galangal. After being cooked into a supple, chocolaty dough, the mixture is clapped between the large teeth of an *acuan* into dainty lozenges. Fleshed out from *kapur* (or *kapor*) wood and looking at home in a carpenter's tool box, the mould was expressly designed for this purpose.

Interestingly, the circular portion of the traditional mould used for shaping *koya* is known as *pitis*. Although it does not appear to exist in Malay or Indonesian vocabularies, in Tagalog this word means "snugly fitting", as for apparel. Is this pure coincidence? The same may be asked of the relationship between *belutak*, the sun-dried Bruneian beef sausage and the similar-sounding *balotac*, the Tagalog synonym for *longaniza* dating as far back as the early 17th century.

Brunei's position in Southeast Asia has also gifted it with numerous culinary concepts that have been circulating the region for centuries, even millenia. The lack of records and abundance of analogues have made the tracing of their histories a pretty ghastly task. Up till this day, most of their roots remain a mystery, the widely accepted backstories urban legends. One is the aforementioned fermentation of meat, fish and vegetables using salt and roasted or cooked rice, though many seem to credit the Chinese with this. (It is true that the *kawai* regularly used to roast the rice and cook the fermented articles most certainly has Chinese origins.)

Another is the concept of *kueh* and the consensus is that the first of their ilk in Brunei were prepared by the Malay community in Kampong Ayer. There are several *kueh* that seem unique to Brunei, though this could possibly be due to them becoming elusive or extinct everywhere else. *Ampung* are cylindrical, turmeric-tinted, glutinous rice parcels filled with sweetened coconut. *Cakul* are steamed, pumice-like, patties of sugar, freshly ground rice and grated coconut, while *sakul* are griddled discs of sago starch, coconut and dried shrimp. *Kulat* are fried biscuits of wheat flour, sugar and coconut milk, named for the way they resemble mushroom caps, while *roti* are baked, serrated-edged, tiles made with wheat flour, sugar, coconut milk and aerated eggs. *Kuripit* are crisp discs of sago starch, sugar and coconut, their surfaces anointed with slaked lime (*air kapur*) before their quick session over hot embers. *Panganan cincin* distinguish themselves from regular *cincin* with a cloak of batter made from ground rice, turmeric and slaked lime. *Seri rupa* is a steamed two-tier wonder set in cubist boats of nipa blade (*katilapan*), a quaking coconut pudding set atop one of coconut sugar and *air kapur*.

Another ubiquitous concept is that of the portable meal. Every country in Southeast Asia has some kind of leaf-wrapped, rice-based meal, designed for brisk, often ambulant, consumption. In the case of Brunei, it is *nasi katok*, a banana leaf parcel of boiled white rice and *sambal* that was prior to the 1980s known as *nasi bungkus* – "wrapped rice". Its present name was derived from its popularity among those working the night shift in Kampong Ayer, who had to knock on the doors of *bungkus* vendors in order to receive their evening meal. *Katok*, in Bruneian Malay, means "knock".

THANKSGIVING AND A CROCODILE

The following afternoon, I find myself at the Eco Ponies Homestay, in the warm and bright company of owner Eyon Ukoi. Of Dusun blood, Eyon knows her *piyay* from her *lemiding*. As she takes me on a guided tour of her estate on the fringes of a jungle, she snaps fruit off stalks and tender leaves off stems, bringing my attention to their culinary potential. She harvests *kulimpapa* shoots (*Vitex pinnata*), traditionally used to treat jaundice, dysentery and stomach diseases. Her mother used to eat these with shallots and tinned sardines. "Those tins have been around for over a century," she says, noticing my furrowed brow.

She picks some broad, waxy leaves of *natol bubur* that darkly green and thicken broths of slivered bamboo shoot, and a couple of guava-like *buah sulang* that is occasionally used to impart a striking canary colour to *Phrynium* parcels of glutinous rice cake (*kelupis*). "You do not use the flesh but its seeds," she enlightens me, gingerly slicing one open for me to behold with gloved hands. The fruit's interiors, from its core of small, loose seeds to its chalky, densely woven flesh, is smartingly vermillion, boldly contrasting against its uninspiring pale jade skin. The absurdly hued elixir produced by mixing some of its seeds into water may be used to tint whatever dish one fancies, as long as it does not involve chicken – the combination is believed to be

toxic.

As we amble back towards the kitchen, Eyon mentions other noteworthy botanicals. Turmeric blossoms (*bunga kunyit*) and the tender leaves of *tambilikan* that make superb *ulam*. *Pawas* (*Litsea elliptica*) that is also eaten as *ulam* and used to treat fevers and stomach ulcers. *Lamba* (*Eleutherine palmifolia*), sometimes called *bawang jabu*, a red-skinned, shallot-like allium with foliage as rigid as paper fasteners, that are said to be good in soups. *Telur tebu* (*Saccharum edule*), the roe-like fruit from a plant that grows near the river, named for its resemblance to sugarcane. *Umbut bangkala* from deep within the jungle. The leaves of *batat*, ovalish yellow cucumbers grown by paddy farmers in the mountain terraces while they wait for their harvests to be ripe and ready. Mildly sour, these leaves are wonderful fried, quite simply, with garlic and dried anchovies.

On handing her gleanings to head cook Fatimah to manage, Eyon runs me through the menu for the day. Besides the *kulimpapa* and *kelupis sulang*, there is a stir-fry of common purslane (*gelang pasir*; *Portulaca oleracea*), its leaves, tasting of pea shoots, believed to promote lactation in mothers; succulent *ginjir* (*Limnocharis flava*) fried with fermented soy beans (*taucheo*); mangrove red snapper (*ikan berahan*) cooked in a soup of turmeric, *terung Iban* and Vietnamese mint; and *nasi sumboi-sumboi*, glutinous rice cooked with coconut milk in pitcher plants, zaftig, maroon and thick-lipped. Certain species of *Nepenthes* are sadly on the verge of becoming endangered.

While lunch is being tended to, Eyon leads me to another section of the farm to witness *ngal amping*, the making of *amping*, which she describes as "rice oatmeal". Although several species of glutinous rice may be used, today Eyon has plumped for *pandan pulot*, named for the perfume released as the grains sweetly cook.

Ngal amping begins with recently picked rice. This particular batch was harvested not five days earlier and was put out to sun for a day before being boiled to soften the grains sightly. They were then sunned one more time. Puan Sikat Dungok, a seasoned *amping* maker, lights a small fire beneath a large wok and flings in the sunned grains, pushing them around until nuttily aromatic, which takes a solid twenty minutes. "They are ready when they *malaput*". *Malaput* means "pop". The grains, hot and burnished, are then conveyed in batches to a huge pestle and mortar (*lasong*) of *kulimpapa* wood where they receive a good pummelling. This step separates the troublesome chaff from the grains, which a brief, fan-assisted winnowing session efficiently removes.

Puan Sikat Dungok proudly presents me with the basket, bearing a collection of grains, warmly fragrant and lightly bruised. The *amping* is ready to be kept in jars where it will last for months. Eyon highly recommends dousing bowls with coconut water, which softens and sweetens them slightly, and eating them like oatmeal. This, she tells me, will be our dessert later.

For the Dusun, *amping* provides more than pleasure or sustenance, carrying with it cultural significance. It is an essential component of *Acara Melepaskan Niat*. During this ritual, an individual serves the *amping*, along with other foods, to a (usually small) group of attendees as a way of demonstrating gratitude and integrity to the powers that be for having their wishes granted. It can also serve as a component, albeit a non-mandatory one, on ceremonial platters (*dulang*) for thanksgiving rituals known as *tamarok*, which have in recent decades been curbed by Islamic authorities in the country.

There are several kinds of *tamarok*. There are small ones, such as those conducted to celebrate an individual's recovery from illness, and large ones, like the *tamarok gayo*, held at the end of paddy harvest season. The ritual is always held in the evenings, around dinner time, as this is when the *derato*, supernatural beings in the *pagun sawat* or upper world, are believed to be awake. Behind closed doors, on the floor of the largest room in the selected house, new rice is used to form the shape of a crocodile, with candle light as the sole source of illumination. The size of the crocodile hinges on the magnitude of the propitiation. Eyon shares that an especially lavish *tamarok* may have a reptile formed with up to a hundred gallons (*gantang*) of rice. A pair of hardboiled eggs will serve as eyes, clusters of ambrosial Lady Finger bananas (*pisang mas*) or *pisang nambak* teeth and feet. The *dulang* are then artfully arranged around the beast's tail. Besides *amping*, these trays must each contain seven *tabo'oh* or *ketupat*, four shaped like hens, three like roosters; a bunch of the aforesaid bananas; and a small plate (*suwek*) holding seven pieces of *taji*, dumplings of ground rice and crushed bananas, again those used on other parts of the crocodile, cooked in heat-split coconut milk.

To the beating of gongs (*canang*) and drums (*dombak* and *gendang*), a group of women known as *belian*, dressed in black blouses, red skirts and headbands (*asyik*), would then dance around the reptile in a state of trance. "This is best done in a concrete house," Eyon tells me. "A wooden one could collapse." The percussions have to be steady and continual, as the women are to continue moving in their altered state into the depths of night. Before *tamarok* was outlawed, entire villages would gather and take turns with the drum work, lest the performance is interrupted, the spirits possibly displeased.

The following morning, the crocodile would be dismantled, the tray-borne food consumed.

The *buah pedada* or mangrove apple, with its firm, fig-like interiors, adds sourness and a faint, cheese-like aroma to this refreshing, crunchy number.

KERABU POKOK PAKU KUBUK

SERVES 4

2 tbsp dried shrimp, washed
   and toasted (page 521)
1 garlic clove, peeled
2 shallots, thinly sliced
4 red bird's eye chillies, sliced
2 tsp fermented shrimp paste, grilled
   (page 522)
1 mangrove apple, peeled
   and chopped
Juice of 4 calamansi limes
250g young creeping sword
   fern, trimmed
Salt, to taste

1 Pound the toasted dried shrimp with a pestle and mortar into floss. Work in the garlic, shallots, chillies and fermented shrimp paste. Pound in the mangrove apple and lime juice. You should get a nubbly but cohesive and moist paste.

2 Blanch the trimmed fern in lightly salted water until tender-crisp. Drain, rinse under a cold tap and gently squeeze to remove excess water. Then pop them into a bowl and mix in the pounded ingredients. Taste and adjust seasoning with salt.

It was at an *ambuyat* restaurant in Brunei that I detected the use of *sambal mambagan* in their version of Asiatic pennywort salad. Even in its absence, this will still be lovely.

KERABU PEGAGA

SERVES 4

1 tsp fermented shrimp paste,
   grilled (page 522)
1 tbsp lime juice
1 tbsp *sambal mambangan*
   (page 495)
Pinch of sugar
150g Asiatic pennywort leaves,
   shredded
3 shallots, thinly sliced
2 red chillies, deseeded and
   finely sliced
Salt, to taste

1 In a medium-sized bowl, dissolve the fermented shrimp paste in the lime juice. Stir in the *sambal mambangan* and sugar. Finally, toss in the pennywort, shallots and chillies. Taste and adjust seasoning with salt. Serve at once.

The *kulimpapa* leaves are not incredibly aromatic but have a delightful, mildly tart, flavour, with notes of tropical citrus and unripe peppercorns.

ULAM KULIMPAPA NAA SARDIN

SERVES 4

1 x 250g tinned sardines in
   tomato sauce
1 garlic clove, finely minced
4 shallots, finely sliced
2 red chillies, finely sliced
Juice of 2 calamansi limes
A handful of young *kulimpapa* leaves
Salt, to taste

1 Tip the sardines into a bowl and break them up with a fork or your fingers. Add the garlic, shallots, red chillies and calamansi juice. Tear in the *kulimpapa* leaves and stir to combine. Taste and adjust seasonings with salt.

Young, tender, waxy tongues of *mambangan* leaves, some pale green, others flushed pink, are the only ones to be contemplated. (They are probably the only ones ever found in markets.) With a taste reminiscent of green mangoes, they are the perfect foil for the dried shrimp filling, brimming with umami and red spice.

ULAM MAMBANGAN

SERVES 4

100g dried shrimp (page 521)
2 tbsp vegetable oil
4 shallots, peeled and finely chopped
4 bird's eye chillies, finely sliced
1 tbsp calamansi lime juice
½ tsp light brown sugar
¼ tsp salt, plus more to taste
A handful of young *mambangan* leaves

1 Begin with the filling. Soak the dried shrimp in a bowl of water for 5 minutes to remove excess salt. Drain, dry thoroughly and pound into a floss with a pestle and mortar. Tip out into a bowl. You may use a cosy blender instead, if you prefer.

2 Heat the vegetable oil in a large frying pan over medium-low heat. Add the pulverised dried shrimp and fry, stirring, until fragrant and light gold. This will take about 5-7 minutes.

3 Transfer the fried dried shrimp to a bowl. Cool slightly, then mix in shallots, bird's eye the chillies, calamansi juice, light brown sugar and salt. Taste and adjust seasonings, then serve with the young *mambangan* leaves.

In West and Northern Borneo, torch ginger, with citrussy undertones and an appetising astringency, is regarded more than an aromatic but also a vegetable in its own right. Bruneians make it into a salad or *sambal*, often in the company of green mango and poached shrimp. (In Brunei the Dusun, Bisaya and Kedayan use the word *sambal* to refer to what the West would call salads. Unlike the Malays, they do not use the word *kerabu*.) They also stir-fry it with pounded dried shrimp or fermented shrimp paste for much desired umami. For this recipe, I have plumped for the latter, also adding a modest handful of small, pale jade, chillies that locals have poetically named *lada susu*, "milk chillies".

In markets, one will find two kinds of torch ginger inflorescences, tone notwithstanding: those as voluptuous as minarets and those slim as parasols. The first sort, comprising fine, tender bracts and fine buds, are easily dismantled. The second, comprising wide bracts interspersed with the odd bud, tends to be more fibrous and has to be thinly sliced. Although I have used the former in the photograph, it is the latter that I shall assume you shall be using as it is more widely available.

SAYUR BUNGA KANTAN

SERVES 6

6 torch ginger buds, approx. 200g
150g small shrimp
3 tbsp vegetable oil
4 garlic cloves, finely chopped
5 shallots, finely sliced
1 tsp fermented shrimp paste, grilled
  (page 522)
50g small white chillies
½ tsp salt, plus more to taste
4 tbsp chicken stock

1 Trim the bases off the torch ginger buds, slice them thinly and set them aside. Peel the shrimps, leaving their tails intact, then devein them and set them aside as well.

2 Heat the oil in a large saucepan over medium heat. Once hot, add the chopped garlic and shallots and fry until lightly coloured and fragrant.

3 Add the grilled fermented shrimp paste, crushing it in with your frying implement until it intensifies in aroma.

4 Stir in the prepared shrimp. Once they curl up and turn slightly opaque, add the torch ginger, white chillies and salt. Fry for 2 minutes, then pour in the chicken stock and continue cooking until the torch ginger is tender. Taste and adjust seasoning with salt.

Almost any kind of vegetable, fruit and fungi works in this gatherer's dish. I have used *tunjuk langit* (*Helminthostachys zeylanica*), *sayur bagu* (*Gnetum gnemon*) and enoki mushrooms. Bamboo shoots, peeled, sliced and boiled first to rid them of bitterness, are a fine addition, as are shaved corn kernels.

Some versions of *sayur bedudun* include coconut milk.

SAYUR BEDUDUN

SERVES 4

700ml dried anchovy stock (page 520)
1 garlic clove, peeled and crushed
2 shallots, peeled and finely sliced
350g *Helminthostachys zeylanica* leaves, roughly chopped
200g *sayur bagu* leaves, roughly chopped
200g enoki mushrooms, tough bases trimmed
Salt, to season

1 Bring the stock to a boil in a saucepan over medium heat. Add the garlic and shallots, cover, lower the heat and simmer for 5 minutes. Pile in the prepared vegetables, cover and cook until the vegetables are tender. Taste and seasoning with salt.

As its title suggests, this dish is boiled into life, which makes for something easy on the nerves and palate. For something more rounded and emphatically spiced, grind the spices without (or with very little) water into a smooth paste then fry it in 5-6 tbsp vegetable oil until it splits and deepens in colour. Add the lemongrass and chicken, cover and leave to steam for 10 minutes over a low heat. Then add the remaining ingredients and cook for 40 minutes or so until the chicken is tender.

Masak rebus kunyit is recognised as a Kedayan preparation that may also be made with beef and fish. Shrimp may be used but without the aromatic roots and rhizome. The finished article is known as *rebus putih*. I once asked a Kedayan cook if vegetables may be added and her eyes told me everything before her lips could so much as part. They said: absolutely *not*.

I sometimes make a fish version of this by replacing chicken with 750g cleaned *ikan rumahan*, chub mackerel. Add it with the *asam aur-aur* and cook it for just 5-7 minutes.

AYAM MASAK REBUS KUNYIT

SERVES 6-8

20g shallots, peeled
3 garlic cloves, peeled
15g galangal, peeled
15g ginger, peeled
5g turmeric, peeled
3 red chillies, sliced
½ tsp fermented shrimp paste, grilled (page 523)

750ml water
2 lemongrass stalks, bruised
1 tsp salt
2 tsp sugar
1½kg free-range chicken, cut into eighths
8 dried *Garcinia forbesii*

1 Blend the shallots, garlic, galangal, ginger, turmeric, chillies and grilled fermented shrimp paste with the 750ml water, producing a smooth, deep orange liquid. Pour this into a large saucepan and place over medium-high heat. Once it boils, add the lemongrass, salt and sugar. Lower the heat, cover and simmer for 20 minutes.

2 Stir in the chicken pieces and *Garcina forbesii*. Cover and continue simmering gently for 40-45 minutes or until the chicken is tender. Taste and adjust seasoning with salt and sugar. If you prefer your sauce a bit thicker, then uncover, raise the heat and bubble away for 5 minutes or so.

Nobody knows the origins of *belutak* but everybody agrees it is ancient. From a correspondence with Philippine Food Historian Felice Prudente Sta. Maria, the word may be related to *balotac*, the Tagalog term for sausage as far back as 1609, predating the Hispanic *longaniza*. While it was once the flesh, fat and intestines of the carabao that were used, these days it is cattle that does the job. Some of the country's top *belutak* producers have intimated a preference for topside and blade. After being hewn into pieces and mixed with fat, also cut into similarly robust dimensions, the meat is seasoned with salt and sugar, often chilli and garlic, fed into casings, manipulated into knotted serpents and dried for several days under a hot sun. These days prominent *belutak* manufacturers consult dehydrators. Some cottage industries smoke theirs.

Belutak is simply cooked, snipped into a pan with garlic, onion, chillies and water and simmered until the liquid has evaporated, the meat is tender and the fat has rendered down. Tomatoes are sometimes added. It may be added to fried rice, too. This recipe, which combines it with yam stalks and coconut milk, was given to me by Eyon Ukoi of Eco Pony Homestay. It is quite sensational. One word of caution, though: use *belutak* that is not too sugary, though exuberant with garlic and chilli. If you can get them smoked, so much the better.

BELUTAK MASAK LEMAK

SERVES 6-8

FOR THE SPICE PASTE
2 garlic cloves, peeled
20g shallots, peeled
20g galangal, peeled
1 red chilli, sliced
2 bird's eye chillies

TO FINISH
5 tbsp vegetable oil
250g *belutak*, cut into 1cm rounds
1½ tsp salt
600ml coconut milk
 (second extract, page 521)
250g young taro stalks, cut into
 10cm lengths
100ml coconut cream

1 Pound the ingredients for the spice paste with a pestle and mortar until fine and smooth. Alternatively, grind them in a cosy blender with a tiny bit of water if necessary.

2 Heat the vegetable oil in a medium frying pan over medium-high heat. Add the spice paste. Fry for a minute, stirring to prevent burning, then lower the heat and continue frying until aromatic, deeper in hue, and it has just begun to split from the oil.

3 Add the *belutak* and salt. Turn the heat to its lowest setting and fry for 10 minutes to help its fat render down. Pour in the coconut milk, cover and simmer for 30 minutes or until the meat is tender.

4 Meanwhile, blanch the yam stalks in a saucepan of boiling water until tender. Drain and rinse under a cold tap. Massage with a little salt, leave for 5 minutes, then rinse and squeeze to remove excess water. Add these to the pot and simmer for 5 minutes. Add the coconut cream and cook for a final 5 minutes. Taste and adjust seasoning with salt.

In Borneo, making *ambuyat* is simple, straightforward. The *ambulong* simply needs to be put in a sturdy bowl, thinned with regular water to the consistency of cream and have boiling water beaten into it. As *ambulong* is unavailable where I am, this recipe uses sago flour that is first hydrated.

Ambuyat with the odd streak of white is a common sight. Such servings, however, tend to wrap inelegantly and brittly around the bamboo *chandas*, the customary eating implement for the jellified starch. I prefer my *ambuyat* more gluey and elastic and so heat it up in a double boiler, stirring until all the white has been vanquished and the mixture loses even more opacity.

The *ambuyat* in the photograph (page 493) is served with *ikan masak rebus kunyit* (page 485), *belutak tumis* (fried with onions, chilli and tomatoes), *belutak masak lemak* (page 487), *kerabu pegaga* (page 477), *sambal tahai* (page 494), *sambal mambangan tempoyak* (page 495) and *hati buyah* (page 491). There is a local Bruneian saying to the effect of "those who think of *ambuyat* must eat it", the implication being that something unpleasant may otherwise occur. If you have made it this far down the page, I highly recommend getting on with it.

AMBUYAT

SERVES 8

400g sago flour
500ml water
600ml boiling water

1 Combine the sago flour and water in a sturdy bowl. Stir until you get a thick, viscous paste that seems caught somewhere in between solid and liquid. Cover and leave overnight or for at least 12 hours.

2 The following day, you will find the sago flour to have solidly settled at the bottom of the bowl, serenely veiled by a thin layer of water. Create some disturbance with a wooden spoon, stirring until you get a smooth white liquid. This will require a modicum of elbow grease and around 2-3 minutes of your time.

3 Pour the boiling water straight into the bowl, stirring all the while. Whatever starch that has come into contact with this vicious heat will be stunned translucent. Once all the water is in, beat the mixture feverishly so that you get a thick, smooth, translucent goo. There may be the odd streak of white. Convey this to a double boiler, stirring, until all the white has been removed and the mixture gets more translucent.

Numerous versions of this exist, varying in spices and the number of frying processes – some like them extra crisp. Some cooks also add a sluicing of *kecap manis*, which adds treacly sweetness and an inky colour.

If you have deep-fried your lungs in advance and discovered they have gone cold at serving time, there is a way to resuscitate them: warm some sliced yellow onion and red chilli in a tiny bit of oil in a pan, just to vaguely soften them, then add the lungs. Fry them for 2-3 minutes, just to reheat.

HATI BUYAH

SERVES 8

350g cow lungs	FOR THE SPICE PASTE
2cm ginger, crushed	2 garlic cloves, peeled
1 tsp salt	30g red onion, peeled and sliced
½ tsp sugar	40g galangal, peeled and sliced
Vegetable oil for frying and	10g ginger, peeled and sliced
deep-frying	5g turmeric, peeled
	1 red chilli, sliced

1 Cut the lungs into 8cm chunks or thereabouts. Place in a bowl and rinse several times until the water is only slightly reddish. Drain well.

2 Bring a medium-sized saucepan of water to a boil, then lightly season with salt (not the 1 tsp listed) and drop in the crushed ginger. Add the washed lungs, cover, lower the heat and simmer until just tender, which usually takes about an hour or so.

3 Meanwhile, make the spice paste by either crushing the ingredients with a pestle and mortar or grinding them in a cosy blender with a teeny bit of water to help them along.

4 Drain the lungs. Let them cool before cutting into ½cm slices. Heat 4 tbsp of vegetable oil in a deep frying pan or wok over medium-high heat. Once hot, add the spice paste. Fry for 30 seconds, stirring, then lower the heat and continue cooking until it deepens in colour and becomes aromatic. Add the 1 tsp salt, sugar and the sliced lung. Cook for just a minute then turn off the heat completely. At this point I let the lungs cool and leave them to marinate in the fridge overnight, but an hour at room temperature should suffice.

5 Remove the lungs from the cold and give them a stir. Heat 4cm of vegetable oil in a deep frying pan or wok (the same used earlier, possibly) over medium-high heat. Once hot, but not smoking, fry the lungs in batches until crusty and dark brown. They swell magnificently as this happens, which is very satisfying to behold (though they will deflate after). Drain them on kitchen towel and serve as fresh as possible.

Tahai is made from juvenile *ikan tamban*, silver-stripe round herring, commonly caught in the waters off Lawas in Sarawak. The fish is cleaned, salted and smoked over fires kindled by *bakau* wood (*Rhizophora*) for 2 days, getting turned over several times. The barky, coppered fish keep quite happily in a dry, cool place for several months.

Tahai is either sold whole or as skinned shards. I use the latter for this *sambal*. Round herring is by nature fraught with the most impossible bones, so just focus on removing the central ones and any visible pins that you reckon will cast a pall over the consumer.

SAMBAL TAHAI

SERVES 6-8

FOR THE SPICE PASTE
3 garlic cloves, peeled
100g shallots, peeled
50g red chillies, sliced
6 large dried red chillies,
   softened
2 candlenuts

TO FINISH
100ml vegetable oil
100g *tahai*, flaked and
   deboned (see above)
¾ tsp salt
1 tbsp sugar
2 tbsp tamarind water (page 524)

1 Crush the ingredients for the spice paste with a pestle or mortar until fine and smooth. Alternatively, grind them in a cosy blender with a tiny bit of water to help them along if necessary.

2 Heat the oil in a large saucepan over medium heat. Once hot, add the spice paste and fry for a minute, stirring. Lower the heat and continue frying until it turns a deep red and begins to split from the oil.

3 Add the flaked *tahai*, salt and sugar and continue frying for 10 minutes or until the spice paste, thick and brick red, clings to the shards of dried smoked fish. Finally add the tamarind water, fry for 2-3 minutes, just until it is absorbed by the *sambal*. Remove from the heat. Taste and adjust seasoning with salt and sugar.

The smooth ivory flesh beneath the russet skin of *Mangifera caesia* (also *kemanga*), known in Sabah, Sarawak and Brunei as *belunu*, and West Malaysia as *binjai*, may replace the *mambangan*. This makes a chunky *sambal*, so put less of the fruit's fibrous flesh for something more liquid. For *sambal mambangan tempoyak*, add a dollop of fermented durian (page 75).

SAMBAL MAMBANGAN

MAKES APPROX. 200G

1 *mambangan*, approx. 300g
50g red chillies, sliced
6 red bird's eye chillies
1 tsp fermented shrimp paste, grilled
  (page 522)
¼ tsp salt
½ tsp sugar
2 tbsp tamarind water (page 524)

1 Free the *mambangan* flesh from its skin as described on page 156 (where it is referred to as *bambangan*), slicing its flesh into small pieces. Do not worry about exact dimensions.

2 Crush the 2 kinds of chilli into a fine paste with a pestle and mortar, then work in the fermented shrimp paste. Mix in the salt, sugar and tamarind water and thump in the *mambangan* flesh, to release its juice. Taste and adjust seasoning with more salt and sugar.

One of the most spectacular *belacan* I have had came from Kampong Batu Marang. After being harvested from the river, the *Acetes* are cleaned, mixed with salt and fermented for 1-2 days, then drained and sunned for 4 hours before being ground into a greyish pink mortar and shaped into patties. Many *belacan* manufacturers in the area also sell *ikan liking*, most commonly made with shortnose gizzard shad (*kuasi*), feverishly scoring the bony fish, marinating them with salt and tamarind and drying them out slightly for night or so, depending on the weather. A pan of gently simmering oil sends them off onto another plane.

SAMBAL BELACAN / TERASI

MAKES APPROX. 90G

50g red chillies, sliced
8 red bird's eye chillies
1 tbsp fermented shrimp paste, grilled
  (page 522)
¼ tsp salt, plus more to taste
½ tsp sugar, plus more to taste
1 tbsp calamansi juice, plus more to taste

1 Crush the 2 kinds of chilli into a fine paste with a pestle and mortar, then work in the fermented shrimp paste. Work in the salt, sugar and calamansi lime juice, then taste, adding more of each to suit your fancy.

This is a fairly recent addition to Brunei's culinary sphere. It is a fine way of using up leftover *ambuyat* that has solidified into a quivering mound. And while *ambuyat* may not be everyone's cup of tea – this is even true for Bruneians – I have not met a single soul who does not enjoy this.

This recipe is a conflation of several I have found online. I have made a couple of adjustments. I add fish sauce, for an injection of putrid umami, and pickled radish, (*chye poh*) as I lacked the requisite chicken when I first made it. A blessing in disguise.

AMBUYAT GORENG

SERVES 2

250g *ambuyat* (page 490)
2 tsp fish sauce
2 tsp sweet soy sauce (*kecap*)
2 tsp light soy sauce
2 tsp dark soy sauce
1 tbsp garlic-chilli sauce
2 tbsp pickled radish (*chye poh*),
   finely chopped
2 tbsp vegetable oil
2 garlic cloves, finely chopped
25g garlic chives, cut into 2cm sections
30g beansprouts
Salt

1 Cut the *ambuyat* into approx. 2cm pieces with a sharp and lightly oiled knife. Gently pull them apart and arrange them on a lightly oiled tray.

2 Combine all the five sauces in a little bowl or jug and mix well. Soak the pickled radish in a bowl of water for 5 minutes to remove excess salt, then drain thoroughly, squeezing well. Spread it out over a sheet of kitchen towel to dry.

3 Place a medium-sized saucepan or wok over medium-high heat. Add the pickled radish and chase it around the wok, until dry and on the cusp of being scorched.

4 Add the vegetable oil, which will heat up immediately, followed by the garlic. Stir until the garlic is fragrant and light brown, then pour in the combined sauces. The liquid will bubble up at once, so add the sliced *ambuyat* and fry, shaking the pan and stirring all the while, until all of the liquid has been absorbed. Fling in the garlic chives and beansprouts. Stir for just several more seconds, then take off the heat. Taste and adjust seasoning with salt.

Preserving raw ingredients such as meat, fish and vegetables with salt and pounded roasted rice is common throughout Borneo.

Before using, the prickly *bungar*, *Lasia spinosa*, has to be treated to remove irritation-causing hydrocyanic acid and calcium oxalate. There are a couple of techniques. One is to cut it up, blanch it in salted water and drain thoroughly. Another is to massage it vigorously with salt and then rinse it with water – not so great for people with sensitive skin. Yet another is to only use the very young, tender shoots. For this ferment, I have used the first method.

JERUK BUNGAR

MAKES APPROX. 250G

250g *Lasia spinosa*
50g jasmine rice
2 tsp sea salt flakes

1 Bring a medium saucepan of lightly salted water to a boil. Trim away any tough portions of stalk from the *Lasia spinosa*, then cut the healthy portions into 7cm sections. Blanch them in the boiling water for just 2-4 minutes, or until tender crisp. Drain thoroughly and rinse under a cold tap. Give the blanched vegetables a brief squeeze – they should be safe to handle now – and place in a bowl.

2 Wash the jasmine rice three times or until the water runs clear. Drain thoroughly in a sieve, then toast in a dry frying pan over medium-low heat, stirring to prevent burning. You want them to be pale gold. Allow them to cool slightly before crushing into a powder with a pestle and mortar.

3 Sprinkle this powder and the sea salt flakes into the cooked prepared vegetables. Mix well and then pack into a sterilised 500ml Kilner jar. Cover and keep in a cool, dark place for at least 1 week before eating. The vegetables will continue to soften, releasing a modicum of liquid in the process.

For regular *kelupis*, omit the *sulang* seeds and boiling water and use 200ml coconut milk. By all means use softened banana leaves instead of the *nyirik* (*Phrynium*) ones if they elude you, snipping them into 12x20cm rectangles or thereabouts and softening them as described on page 520. It should be noted that when mummified in coconut blade, *kelupis* tends to be called *lamban*, especially among the Bruneian Malays in Labuan.

Kelupis may be stuffed with spiced pounded dried shrimp, producing *kelupis berinti udang*. The glutinous rice may also be ground with regular rice, made into a dough with water and wrapped around beams of lightly sweetened coconut. Wrapped in *nyirik* leaves and steamed, the result is known as *kelupis petani*.

KELUPIS SULANG

MAKES 8

1 tsp *buah sulang* seeds
60ml boiling water
150ml coconut milk
   (second extract; page 521)
200g glutinous rice, rinsed thrice
   and soaked overnight
50ml coconut cream
1 tsp sugar
½ tsp salt
8 *Phrynium* leaves, cleaned

1 Place the *buah sulang* seeds in a jug. Stir in the boiling water, which will be immediately tinted orange by the seeds. Then add the coconut milk and leave to steep for 10 minutes.

2 Drain the glutinous rice and put into a medium saucepan. Strain over the yellow-tinted, slightly thinned, coconut milk. Put the pan over medium-low heat and cook, stirring, until the glutinous grains absorb all the liquid. Stir in the coconut cream, sugar and salt and remove the pan from the heat.

3 Prepare your steamer. Divide the half-cooked rice among the *Phrynium* leaves. Bring both sides of the leaf over the cargo of rice such that one side is larger than the other. Fold this larger side of leaf over the shorter side and continue doing so until you reach the cargo-loaded body. Fold excess leaf under this filled portion on either side, thereby creating slender parcels.

4 Steam the parcels for 30 minutes. Allow to cool before eating.

Do not underestimate the power of 3 tablespoons of peanut butter. It provides all the aroma and flavour needed. Also, no need for Organics: regular PB will work fine.

I used *sulang* water to gild the peanut layer of this *kueh* as I had leftover pulp from my *kelupis* cooking session. Use whatever yellow food dye or colouring you have.

TALAM KACANG

SERVES 8

FOR THE COCONUT LAYER
35g rice flour (page 523)
2 tbsp water, plus 200ml
1 tbsp tapioca starch
1 tbsp wheat starch
50g caster sugar
¼ tsp salt
100ml coconut cream

FOR THE PEANUT LAYER
35g rice flour (page 523)
2 tbsp water
2 tsp tapioca starch
2 tsp wheat starch
60g caster sugar
1 tbsp *sulang* water (page 505)
150ml evaporated milk
150ml milk
2 egg yolks
A few drops vanilla extract
3 tbsp peanut butter
2 tbsp roasted peanuts, chopped
 (page 522)

1 Combine the 35g rice flour with 2 tbsp water for *both* coconut and peanut layers in 2 small separate bowls. Work into cohesive doughs, then cover and leave overnight or for at least 12 hours.

2 Begin the following day by preparing your steamer. Also grease and line the base and sides of a 10x22x7cm loaf tin with baking paper.

3 Now, tend to coconut layer: place the rice flour dough, tapioca and wheat starch, sugar, salt and remaining 200ml water in a medium saucepan. Stir gradually until you get a smooth liquid. Cook over medium-low heat, whisking, until it just begins to seize and thicken. Remove from the heat, whisk to expel any lumps, then mix in the coconut cream. The result should have the consistency of thick custard. Pour into the prepared tin and steam over medium-low heat for 20 minutes or until springy to the touch.

4 Meanwhile, take care of the peanut layer. Place the rice flour dough, tapioca and wheat starch, sugar, *sulang* water, evaporated milk and milk in a medium saucepan, whisking until smooth. Cook over medium-low heat, whisking, until it begins to seize and thicken. Remove from the heat, whisk to expel any lumps. Stir in the egg yolks, vanilla extract and peanut butter. The resultant batter should be spoon-coatingly thick. Stir in the chopped peanuts.

5 Once the first layer is cooked, use a sheet of kitchen towel to remove any moisture on its surface. Carefully pour over the peanut batter, give the tin a little shake, cover and steam over low heat for another 20 minutes, or until springy to the touch. Remove from the steamer and cool completely before removing from its tin and slicing.

Traditionally these are steamed in *katilapan*, elegant, straw-coloured cradle-shaped moulds fashioned from nipa palm blades. These days, it is common to find them cooked in large trays. And it is this latter path that I have taken.

I have experienced *biraksa* as hard as yoga mats, some so soft that they trembled at the faintest suggestion of a spoon. I reckon that it is at its zenith when bouncy to the touch, and tender, almost yielding, in the mouth. It is at these coordinates that the aromas and flavours of the toasted coconut, molasses and spices seem to be at their burningest.

BIRAKSA

SERVES 8

50g rice flour (page 523)
425ml water
½ tsp coriander seeds
½ tsp fennel seeds
¼ tsp cumin seeds
¼ tsp ground cinnamon
60g dark muscovado sugar
75g caster sugar
¼ tsp salt
1 tbsp mung bean starch
   (*tepung hoen kwe*)
25g roasted mung bean flour
100g grated coconut, made into *kerisik*
   (page 521)

1 Combine the 50g rice flour with 50ml of the water in a medium-sized bowl. Work into a cohesive dough, then cover and leave overnight or for at least 12 hours.

2 The following day, prepare your steamer. Also grease and line the base and sides of a 10x22x7cm loaf tin with baking paper.

3 Lightly toast the coriander, fennel and cumin seeds in a small, dry saucepan over medium heat. Once aromatic and faintly coloured, pound into a fine rubble with a pestle and mortar. Stir in the ground cinnamon and set aside.

4 Place the rice dough in a medium saucepan. Add the remaining 375ml water, both sugars, salt, mung bean starch, roasted mung bean flour and *kerisik*. Stir gradually until a smooth liquid is produced. Cook this over medium-low heat until it just begins to seize and thicken, then remove from the heat, whisk to expel any lumps. Expect the pourable consistency of runny yoghurt.

5 Stir in the ground spices and pour into the lined tin. Steam for 45 minutes or until set. It should not feel hard; beneath its springy firmness should be a detectable hint of wobble. Remove it from the steamer. Let the *biraksa* cool completely, during which time it will set further, before freeing it from its tin and slicing it into dainty portions. This is quite lovely nibbled on alongside cups of hot, milky, coffee.

It is the conjunction of sticky rice, husky spice and sweet filling that I find quite irresistible. In place of the *palas* palm leaves, feel free to use banana leaves.

AMPUNG

MAKES 8

FOR THE GLUTINOUS RICE
200g glutinous rice
500ml water
1 tsp turmeric powder
200ml coconut milk
  (second extract; page 521)
50ml coconut cream
1 tsp sugar
½ tsp salt
8 *palas* palm leaves, cleaned

FOR THE FILLING
40g coconut sugar, shaved
  (page 524)
1 tbsp caster sugar
Pinch of salt
5 tbsp water
100g grated coconut

1 Rinse the glutinous rice three times or until the water runs clear. Place the washed grains in a medium-sized bowl, then add the water and turmeric powder. Cover and set aside overnight or for at least 8 hours.

2 In the meantime, make the filling. Combine the shaved coconut and caster sugars, salt and water in a saucepan. Over medium heat, simmer until the sugars dissolve, then stir in the grated coconut and cook until you get a fluffy, faintly moist, mixture. Leave to reach tepidity.

3 Drain the glutinous rice of its yellow liquid and put it into a medium saucepan. Add the coconut milk, then put the pan over medium-low heat and cook, stirring, until the grains absorb all the liquid. Stir in the coconut cream, sugar and salt. Once these have too been absorbed, remove the pan from the heat.

4 Prepare your steamer. Divide the half-cooked rice among the *palas* palm leaves. Pat each portion into rectangles, vaguely 3x9cm in dimension. Divide the coconut filling among these, forming beams down their middles. Lift one side of leaf over the cargo and roll into a firm, fat cigar shape, tucking both ends of excess leaf under the formed parcels.

5 Steam the parcels for 30 minutes. You should cool them completely before defrocking and eating, but I quite like these warm.

Three kinds of *wajid* exist in Brunei. The first is prepared with glutinous rice, the second taro yam. The third, unique to Temburong, uses *padi jawa*, a variety of millet, the sand-toned grains as fine as *tobiko* roe. Foxtail, non-glutinous proso, kodo and little varieties of millet, available at Indian or health food shops, should work.

As I discovered during a session with a group of Kedayan cooks, these are barely sweet, made not with coconut sugar but white sugar taken deep into amber territory in heat-split coconut cream or milk. The stern breath and colour of the burnt sugar imbues the cooked beads, so that the *wajid* resemble plump fingers of aged roe in their leaf purses.

The caramelised sugar and coconut mixture will solidify startlingly hard if made in advance. The solution is easy, however: add a little water to the pot and heat it up over medium-low heat, stirring until all the sugar has melted.

WAJID JAWA TEMBURONG

MAKES 8

150g millet
525ml water
250ml coconut cream
125g sugar
¼ tsp salt
8 *Phrynium* leaves, cleaned

1 Prepare your steamer. Rinse the millet several times to remove any impurities. Drain well, place in a 20cm round cake tin with 225ml of the water. Lower the dish into the steamer and cook for 35-40 minutes, or until the grains have swollen and are tender. Remove and allow to cool completely.

2 Place the remaining 300ml water with the coconut cream in a large shallow saucepan or a wok. Bring the liquid to a boil over high heat, then turn the heat down to low and cook, stirring lazily, until the mixture begins to split into fluffy curds and oil.

3 Stir in the sugar, which will combine with the freshly seized, and still runny, curds. Continue cooking over low heat, stirring slowly but constantly, until the curds deepen in colour, eventually turning chocolaty, sizzling in a pool of coconut oil. Remove all but 2 tbsp of this rendered fat.

4 Give the cooled millet a brief stir, to break up the grains, and tip into the caramelised sugar mixture. Gently and patiently stir the mixture over low heat until you achieve a beaded and uniformly brown mass. Add 1-2 tbsp water if you feel the mixture needs some coaxing. Let the millet cool completely, then divide among the *Phrynium* leaves and fold them into svelte parcels as described on page 505. The *wajid* is now ready for consumption and is best eaten on the day it is made.

For reasons that remain unclear, some Dusun call this delicacy *taji apam*, *taji* referring to the split coconut cream, *apam* the free-form dumplings of banana and ground rice. Some cooks prefer their dumplings firm and so use mostly rice flour, but I belong to the camp who likes theirs soft and slippery. You taste more of the banana this way, too. Speaking of which: use the ripest Lady Finger bananas (*pisang mas*) possible. It is, after all, the dish's only source of sweetness.

TAJI

SERVES 6

125g glutinous rice flour
50g rice flour (page 523)
375ml water
175g Lady Finger bananas, peeled weight
700ml coconut cream

1 Combine the 2 rice flours in a bowl and mix in 125ml of the water to produce a damp, crumbly rubble. Cover and set aside for at least 8 hours or overnight.

2 Place the banana flesh in a medium bowl and crush it with a fork into a paste. Add the hydrated rice flours and mix very thoroughly to achieve a thick, sticky batter. Cover and set aside for 30 minutes.

3 Place the coconut cream and the remaining 250ml water in a large wok or deep saucepan. I use one that is approx. 22cm wide. Bring to a simmer over medium heat, then lower the heat and continue cooking just until the liquid thickens and begins to split into curds and oil.

4 Give the batter a stir, then drop tablespoonfuls into the simmering coconut liquid in various areas, juddering the pan to prevent them from sticking to one another. Half-cover the pan and let the dumplings simmer for 3-5 minutes or until cooked. I usually give the contents brief, gentle stirs to prevent them from catching, basting the dumplings with the hot liquid in the process. The sauce will thicken and split even further with time, but if it looks a bit dry, just splash in a little water. Dish out the dumplings, which should be soft, swollen and golden, and dribble over just a little of the split coconut sauce.

Analogues of this, glutinous rice dumplings filled with sweetened coconut, are found throughout Southeast Asia. In Brunei, they are shaped into the fruit *pengalaban* (*Litsea garciae*), their namesakes, and appear on trays during all sorts of celebrations. Instead of the spinach and beetroot powders, you may use food dyes, as long as they are thick and potent. Anything too dilute will affect the pastry's consistency.

PENGALABAN

MAKES 16

FOR THE PASTRY
100g glutinous rice flour
110ml water
1½ tsp rice flour (page 523)
75g boiled sweet potato flesh, crushed
1 tbsp vegetable oil, plus more for brushing
Approx. ¼ tsp spinach powder
Approx. ½ tsp beetroot powder

FOR THE FILLING
25g coconut sugar, shaved (page 524)
1 tbsp caster sugar
Pinch of salt
3 tbsp water
75g grated coconut
Banana leaf, cut into 16 x 3cm coasters, lightly greased

1 In a medium bowl, combine the glutinous rice flour with 75ml of the water, mixing until you get a cohesive but slightly crumbly dough. Cover and set aside overnight, or for at least 8 hours.

2 Begin the following day by making the filling. Combine the shaved coconut and caster sugars, salt and water in a saucepan. Over medium heat, simmer until the sugars dissolve, then stir in the grated coconut and cook until you get a fluffy, faintly moist, mixture. Leave to reach tepidity.

3 Combine the rice flour with the remaining 35ml water in a small saucepan and cook until you get a thick paste. Tip this paste into a small bowl and leave to cool before mixing with the crushed sweet potato and oil into the hydrated glutinous rice flour, working until you get a smooth but firm dough. Cover and set aside for 30 minutes.

4 Pinch off a walnut-sized lump, about 20g, from the dough. To it, add the spinach powder and massage it in until uniformly green. Work the beetroot powder into the remaining dough and divide it into 16 pink balls.

5 Prepare your steamer. Take a pink ball, shape it into a 3cm disc with your fingers, then drop 1 tsp of filling onto its centre. Bring the sides of the pastry over, press to seal the edges, then carefully roll back into a ball. Fill the remaining 15 pink balls this way, arranging them on their banana leaf coasters in the perforated steamer compartment.

6 Divide the green ball into 16 smaller ones, then pinch and fasten these onto the tops of the pink orbs. Steam for 5-7 minutes over lowish heat. Gingerly remove the *pengalaban* from the steamer tray and lightly brush them with oil. Leave to cool before eating.

This is essentially a sweet leavened rice cake, traditionally cooked over hot coals. *Calak* refers to a particular single-handled mould with flower-like identations (which I substitute with the more widely available *bahulu* mould). *Lambai* means "to wave" and is thought to refer to how soft the resultant cake should be.

While Bruneian Malays will likely use a single kind of rice, which may vary from family to family, I use a combination of jasmine and basmati. Relying on the fermented tapioca (*tapai ubi*) to do the leavening demands patience. The process can sometimes take up to 3 days, depending on the environment. It is essential, however, to prevent it from over-fermenting and becoming sour. Sometimes, I let ½ tsp easy-blend instant yeast do the raising instead. Speed in exchange for tang and nuance.

This is sometimes served with a pandan-green, custard-thick, sauce. For this, combine 2 tbsp cornflour and 125g caster sugar in a saucepan, then whisk in 250ml water. Bring to a bubble over medium-low heat, stirring until it thickens. Then add 1 tbsp fresh pandan extract (page 522) and 100ml coconut cream. Simmer for just a few seconds, then remove from the heat. The sauce will thicken further upon cooling.

CALAK LAMBAI

MAKES 5-6

425g jasmine rice
75g basmati rice
Approx. 350ml water
40g fermented tapioca (page 379)
275g sugar
½ tsp salt
Vegetable oil, for greasing

1 Wash the 2 kinds of rice together three times or until the water runs clear. Drain well, place in a bowl, cover in 2cm of water and leave to soak overnight.

2 The following day, drain the rice. Put into a wet grinder with the 350ml water and grind until a smooth cream is obtained, around 10-15 minutes. Crush the fermented tapioca, removing any hard fibres, and add to the grinder with the sugar and salt. Grind for a further 5-10 minutes. The result should be a pourable batter with the consistency of double cream. Scrape this into a large bowl, cover with clingfilm and leave for 24-36 hours in a cool place or until the batter's surface is speckled with tiny bubbles. It should smell pleasantly alcoholic. Tangy but not sour.

3 Preheat your oven grill to its highest setting. Lightly lubricate the *calak* or *bahulu* mould with vegetable oil and place over medium flames at the stove. Once hot, give the batter a mix and pour approx. 150ml into the mould, making sure to fill its indentations first. Once you see bubbles appearing on its surface, gingerly convey the mould with gloved hands to the preheated oven. Leave it there until its surface is dry and springy, 3-5 minutes. Remove it from the oven and lightly paint its surface with oil before knocking it out of its mould onto a lined platter or tray. Make the remaining *calak lambai* this way.

GLOSSARY

ANCHOVY

In the Southeast Asian kitchen, anchovies are most commonly used in their dried state. They make an excellent stock that may be used as a base for soups and braises, and even applied to stir-fries for both flavour and moisture. Or they may be deep-fried to a crisp to add texture to foods.

ANCHOVY STOCK Weigh out 50g dried anchovies. A variety may be used for stock; if using large, so-called "Grade B" ones, or those about 2cm in length, remove their heads and innards as they can make the stock bitter. Place these in a bowl and rinse in several changes of water to remove surfeit salt. Then put them in a large saucepan with 1½ litres water, 2 bruised garlic cloves and 2 thin slices of ginger. Bring to a boil over high heat, then lower the heat, cover and simmer for just 15 minutes. Allow to cool slightly and strain.

CRISP-FRIED ANCHOVIES "Grade A" anchovies are the best to use here. Place the required amount in a bowl and rinse in several changes of water to remove surfeit salt. Drain them thoroughly and dry them on kitchen towel. Heat 3cm of oil in a large saucepan or wok over medium heat. Once hot, but not smoking, introduce the dried anchovies. Stir for several seconds, then lower the heat slightly and continue frying until light gold and crisp, stirring languidly. Remove them with a slotted spoon to a sheet of kitchen towel to drain off excess oil. They crisp up as they cool. These are best consumed fresh, but will keep for a couple of days in an airtight container in the refrigerator.

BANANAS

Several banana species are brought to attention in this book. The two most commonly used in the Bornean kitchen are the ambrosial *pisang mas*, *Musa acuminata*, also known as Lady Finger bananas, and the creamy, starchy *pisang kepok*, *Musa acuminata x balbisiana*, commonly known as the *saba* banana.

BANANA LEAVES

All over Southeast Asia, banana leaves are used to wrap many foods, from rice-based meals to pudding-like snacks. They generally need to be softened first, which can be done by running them briefly over a ring of flames until they are glossy and a more vivid green. Alternatively, they may be briefly immersed in a large wok or saucepan of boiling water.

CHILLIES

Several chilli peppers are used in the cooking of Borneo. In Malay, they are known as *cili* or *lada*, the latter term also referring to the peppercorn, while in Indonesian they are called *cabe*.

Across the island, the most widely used are cultivars of *Capsicum annuum*, smooth red or green fingers that grow up to 15cm in length and are mild in heat. In Sabah, Sarawak and Brunei, these are known as *cili merah*. In Indonesia, they are named *cabe merah* or *cabe besar*. These are also enlisted in their dried state, especially in spice pastes for braises, that have their fruity spiciness framed with an aged smokiness. They usually require a brief immersion in boiling water to soften, first. Simply put the desired quantity in a bowl, cover generously with freshly boiled water and leave for 10-15 minutes, until they swell, lighten in red, and feel more yielding and tender between the fingers.

In Kalimantan, another cultivar of *Capsicum annuum* is also used, *cabe merah keriting*. Meaning "curly chilli", these fruits are finer and a rich scarlet, registering higher on the Scoville scale than their more ubiquitous, juicier, counterparts.

Then there is the bird's eye chilli, *Capsicum frutescens*, the latter word meaning "bushy", referring to the stature of its plant. In Indonesia, bird's eye chillies are called *cabe rawit*, and come in various colours, from mustard to orange, pale green to engine red. In Sarawak and Sabah, a cream-coloured variant of *cili padi* is especially adored. Its name is *lada puteh*, "white chilli". Fiery and loud, a little of these go a long way. This is even truer for the habañero, *Capsicum chinese*, which in recent years has become increasingly common in the kitchens of Sarawak. In Malay, this is called *cili goronong*, in Indonesia, *cabe perangi*. *Perangi*, in Indonesian, means "fight".

COCONUT

In Borneo, both young and mature coconut (*kelapa*) have their place in the kitchen. Young coconut tends to be added to sweet dishes or snacks. Mature coconuts are prized for the fragrant white liquid their flesh yields. Almost anything in this part of the world may benefit from the mellow, delicately enriching powers of coconut milk. For the recipes in this book, I strongly recommend using fresh coconut cream and milk for the best results. If you have to settle for tinned or boxed stuff, ensure they contain no colourants or stabilisers.

The grated flesh of mature coconuts may also be toasted and crushed into a fine, aromatic rubble, known in Malay as *kerisik*. The Suluk and Ubian are especially keen on *pamapa itum*, a spice paste whose star component is a whole coconut kernel, sans testa, blackened over an open fire. Dishes that require grated coconut meat for heft tend to use what I call "teenage" coconuts — ones in the middle.

BURNT COCONUT PASTE It is best to ask your coconut seller to remove the testa from the kernel and relieve it of juice. Back home, snap it into smaller pieces and leave to dry slightly either under a hot sun or in an air conditioned room. You then pop these on a lit barbecue and cook until totally black, turning them regularly. They should feel hollow and light. In Mindanao, I have seen these being chucked straight onto live coals. I have attemped this over several lit burners on my stove. Effective but messy. All that is left to do is let the charred kernels cool slightly, then pound them into a black, slightly oily, powder. It is difficult to be precise about the yield as kernels vary in size. The only recipe using this is *kullia* on page 199, and for this 250g white kernel should more than suffice. Any surfeit powder will keep well in the freezer for up to 2 months.

COCONUT CREAM When the grated flesh of an adult coconut is wrung in muslin without water, one gets thick coconut milk, sometimes called coconut cream, or in Indonesian, *santan kental*. 300g of grated coconut usually yields 125-150ml.

COCONUT MILK There are some recipes that require *santan* or coconut milk that has not been relieved of its thick, volatile cream. This can be achieved by pouring 250ml water over 300g grated coconut and squeezing the moistened filings in muslin. This yields approx. 300ml coconut milk.

For recipes that need coconut cream and coconut milk separately, two steps are required. The first is to squeeze 300g grated coconut with muslin, to extract the cream, as above. Then add 250ml tepid water to this once-used flesh and squeeze to obtain the second extract, the coconut milk. You should get 250-300ml. A recipe may specify the use of warm or hot water.

KERISIK Toast the required amount of grated coconut in a large wok or frying pan over medium heat, stirring constantly, until uniformly tanned. You are looking for a rich gold colour. Remove the coconut from the pan before it gets to brown any further, then pummel with a pestle and mortar. While on the Malaysian Peninsula *kerisik* is often crushed into an oily paste, as for *rendang*, a fine rubble will suffice for most recipes in this book. The two exceptions are the *asam pedas belulang* (page 440) and *biraksa* (page 508).

DRIED SHRIMP

Udang kering is a store cupboard must-have if one wishes to cook anything remotely Southeast Asian. Making them is a labour-intensive process. The shrimps are first cleaned and boiled in a saline solution until tender and orange. After being drained, their heads are removed and their bodies are spread out on trays or winnowing baskets and left to bake beneath a hot sun until they shrivel in size and their shells turn papery and crisp. Sometimes, the boiled shrimp are dried out on a large metal pan, gently heated from beneath by firewood. This hastens the drying process, turns their shells a deeper coral and imparts an especially appetising aroma.

Once dry, a quick session of gentle abrasing helps loosen and free their bodies from their shells, which are then expelled with the help of moving air, either wind, as is done in many a kampong, or an electric fan. Good quality dried shrimp should not be damp or smell musty. They should be a peachy to rosy orange in colour. They normally require softening before being added to dishes like salads or stir-fries or getting pounded into spice pastes. To do this, simply immerse the desired quantity in warm water for about 10 minutes, drain thoroughly and use as desired. Do note that the soaking time will depend on the size of your shrimp and just how thoroughly they have been dried out.

Shrimp of various sizes may be dried through the method described. *Udang rebon* is the name given to *Acetes*, a diminutive species of shrimp that many, erroneously, refer to as krill. Because of their size, they are neither beheaded nor peeled. These fine, deep orange darlings *may* be added directly to dishes without soaking. (Some recipes do involve soaking them.) They are sublime lightly heated in a pan and sprinkled onto hot rice.

FERMENTED SHRIMP PASTE

This notoriously pungent substance is known in Malay as *belacan*, Indonesian *terasi*. It is made by sunning *Acetes* on winnowing baskets until half-parched, pounding them with salt to form a puce-grey mortar, shaping this mortar into bricks or patties, and then leaving them to ferment and dry out under a hot sun. A mere nugget is enough to transform any dish, be it a salad or braise, with its characteristic brand of fetidity and savouriness.

Before being applied to foods, it should be grilled or toasted. Ideally, this will involve pressing the required amount beneath two squares of banana leaf, containing this in a grill frame and turning it over a lit burner. The idea is to get this 'cake' dry, matte and scorched in parts, its insides slightly parched and crumbly. Its aroma should also have shifted from that of sewers to hot beaches. Most often, I wrap it in banana leaf and then stick it into a hot oven. If only a tiny amount is required, like a tablespoon or so, I usually wrap it around a metal skewer and turn this over a gentle ring of flames on the stove.

GARLIC

Crisp, golden-fried chips of garlic are often used to complete soups, and noodle and rice dishes, especially Chinese-influenced ones. They may be bought from Asian grocers but are best home-made.

FRIED GARLIC Finely chop 10 cloves of peeled garlic. Heat 2cm of vegetable oil in a medium-sized saucepan over medium-low heat. Once hot, shoot in the garlic and fry, stirring, until they are pale gold, fragrant and feel light. Immediately tip the lot into a sieve suspended over a bowl. Spread the drained chips over some kitchen towel, to cool and crisp up. If not using within the next couple of hours, these should be kept in an airtight container in the refrigerator, where they will last for a couple of weeks. The fragrant oil may be kept for other uses as well.

LIMES

Several limes are used in Borneo. In Sarawak and Sabah, limes are *limau*, in Indonesia, *jeruk limau*. *Jeruk* means sour. In Malay, the word *jeruk* is also used to mean pickle or ferment.

The most commonly used lime must surely be the calamansi, *limau* or *jeruk kasturi*. Its juice, both sharp and honeyed, is frequently squirted into salads, soups and drinks. In these parts, a halved ball of calamansi commonly accompanies grilled or fried fish and meats, bowls of rice porridges and plates of fried noodles. Its ubiquity is such that the Indonesians also refer to it, rather plainly, as *jeruk*. The thin-skinned *limau* or *jeruk nipis*, a variety of *Citrus x aurantifolia*, may be used similarly. The same goes for *Micrantha*, the "native lime", sold in many a market and *tamu* across Sabah. Slightly elongated in shape, its aroma is especially striking and suffusive, with notes of jasmine and lemongrass, like a scented candle lighting up a spa in a tropical beach resort.

The makrut lime, *Citrus hystrix*, is also used in Borneo, but mostly in Kalimantan, where it is called *jeruk purut*. *Purut* means stomach, and here the word is used to summon to mind the ridges covering the inside of the stomach wall. It is what the fruit's rough, undulating exterior is thought to resemble. The zest of the makrut has a more piercing ring than the other two limes, its juice shriller in astringency.

PANDAN

Pandanus amaryllifolius is often regarded as the vanilla of Southeast Asia in the way it is used to add fragrance to foods. Unlike vanilla, however, pandan is commonly applied to both savoury and sweet items. A knotted blade may be dropped into a pot of rice or coconut sugar syrup as they simmer, imbuing them with its fragrance. Sometimes, and this is especially true for sweets, it is its extract that is used.

PANDAN EXTRACT Snip 100g pandan leaves into short sections and blend with 400ml water into the finest possible mulch. Strain the mixture through a muslin, squeezing to extract every last bit of juice from the fibres, into a suitably sized jug or jar. Seal and refrigerate for 16-24 hours, or for as long as it takes for the liquid to separate. The residue that would have settled at the bottom of the vessel is what you use; you should obtain approx. 3-4 tbsp. A little goes a long way. This extract will keep well in the fridge for up to a week. Do not, however, attempt to freeze it.

Those who seek a richer hue but not any of the bitterness that comes with overdoing the pandan extract, may replace some pandan leaves with the scentless but intensely green *Dracaena angustifolia*, recognised in these parts as *daun suji*.

PEANUTS

Peanuts can bring a wonderful richness, fragrance and texture to many foods.

ROASTED PEANUTS Spread the desired quantity in a single layer over a suitably sized baking tray or shallow tin and bake on a centre shelf of an oven preheated to 170°C for 15-20 minutes, or until light gold and fragrant; they deepen in colour and crisp up as they cool. This technique applies to both skinned and unskinned nuts, though the latter party will require slightly more discernment on your part. The best way to check is to remove one to a plate, cool it for about half a minute and taste it. They may not be crisp, but should taste warming and rich.

FRIED PEANUTS The recipes that use fried peanuts in this book require them to be unskinned. Heat about 1cm vegetable oil in a wok or wide and deep frying pan over medium-low heat. Once hot, add the peanuts and cook, stirring, until they are fragrant, their papery jackets have deepened in tone, and any visible cleavage is light gold. The best way to check for doneness is to remove one to a plate, cool it for about half a minute, and taste it. You should experience warmth, not rawness.

PETIS UDANG

Also known by its Hokkien name *hae ko*, this thick, sticky paste is made by boiling and reducing the slurry of leftovers from shrimp processing. The addition of molasses makes it treacly both in sweetness and colour. In this book, it is only enlisted in one dish, the cucumber *rujak* (page 424) of Singkawang, West Kalimantan.

PRESERVED FISH

Preserving fish in Borneo is an ancient tradition. There are several classes of preserved fish here. There is fish that have been gutted, salted and dried, *ikan masin*. A wide array of fish succumb to this treatment, from freshwater snakehead murrel to marine shark and Spanish mackerel. Many of these require an immersion in water before cooking, to rid them of surfeit saltiness. The *ikan liking berlada* of the West Coast Bajau in Sabah, for which doublespotted queenfish is filleted and rubbed with salt and chilli paste counts as a form of salted fish, although it is not entirely dehydrated and may be cooked without any preliminarily preparation.

There is *ikan kering*, fish that have been cleaned and dried, like the octopus and stingray adored by the Bajau, and even the *tripang* or sea cucumber, that has been highly sought after by the Chinese for centuries. While it is true that certain kinds of dried fish may contain salt, it is seldom to the same extent as *ikan masin*.

Borneo is also home to several kinds of smoked fish, a fine example being the *ikan salai lumek*, smoked Bombay duck, that the Iban of Sarawak add to a broth soured with *Solanum ferox L.*.

Fish may be preserved with salt and cooked rice, to varying degrees of moistness. This includes the *bosou* of the Kadazandusun, *tamba* of the Murut, *sinamo* of the Rungus. In some cases, fruit and tubers, like unripe papayas and cooked sweet potatoes and tapioca, are used in place of cooked rice. Powdered rice may be used instead too, as in the *pekasam* of the Ibans in Sarawak, the *samu* of the Banjarese in South Kalimantan and the *wadi* of the Ngaju of Central Kalimantan. (*Samu* and *wadi* in fact just mean *pekasam/pakasam* in the respective local dialects). Rice used for *samu* and *wadi* are usually dry-roasted first.

In Brunei, there exists a condiment known as *lusip*, made by fermenting shucked *kujang* (small mussels) with salt.

RICE

Rice is grown in many areas across Borneo, both in the lowlands and uplands. Non-glutinous rice are of short, medium and long grain varieties, and come in many shades, from white to dusty red, black to purple. A trip to Sarawak would be incomplete without a taste or purchase of Bario rice. Although the name may refer to any variety of *Oryza sativa* grown in the vicinity of Bario in the Kelabit Highlands, the grain that usually comes to mind is white as alabaster and fine, like the teeth of baby mice. They swell gorgeously when cooked, releasing a perfume of pandan and hot dewy mornings.

Another famous rice is the short-grain Adan, grown in the Krayan Highlands in Sarawak and North Kalimantan, that has a faint stickiness when cooked. Though available in red and black, it is the white variety that is especially popular.

Glutinous rice is also grown in these parts, primarily in shades of white, black and purple, featuring prominently in snacks and sweet dishes. They are also used to make various kinds of rice wine. These days, a decent percentage of the glutinous rice on sale in Borneo is imported from Thailand.

Unless specified, I use regular jasmine and glutinous rice from Thailand as that is what is most easily available to me.

RICE FLOUR

Likely due to the use of different varieties of rice (and their varying levels of amylose and amylopectin), and manufacturing methods, different brands of rice flour can produce vastly different results. Grabbing the wrong bag may result in a pudding that will not set, or a fritter batter that is chewy and leathery. Unhelpful as it sounds, you may need different rice flours for different occasions. Very broadly speaking, the rice flour I use for puddings is usually of Thai make, a bright white and fine and soft as talcum powder. The ones I prefer for batters are bought from Malay grocers, in bags labelled *tepung beras*, that seem to be off-white and a little coarser and feel less slippery.

SHALLOTS

Shallots are part of the foundation for many savoury dishes in this book, in particular spice pastes. The ones I use are, roughly speaking, the size of large marbles. Fried shallots are often used to finish dishes, providing texture, aroma and flavour.

FRIED SHALLOTS Peel and thinly slice the desired quantity of pink shallots and spread them over a sheet of kitchen towel. Leave them for 30 minutes so that excess moisture may be absorbed. Heat 2cm of vegetable oil in a wide, deep, frying pan over medium-low heat. Once hot, scatter in the sliced shallots and fry, stirring, until they are pale gold and fragrant. Quickly retrieve them with a slotted spoon and spread them over yet more kitchen towel, where they will cool and crisp up. Whatever that is not used within the next couple of hours should be stored in an airtight container in the refrigerator, where they will last for a week or so.

SLAKED LIME

Also called limestone paste, this is bright white and medicinal in scent, derived from cockleshells that are baked, pulverised and hydrated with water. I get mine from Thai grocers. They are also sold pink, thanks to the addition of turmeric.

Air kapur imparts bite to many steamed and boiled rice cakes in Southeast Asia. Vegetables for salads can be steeped in cold baths of water faintly clouded with it so that they retain their crispness. It is also added to fritter batters, affording the fried article with a lasting, sonorous, crunch.

Most of the time, cooks would add a soupçon of *air kapur* straight into whatever they are making. Depending on the dish, there is a noteworthy risk of a soapy aftertaste coming through, which is why a clear limestone solution is sometimes preferred. This is made very simply by mixing 25g of *air kapur* with 150ml water and leaving the resultant liquid for several hours to settle and separate. The white calcium substance should sink to the bottom, beneath a column of clear liquid. This clear liquid is what is to be used. Besides being less abrasive, using this also reduces the chance of the article acquiring a yellowish tint.

SUGAR

Everybody is familiar with the transformative powers of white cane sugar – it is the unrefined ones that probably need elucidation. *Gula tebu*, unrefined sugar derived from the reduction of sugarcane juice, is commonly used in Sabah. *Gula merah*, "red sugar", made by reducing the sap collected from the flower buds of various palms, usually coconut in these parts, is a big favourite, added to sweets, sometimes soups, stews or whatever item that would benefit from both sweetness and depth in flavour.

Gula merah is an umbrella term. Those from Java are called *gula Jawa*, Malaysia *gula Melaka*. *Gula aren*, made from the aren palm, *Arenga pinnata*, is sometimes used in Kalimantan. *Gula apong* is made from the nipa palm.

It is important to remember that these sugars vary from batch to batch in flavour, aroma and sweetness. A rich, floral and almost toffee-like fragrance, and a faint stickiness, are desirable qualities. Those that are rock hard and smell of nothing may well have been corrupted with caster sugar. They are far more suited to self-defense than the kitchen.

Also, depending on manufacturer, they may contain undesirable materials, from pebbles to basket fibre, and are thus best diluted in some water and strained. When a mere lump is required for a dish, however, I usually just crush it between my fingers or chop it up with a knife (depending on how firmly it has been set) and add it straight to the pot.

TAMARIND

Pulp gouged out from the fruit pods of *Tamarindus indica* is a common souring agent throughout Southeast Asia. Those who seek a green hit of acidity may use unripe ones, crushing them (often without peeling) and then allowing these broken bodies to infuse warm water, that may in turn be added to whatever requires sharpening. Most of the time, however, the flesh of ripe pods is used. When I prepare tamarind water, I use store-bought blocks of this ripe pulp, fraught with seeds. Colour and texture are usually fair indications of quality. You are looking for something caught in between amber and umber, and the contents of the packet should feel moist and heavy when held.

TAMARIND WATER To produce approx. 125ml of tamarind water, dissolve 40g of shop-bought tamarind pulp in 125ml boiling water and strain.

BIBLIOGRAPHY

Bellwood Peter, Fox, James J, Tyron Darrell (ed), *The Austronesians: Historical and Comparative Perspectives* (ANU Press, 2006)

de Vienne, Marie-Sybille, *Brunei: From the Age of Commerce to the 21st Century* (NUS Press, 2015)

Harrison, Tom, 'Gold & Indian Influences in West Borneo', Journal of Malayan Branch of the Royal Asiatic Society, Vol. 22, No. 4(150), September 1949 (Malaysian Branch of the Royal Asiatic Society)

Hussin, Hanafi, *Buwas Kuning (Yellow Rice) and its Symbolic Functions Among the Sama-Bajau of Malaysia* (SAGE, 2019)

Janowski, Monica, *Rice, Work and Community among the Kelabit of Sarawak, East Malaysia* (SOAS, University of London, 1991)

Jehom, Welyne Jeffrey, 'Ethnicity and Ethnic Identity in Sarawak', Akademika 55 (Julai) 1999: 83-98

Ju-Kang, Tien, 'The Chinese of Sarawak: Thirty Years of Change', Southeast Asian Studies, Vol. 21, No.3, December 1983

Lamb, Anthony, *A Guide to Wild Fruits of Borneo* (Natural History Publications (Borneo), 2019)

Owen, Sri, *Indonesian Regional Cooking* (St. Martin's Press, 1995)

Stenross, Kurt, *Madurese Seafarers, Prahus, Timber and Illegality on the Margins of the Indonesian State* (Asian Studies Association of Australia: Southeast Asian Publication Series, 2011)

The Traditional Cakes of Brunei (Dewan Bahasa, Pustaka, Malay version in 1986; English version in 2006)

Traditional Cuisines of Sabah, A Culinary Heritage (BAKISA, 1999)

Wan Kong, Ann, 'Examining the Connection between Ancient China and Borneo through Santubong Archaeological Sites, Sino-Platonic Papers' (Department of East Asian Languages and Civilisations, University of Pennsylvania, 2013)

Zepp, Raymond, 'The Chinese in Sarawak', Bulletin de Sinologie, Nouvelle Serie, No.53, Mars 1989 (French Centre for Research on Contemporary China)

ACKNOWLEDGEMENTS

To describe this book's conception as arduous and tedious would be sorely understating things: it often seemed that it would never see the light of day. In the preface I spoke of awaiting consent from the Gods that be, waiting for spirits to channel and for colours and shapes to take over. When they finally did, I got the whole business and was overwhelmed. And I have the following individuals to thank for it...

SARAWAK Big, heartfelt thanks to Amy Ting, Ting Kew Ming and his wife Lau Ling Huong for taking terribly good care of me, for driving me around the state and introducing me to the Iban and Bidayuh communities there who, in turn, gave me a proper education on their food. I am grateful to Basil Thomas for similar reasons. I send warmth in the directions of Eugene Chin, Neyna Radzuan for the wonderful time in Kuching, and to Alena Murang and Grace Balan for the assistance they so graciously rendered on the Kelabit chapter.

SABAH Without the likes of David de la Harpe, Andreas Angkaus, Joe Matius and Kenneth Lim, I would have been lost. They afforded invaluable advice, planned itineraries with me and enabled correspondences with numerous communities across the state. My gratitude is extended to Sylvian Chong, Dino Datu, Fairul Pat Lingham for similar reasons, and also to Herman Scholz, who taught me plenty about the cultures of the myriad ethnic groups in Sabah and inspired me with his resilience, hardiness and adoration for the bottle. I am also thankful for the friendship of Pison Jaujip, who sheltered me in Kota Belud and took me to my first *tamu*.

There are more to thank. Samwise Loh and the Murut community at Marais for granting me a glimpse into their lives. William Lee and Hendretha Shamfuk from the Koposizon Homestay in Papar for the proper education on Dusun food. Susan Angkap from the Bavanggazo Longhouse for the Rungus cookery lesson. Fajian from Kinabatangan and Juans bin Tikuson from Pitas for enlightment on the food cultures of the Orang Sungei and Tombonuo. Nasirah binti Lamanna and Rasmi binti Anwar in Sandakan for the scrumptious *barobbo* and *perkedel*. Rukiah Tampi and Hajah Zulianah in Semporna, for rustling up an unforgettable East Coast Bajau feast. Ismail bin Yusuf, Hj. Annuar, Mabulmaddin bin Shaiddin and Liaisin Bin Kaloh in Kota Belud, for patiently sharing all they know about the cuisines of the West Coast Bajau, Kagayan, Ubian, Iranun and Suluk.

KALIMANTAN If it were not for my friend Duta Alamsyah who connected me with Pontianak-based Chef Yudha Indra Pramanto, I would not have been able to touch any of Kalimantan, which occupies a formidable chunk of Borneo. That it was the first region to be completed leaves me astounded still. Gratitude must certainly be extended to Hefni Effendi, Syahrullah Arul and Baro, my brothers from Banjarmasin, who were generous with their knowledge and time. The evening spent in Hefni's mother's home learning about the local *wadai* remains a precious memory. I am also thankful to Datu Norbeck and Enny Asrinawati for enlightening me on the foods of North Kalimantan, and to Chef Joko Utoro in Bontang, for the exquisite *sambal gami* and *ayam cincane*.

BRUNEI I find myself entirely indebted to Wan Zainal and Salinah Salleh for enabling this section of the book, which miraculously came to fruition in the thick of the COVID-19 crisis. Luscious swathes of gratitude to Eyon Ukoi and Fatimah Jali from Eco Ponies Homestay, and to Haji Mohammed Syafien bin Yandol and Samhan Nyawa from Alai Gayoh, for teaching me the foundations of Bruneian Dusun food and answering my insufferable queries. I am also thankful to Roslinah binti Haji Mohsin and Hajah Rogayah binti Md Yassin in Jerudong for the *belutak* lesson; Zarifah Omar Ali, Fatimah Said, Hjh Munah bte Samat and Nurul Ayuni bte Abdullah in Temburong for teaching me about Kedayan cookery; Pg Basmalati Pg Hj Abbas for the delicious *talam kacang*; Chef Rizal and his wife for the memorable *pengalaban* and *biraksa* demonstration; Dk Kemariah Pg Hj Duraman for the guided tour around Kampong Ayer; Chan Su Jee for the delicious *ulam mambangan*; and Datin Soraya Hamid for the advice and encouragement.

To my graphic designer, Nay Zaw Lin and editor Meena Mylvaganam, thank you so much for your tireless efforts these past few years. To Wilson Wang, I owe you several internal organs for your sumptuous map. You have surpassed yourself. To Darren Gabriel Leow for taking my picture and making me look less monstrous. And last but not least, to mom, Dawn and Zhiyong, for the support and for accommodating my many moments of madness. I fear there are more to come.

INDEX

THE AUTHOR

Bryan Koh is an award-winning author of three cookbooks. His breakthrough, *Milk Pigs & Violet Gold* (2014), won the Best Food Book Award at the Philippine National Book Awards. Its second edition *Milkier Pigs & Violet Gold* was released in 2020.

His second book, *Mornings are for Mont Hin Gar, Burmese Food Stories* (2015), won third place in the Best Asian Cookbook category at the World Gourmand Cookbook Awards 2016. His third book, *Bekwoh* (2018) focused on the food of East Coast Peninsular Malaysia.

Bryan majored in Mathematics at the National University of Singapore and has a Masters in Management Hospitality from Cornell University. He lives in Singapore and is co-owner of cake company Chalk Farm.

OTHER RELEASES BY THE AUTHOR

MILKIER PIGS & VIOLET GOLD
Philippine Food Stories

MORNINGS ARE FOR MONT HIN GAR
Burmese Food Stories

BEKWOH
Stories & Recipes from Peninsular Malaysia's East Coast